Julie Satter

Luther and the Cardinal

A historic-biographical Tale

Julie Satter

Luther and the Cardinal
A historic-biographical Tale

ISBN/EAN: 9783743335349

Manufactured in Europe, USA, Canada, Australia, Japa

Cover: Foto ©Lupo / pixelio.de

Manufactured and distributed by brebook publishing software (www.brebook.com)

Julie Satter

Luther and the Cardinal

CARDINAL ALBRECHT.
From a portrait by A. Dürer in the British Museum.

LUTHER AND THE CARDINAL.

A Historic-Biographical Tale.

GIVEN IN ENGLISH

BY

JULIE SUTTER.

THE RELIGIOUS TRACT SOCIETY;
56, PATERNOSTER ROW; 65, ST. PAUL'S CHURCHYARD;
AND 164, PICCADILLY.

LONDON:
R. CLAY, SONS, AND TAYLOR,
BREAD STREET HILL, E.C.

PREFACE.

THE following is an adaptation from the German of Pastor Nietschmann of Halle. It is not so much a translation as a reproduction in kind with liberty of handling; the object being to give in English what, it is hoped, may be accepted as a worthy picture of the time when the night was dispelling and the broad daylight appearing with the freedom of souls in its wake.

The story embodies Luther's struggle with the most powerful of his adversaries, the Elector Archbishop Cardinal Albrecht of Mainz, Primate of all Germany, and, next to Pope and Emperor, the greatest man in the realm. There are no fictitious characters introduced, the *dramatis personæ* each and all being true to history.

It does not seem to be easy to judge rightly of the great Cardinal himself, or to understand how it was that one naturally gifted with all that is generous, one of whom even Luther had hopes, fell away so grievously. There was a time when the two roads lay before him, when he was "almost persuaded" to turn his back upon Rome; but he could not wean his heart from its weakness, and, as Hutten points out, it is the "way of the flesh" which takes Albrecht to Rome. There is that in his natural disposition which moves one to pity, as from weakness he sinks to wickedness, ending his struggle in defeat. "Thou has conquered, Augustinian," he is brought to own at the last. And the Prince Primate of Germany, the magnificent, luxurious hierarch, the patron of arts and letters, the high-born ruler who, at the outset of his career, had not a little of the amiability that wins men's hearts, dies almost forgotten, and, at any rate, poor and powerless, in his lonely palace at Mainz. The Truth had prevailed, and Albrecht reaped what he had sown.

As the following pages do not trace his life quite to the end, we may add here that he died in 1545, in the fifty-sixth year of his age.

We offer this volume as a tribute to the Cardinal's fearless opponent—the brave, true-hearted Luther—who, in the strength of his faith, took up the conflict with the powerful hierarch, who broke the chains which bound the people to Rome.

It may interest the reader to know that the actual grant of indulgence assigned by Pope Leo X. to Cardinal Albrecht, which may well be called a hinge of this story, as it also was a starting-point of the Reformation, can be seen at the British Museum, King's Library, Show-case XII.

The illustrations are confined to portraits of the chief characters who figure in the story. They are nearly all taken from the best contemporary authorities, and help us to form some idea of what manner of men they were who did the deeds recorded in this story.

J. S.

CONTENTS.

CHAP.		PAGE
I.	DAYS OF PROMISE	1
II.	HIS GRACE OF MAINZ	8
III.	AT THE ELECTOR'S COURT	16
IV.	THE ARCHBISHOP IN DIFFICULTY	26
V.	FALLING AWAY	39
VI.	BOUND FOR MAINZ	48
VII.	DOMINICAN AND AUGUSTINIAN	58
VIII.	THE CARDINAL'S HAT	70
IX.	THE "HERETIC" AT THE BAR	77
X.	CHANGES	87
XI.	THE HORIZON OVERCAST	96
XII.	FRIENDSHIP PARTED	108
XIII.	FIRE FOR FIRE	120
XIV.	WORMS	128
XV.	HE CANNOT OTHERWISE	141
XVI.	FRESH DIFFICULTY AND A NEW EXPEDIENT	160
XVII.	THE IDOL AT HALLE	177
XVIII.	LUTHER VERSUS THE CARDINAL	186
XIX.	THE GREAT CATHEDRAL	204

CONTENTS.

CHAP.		PAGE
XX.—ANOTHER WITNESS FOR THE TRUTH		216
XXI.—STORM-TIDE		227
XXII.—POSSIBILITIES		241
XXIII.—THE PROMISE BROKEN		252
XXIV.—A DEED OF DARKNESS		263
XXV.—CONSCIENCE		279
XXVI.—FRESH ENDEAVOURS		289
XXVII.—TIGHTENING THE REIN		299
XXVIII.—BEHIND THE SCENES		313
XXIX.—CHASTISING WITH SCORPIONS		321
XXX.—RUPTURE		331
XXXI.—COMING TO HIMSELF		338
XXXII.—BROUGHT TO THE GALLOWS		345
XXXIII.—LUTHER RISING IN JUDGMENT		351
XXXIV.—THE LAST STRUGGLE		364
XXXV.—CONQUERED		372

LUTHER AND THE CARDINAL.

CHAPTER I

DAYS OF PROMISE.

A GLADDENED throng of people was pressing through the Ulrichsthor of Halle on the Fifth Sunday after Easter, A.D. 1514. The whole town seemed on foot, crowd after crowd passing the gate and the Judendorf, or Jews' quarter, beyond it, towards the Giebichenstein. Old and young, rich and poor, master and servant—all were there. Just outside the gate a procession formed, headed by the magistrates and town councillors on horseback, exhibiting all the splendour of their official dignity. Next to them, scarcely less imposing in appearance, ranged the clergy both secular and monasterial, having donned their most gorgeous vestments, not forgetting banner and cross. These were followed by the guilds and corporations, notably that of the salt-workers, carrying mace and halberd in honour of the day.

Expectation was written on every face, nor was it surprising, since they were ready to make welcome the new Archbishop. The previous Sunday had witnessed his enthronisation at Magdeburg; the town of Halle, the archiepiscopal residence, having her turn to-day.

A very sunshine of promise gladdened men's hearts, for people hoped great things of the newly-appointed hierarch, fondly looking for a time of peaceful prosperity under his rule. The late Archbishop had left no pleasant memory; his had been an iron sceptre, and, not satisfied with the fortress of Giebichenstein, he had built a strong tower, the Moritzburg, within the town itself, overawing the citizens and succeeding but too well in depriving them of time-honoured political liberties. The result was that, noble or simple, whatever their mutual jealousies, the people of Halle were one in hating his tyranny. Rebellion was but asleep, her wakeful signs becoming apparent here and there; and when the plague had added terror and devastation to general distress, a popular outbreak, headed by a turbulent schoolmaster named Thomas Münzer, showed how little the shepherd could count upon his flock. A conspiracy against his life, which proved abortive, tended nowise towards the healing of deep-seated disaffection. The tyrant's measure, however, was full, and he was called to his account. The funeral rites were befittingly solemn, but grief was expressed by the priests and choristers only, who recited the appointed dirges in lamentation of the dead.

And now Hope spread forth her rose-coloured mantle. Whoever might succeed, a worse ruler than Archbishop Ernest could never be forthcoming. Nor were the people disappointed. News arrived that Markgrave Albrecht of Brandenburg had found favour with the High Chapter of the Archbishopric of Magdeburg; the bells pealed forth the joyful event, and the citizens flocked to churches and chapels to sing a *Te Deum* of praise and thanksgiving. Nothing had ever been heard of the young prince in question but what left room for the joyful expectation that righteousness and peace should kiss each other beneath his rule. The youthful Markgrave was known to be possessed of all knightly graces; he was reported to be clear-headed and high-minded, a lover of art and patron of learning, a man likely to make benevolence and justice the safeguards of his power. And surely he must be specially fitted for high ecclesiastical dignity, seeing that three Chapters almost simultaneously accorded him the palm. For scarcely had he been invested with the see of Magdeburg, when the bishopric of Halberstadt followed in the wake, and within a few months from this a deputation arrived from Mainz praying him to accept the archiepiscopal honours of that town, including one of the seven electorships of the realm.

Something like jealousy at this news could not at first be suppressed within the diocese of Magdeburg, people feeling as though they had lost two-thirds of their Archbishop; and, indeed, who ever heard that one prince could fitly occupy three sees? Misgivings, however, yielded to the fond assurance that if one man was found worthy of having authority over ten cities, power and wisdom no doubt would also be given him for the fulfilment of so great a trust; a feeling of pride eventually rising uppermost, seeing that the Archbishop of Magdeburg now united in his person the highest spiritual and temporal dignity of the empire. As Archbishop of Mainz he was Primate of all Germany, as Elector of Mainz he was Lord High Chancellor of the realm. It was little to be wondered at, therefore, that the good people of Halle were joyously prepared to greet his arrival.

One Nicholas, a worthy master of the pewterers' guild, found himself surrounded by quite a crowd of questioners, for he had been to Magdeburg lately, and had seen all that could be seen of the ceremony there. People wanted to know what it was like; nor was he chary of information, but added description upon description with willing voice.

"I have seen him with my own eyes!" he said. "He is but a youthful prince, he cannot be more than four-and-twenty, but he seems to have reached a maturity beyond his age; there is an earnest manliness about him, and he has the eye of a ruler, but he looked affable and mild, like one who might prove a fatherly guide. And his appearance is striking. How well he sat his horse, as handsome and knightly a figure as ever poet dreamed! I heard him speak, too, and his voice nowise belies his appearance; in it harmony and power are combined."

"And how did the Magdeburghers receive him?" asked one of the crowd.

"How they received him? The town was astir with delight, and so great was the concourse of people that the festive procession could scarcely make its way to the cathedral. For you must know that a bull had arrived from his Holiness the Pope, promising indulgence for sin to all who would hear high mass at the Archbishop's enthronisation; people had come from far and near—the city could scarcely hold them. But the procession was something to behold! At first I saw but an array of horsemen, whose steel helmets and polished cuirasses filled the air with a glitter of dazzling light.

As they approached I recognised the new Archbishop, his brother, the Elector Joachim of Brandenburg, riding on his left ; some two hundred noblemen in scarlet jerkins and glistening breastplates—a goodly sight—acting as his body-guard. The nearing cavalcade was met by a splendid company of welcome from the town. Riding first, there appeared Prince Ernest of Anhalt, with flying colours and a hundred knights clothed in black velvet and silk ; they were followed by the four Counts of Mansfield, with over a hundred horsemen in olive-green apparel, also displaying their banner ; there was Count Barby, with sixteen retainers ; next came the Provost of the Cathedral, Prince Adolphus of Anhalt, and with him the deputies of the Chapter, followed by fifty horsemen, all these again in solemn black. The rear was brought up by the magistrates of Magdeburg with a hundred horse. Beneath a triumphal arch wreathed with flowers the two processions met, and the Archbishop having been received in the name of the town, they turned to gain the cathedral, at the porch of which the Chapter, together with the Bishops of Merseburg, Naumburg, Brandenburg, Havelberg, and Lebus, stood waiting. The Bishop of Merseburg came forward to address the new hierarch in the name of the Chapter, and having offered his congratulations he put upon him the insignia of his high position—the cloak and scarlet mitre. And now, amid the flourishes of drum and trumpet, Albrecht went up the aisle to the high altar, which was ablaze with light and gorgeous with flowers. There he knelt, the choir chanting the *Te Deum ;* after which he was lifted upon the altar, as a sign that he was now indued with the archiepiscopal authority. The ceremony within the cathedral having terminated, the procession moved to the palace, that his grace might there receive the homage due to him as ruler of the land. Nothing was wanting to add to the solemnity; the church bells pealed as he mounted a decorated platform, whence he addressed the magistracy and the thronging people : 'Will you swear allegiance,' he said, with far-sounding voice, 'promising to hold by us faithfully?' 'Yea, yea!' cried the magistrates; and the people held up their right hands in token of yielding their oath. After which the chief official present addressed the Archbishop, asking him in the name of the town : 'Will your lordship promise, in your turn, fidelity to us?' His grace replied with a hearty 'I will,' shaking hands with the magistrates."

The pewterer would have continued, having more to say evidently, but was interrupted by shouts of delight rising from the people more in advance. All heads bared, and in another moment the churches and chapels united in a peal of welcome, the priests adding their solemn chant—silencing for a time the acclamations of the people. There he was, the new Archbishop— indeed a lordly prince; fame had nowise exaggerated his appearance. Beside him rode his brother, Elector Joachim of Brandenburg; behind him his cousin, John Albrecht of Anspach, with the Bishops of Lebus and Brandenburg; these again being succeeded by a retinue of knights.

The Archbishop having been received and made welcome to the town by the assembled magistrates, the procession rearranged to lead him to his palace, the majestic Moritzburg. Proudly waved the colours of Brandenburg together with the archiepiscopal banner from the battlements of the strong-built castle, at the chief entrance of which the youths of the highest families of the town had formed a guard of honour, even now offering a joyous salute to the arriving prelate.

The following day brought new festivity to the township of Halle, calling the people to the market-place for the tendering of their allegiance. On a snow-white charger the Archbishop arrived with his courtly train, and received the homage of the citizens, promising grace and goodwill in his turn.

This ceremony over, the town council presented him with a golden tankard, together with a cask of malmsey, three barrels of Eimbeck beer, and two hundred bushels of wheat. And then, with pipes and kettle-drums, the salt-workers arrived, begging his grace to dismount, whereupon they led the horse round each spring in turn, in accordance with an ancient custom, which also required that the Archbishop must redeem his steed with a gift of twenty gold florins to the salt guild of Halle.

The afternoon of that day was passed amid games and popular sports on the great meadow by the Saale; the people took their fill of pleasure in honour of their new Archbishop, a cloudless sky of May looking down upon all this merriment. And in the evening the men gathered here and there round the social "schoppen," exchanging their ideas concerning the new ruler, when it appeared that there was but one voice among them, since he had gained all hearts by his stately yet gracious bearing.

CHAPTER II.

HIS GRACE OF MAINZ.

AT the meeting of rivers, where the Main and Rhine unite, nestles the ancient fortress whose origin is of the time when the Romans held sway in the land, succeeding centuries adding their spoil—the town and stronghold of Mainz. The middle ages called it the "golden city," not only on account of the wealth accumulated by her merchants and patricians, but also because of the splendour of art adorning her buildings, especially the venerable cathedral, which carried her six steeples proudly beyond clustering houses and churches of lesser degree. Ever since the days of St. Boniface Mainz had rejoiced in the dignity of an archbishopric, the honours of which gained new lustre when the electoral hat was added to the mitre. The Archbishops of Mainz, Treves and Cologne [1] formed part of the august council which disposed of the imperial crown. And more than this, in the course of time he of Mainz had gained a privileged position among his peers, adding to his electoral and archiepiscopal dignities those of Lord High

[1] There were three spiritual and four temporal electors, in whom the right of office was vested to elect a new Emperor at the demise of the crown.

Chancellor of the Empire. And, lest the temporal power should outweigh the spiritual, Rome had stepped in, making the Archbishop of Mainz Primate of all Germany. Thus, then, this favoured hierarch in power and splendour was next to Emperor and Pope—a much-coveted position naturally. There had been a hot contest upon the present occasion: besides Albrecht of Brandenburg, who had come forth victorious, Duke Ernest of Bavaria, Duke Ulrich of Würtemberg, Markgrave Philip of Baden, and Bishop William of Strassburg had solicited the Chapter, outdoing each other in promises. The Emperor's wishes were with the Bavarian Duke, of whose attachment he felt most assured; the Markgrave of Brandenburg, on the contrary, being the very last he desired, not caring that two brothers should sit in the High Council of Electors. But the personal wishes of the Emperor were not respected, since the very one was chosen whom he approved of least.

And was the choice a wise one indeed? Did the Chapter know what it was about? Will a prince of but four-and-twenty summers be equal to the responsible position of Elector Primate, especially as two dioceses were already claiming his attention? And would the Pope give his sanction? Was it not against all precedent to place three mitres upon the self-same head, the head of a young man even who had not reached the canonical age, requiring special dispensation on this account? People at Mainz could but ask and wonder.

Another care added its weight: would the brother of the new Archbishop, the Elector of Brandenburg, really do as he had promised, and pay the price for the archiepiscopal pallium? It was natural if this question troubled the townfolk. The Pope did not grant the white linen strip covered with crosses—the distinctive badge of Archbishops—for nothing. No! Thirty thousand gold florins had to be paid for the same to the "Vicar of Christ." And with whom rested this payment? With the archiepiscopal treasury, of course. But who replenished this treasury? Why, the diocese. Now since Mainz had had the misfortune of losing two archbishops, dying shortly one after another, their resources, in consequence of repeated payments of the pallium tax, were at the lowest ebb; the Chapter therefore had been anxious to direct their new choice to one whom they believed capable by private means to satisfy the papal greed. Albrecht's brother, then, had undertaken to be good for the amount—but will he keep his promise? The people of Mainz could but ask and fear, month after month passing before the newly chosen Archbishop thought of showing himself on the Rhine. "Mainz ought to be of more importance to him than Magdeburg and Halberstadt put together," the people would say, impatiently; their apprehensions being eased at last, when the news reached them that the Elector Archbishop had left Halle with a retinue of two hundred horsemen, and might be looked for at an early date. This was in October.

Acting as a potent charm, the expectation of seeing him allayed all fears; a thousand hands were willing to prepare him a worthy reception.

The Archbishop having expressed a desire to come by ship down the Main, a stately Rhine boat was made ready, decorated with flowers—as many as the late season would yield—and fitted out with all possible convenience. This vessel, followed by a fleet of thirty masts, proudly waving their red and white streamers, sailed up the

Main as far as Höchst, where a deputation of the Chapter, together with the first spiritual and temporal vassals of the archbishopric, awaited the coming of their new lord.

On the sixth of November the cavalcade, headed by Albrecht, came in sight, whereupon the larger vessel hoisted the flags of Mainz and Brandenburg, and a flourish of trumpets greeted the august arrival. As the little fleet sailed down the river the towns and villages everywhere hailed the princely traveller, the church bells pealing forth, that people far and wide might rejoice in the knowledge that the long-expected ruler had now come to his own.

And when the domes and steeples of the "golden city" grew upon the horizon, the mighty cannon raised its voice from her ramparts, and the masses of her citizens pressed through the Fisher-gate. The High Chapter, with the united clergy of Mainz, the Electoral court state, the nobility of the town and neighbourhood, the university, the corporations with their banners, the school children with festive tapers—all had come. The church bells sounded their joyous peal, the trumpets added flourish upon flourish, the people waved their hats in a storm of welcome—the Elector Archbishop Albrecht had landed.

Triumphal arches had been erected, through which the procession moved towards the cathedral; a mounted body-guard in scarlet and gold, with shining helmets and waving plumes, red and white, taking the lead. Then, bearing a cross, came the school children with their masters; the guilds with trumpets and banners; the electoral household in silver-laced scarlet; the priests and secular clergy, the foremost among whom carried the archiepiscopal insignia—the golden crosier and a scarlet mitre covered with pearls. Behind them followed knights and vassals, with pages holding aloft on a gold-broidered cushion the electoral marks of honour, the hat and cloak of red velvet, bordered with ermine. The court-marshal with the electoral sword preceded him who was the central glory of all this pomp and vanity,[1] for now appeared Albrecht, the Elector, in a black silk cassock and surplice of costly Brabant lace, wearing an ermine cape, and on his breast, suspended on a scarlet ribbon, the archiepiscopal cross richly set with diamonds. Four knights in black Spanish costume held a canopy above him, gorgeously worked in gold, silver, and pearls; to the right and left walked a number of satellites in yellow jerkins with halberds, red and white plumes waving from their slouching hats. The Elector himself was supported by the Dean and Provost of the Chapter, one on either hand; behind him followed his chancellor, the grand steward of the palace, and the notables of Mainz, all in black silk capes, with swords and black-plumed caps. The professors in gowns were surrounded by the students of the university in full force bringing up the rear, and followed only by a second division of mounted body-guard.

On the procession went, over carpets and flowers, between banners and wreaths; the eyes of the towns-folk seeking the central figure, who bore himself with majestic dignity, looking about him with winning eyes, handsome in the bloom and power of his youth, the broad forehead not wanting in gravity, as he dispensed the archiepiscopal blessing to the pious multitude.

[1] The description of these festivities is taken from the accounts preserved in the cathedral archives of Mainz.

Arrived at the cathedral, he knelt down by the altar of St. Martin, the patron of Mainz, the choir filling the splendid pile with solemn chant. The capitulation took place in the Chapter room, after which the Elector Archbishop was led in state to his electoral residence, the Martinsburg; and there he met with a splendid reception of purely temporal character. Beside the more exalted office-bearers of his court, there were the Count of Nassau, Lord High Steward of the realm, the Landgrave of Hesse, Lord High Marshal—in fact, quite a galaxy of grandees, the hereditary dignitaries of the empire. His grace of Mainz evidently was considered worthy of honour.

The ceremony of state being over, and before the grand assembly had finally broken up, a young knight forced his way into the Elector's presence, and, gracefully kneeling, he offered a scroll wrapped in a scarlet covering.

Albrecht gave a glance at the kneeling youth, a gleam of delight passing over his face at recognition.

"Thou here, Ulrich mine?" he said. "Friendship is glad to call thee welcome. How full of sunshine is this favoured day! So much happiness and blessing, I am not worthy of it all. But what is this thou bringest me? I guess aright, I think—is it a song of thy lyre to grace thy friend?"

Ulrich von Hutten—for the young knight was he—pressed the Elector's hand with overflowing gladness, pleased not a little with the gracious assurance of unchanged feelings. "Each and all bring their best to-day," he said. "Ulrich is happy if his Elector will not disdain so humble a gift."

Albrecht opened the paper. It contained a long poem

in the Latin tongue, redounding of praise concerning the newly chosen Elector, and congratulating the territory of Mainz at having gained a ruler of such noble birth, whose superior intellectual attainments and high-minded disposition must prove a blessing to the Church, to the Electorate, even to the Empire at large; beneath whose sway arts and letters would flourish to the well-being of his generation.

"Now leave us, Ulrich!" said Albrecht, offering his hand. "I shall look for thee to-morrow, and then we will have a chat, calling back the happy days when we enjoyed our youth at the University of Frankfort. Would thou couldst stay with me always!"

"Far too gracious is the prince to his servant," said Hutten, moved. "But the days are counted which I may spend in happy Mainz: my face is set towards Italy. I mean to study the laws at Bologna."

The Elector smiled. "I did not dream I could keep thee. Thou must be free as the bird in the air, I know. Spread thy wings, then, even as the royal eagle thou art, who seeks the sun. But if ever this town of Mainz can attract thee for a while, be sure that an old friend will delight in thy presence; and who knows whether thou wilt not be glad of him yet!"

Albrecht and Hutten shook hands, the Elector leaving the hall of reception.

Deep into the night the high windows of the Martinsburg were bright with burning tapers, the multitude in the streets, in spite of the now pouring rain, listening to the sounds of feasting in honour of the new ruler. The trustful people felt so glad, so happy, having seen him; for, as at Magdeburg and Halberstadt, he had gained all hearts by his winning presence.

When the last sound had died away, and the lights all had yielded to darkness, Albrecht sat alone in his chamber, thinking. Sleep fled his eyes, and his soul was wakeful with the impressions of the day. He felt lifted up with the worship which had been laid at his feet that day; his hands folded as though he would offer thanks. And, despite his elation, he could not but ask himself with some diffidence: "Shall I be equal to the high calling—I, who after all am young? Sword and crosier—how shall I hold them both? If the right hand wields the sword, there is but the left one for the crosier! Shall I be equal to the holy office?"

CHAPTER III.

AT THE ELECTOR'S COURT.

"WHAT strange occupation is this of yours?" queried Valentine, the steward of the kitchen, of Sebastian, the falconer, in the archiepiscopal palace yard. It was a pleasant day in March, 1515, and the said Sebastian was exerting himself greatly.

"I am trying to teach my bird to take to sparrows," said he bluntly, "seeing he will have little chance of ever proving his training upon a heron again. But the creature is obstinate, and doesn't quite understand the change."

"How should he?" laughed the steward; "you are a fool for your pains, master falconer! Why should you think the days of heron chasing will never return?"

"Why? because I think so, I, the court falconer of Mainz. The blessed days are over. How different it was with the late Archbishop, to be sure! My lord Uriel loved falconry, and Sebastian had a happy time of it. But now we might as well be dead, both I and my bird, for all the new Elector cares for us. Nothing to do from morning to night—I am sick of it!"

"It is a pity you cannot lend us a hand in the kitchen; we have plenty to do, I assure you."

"Yes, you, I dare say," growled the falconer, "since there is no end to dinners and visitors, and extravagance to boot. His grace must have a long purse for all that."

Valentine looked about him cautiously. "Take care of your tongue, Sebastian, it is not well to say all one thinks!" And coming closer, he continued under his breath: "You are right, though; I too keep wondering who is to pay for it all! You have no idea of the expense in the kitchen department. At first I believed it was merely for the sake of novelty, and that his grace thought fit thus to inaugurate his new dignity. But there is no sign of abatement; never a day there is without a host of boon companions—women included, strange to say! This very week we are preparing for a great tomfoolery, no end of ladies being invited. There is going to be a grand game of fortune, and, my stars, you should just see the prizes! Perhaps you have noticed a queer old man about the place; it was a goldsmith of Nürnberg, and a pretty penny no doubt he has made here. Why, his grace is like a child if you show him some glittering trinket. The chamberlain told me that he has seen him pay seven hundred gulden for one single necklace. Good heavens, to think of his throwing away all that money on his lady visitors!"

The virtuous steward was interrupted by a wild halloo from the stable yard—some young gentlemen, booted and spurred, were trying to break in an Arab colt.

"Look at that tribe of dandies," continued Valentine. "It is beyond my understanding why the Elector keeps the like of them at court. They are good only for eating and drinking, and playing at love with the servant girls, torturing the horses and dogs besides. That young fop there, with the carroty hair and milky face, has been sitting up the whole night with some of them drinking and gambling, and a nice picture he looks! It is all the warden of the palace can do to keep the place in order—you can hear his voice now in the servants' hall; I suppose he has to interfere with some of the brawlers there. Nice times these, to be sure!"

"I cry you mercy, gentlemen!" exclaimed a voice behind them; and turning in alarm they perceived a monk, whose face plainly said: "Yes, yes, I heard you!"

The steward bit his lips, and was going to make some covered remark concerning uninvited listeners, but the ecclesiastic anticipated it with a pleasant nod, saying in a half whisper: "Hush, hush, Master Valentine, I could not help being privy to the expression of your feelings, but you are quite safe with me; indeed, you have only ventured to put into words what many others more prudently keep to themselves. It is all true; but it is not the worst. The Elector is but young, and he too must have his time of youthful follies; he will settle down presently. But what good is to come of his predilection for the humanists, I know not!"

"Humanists?" repeated the steward. "Is it Dürer and Kranach you are speaking of, who painted those pictures for the Dom and the palace? Nice to look at, I grant you, but woefully expensive. Why, that single altar-piece in the Dom, representing St. Martin, was paid for with eight hundred gold gulden. Would you believe it—all that money for a bit of coloured canvas!"

"Well, well," said the monk, "the Elector knows where to replenish his coffers, if he drains them."

"Does he!" sneered the steward, "no doubt he does — borrowing of the Fuggers at Augsburg![1] They are pressing him already for the thirty thousand gold florins they have advanced him for the pallium, and which they are not likely to receive back in a hurry. His grace's brother, the Elector of Brandenburg, had promised to be good for the amount, but it seemed more convenient to forget all about it, forcing the Archbishop to have recourse to those usurers. The load of debt, however, does not seem to weigh upon him very heavily, to judge from the waste we witness. Perhaps he is meditating another tax like that first one, when, entering upon office, he claimed of all priests and cloisters the fifth part of their revenues. It created much ill-will even then; I should wonder if it were taken quietly a second time."

"Well," replied the monk, "art is an expensive luxury, but it graces a man's life nevertheless. I would not blame the Archbishop for patronising an Albrecht Dürer and a Lucas Kranach; but his friendship for those others is a hateful thing! It is much to be regretted, too, that he has brought hither his old tutor, Eitelwolf von Stein, and made him his privy councillor."

"Why should he not?" queried Valentine. "He is of noble family, both good and learned, and knows moreover how to speak courteously with plain folk. We all like him for it."

"I dare say you do!" cried the monk, "not perceiving that he is one of those of whom it is written, 'Beware of false prophets, which come to you in sheep's clothing, but inwardly they are ravening wolves.'

[1] The Rothschilds of those days.

You may shake your head, but they are! If this Eitelwolf were the only one—but are they not all coming hither, Erasmus, Herman von Busch, Helding, and the rest of them? Doctor Stromer, the Elector's physician, too, may be considered one of the tribe. And Ulrich von Hutten likewise—what keeps that young adventurer here, I wonder? He was going to Italy, I believed."

"The Elector will not let him depart before he has recovered his health a little," explained the steward; "he looks but poorly."

"Not a doubt of it," rejoined the monk, with an ugly grin; "he looks as he does, methinks, leading a vagabond's life, cursed by his own father as a very Cain. There is little good to be heard of him, I know; his ill looks speak for an ill life, I deem. Would we had seen the last of him! I cannot bear that face of his; I see but scorn on his forehead and a sneer on his lip."

"But what is it that makes you so angry?" inquired the steward. "I have always heard the humanists spoken of as wise and learned men. And our Elector is famed as a patron of learning."

"Yes, yes," said the monk, with ill-suppressed wrath, "so wise is their wisdom, and so learned their learning, that they think they know better than Holy Church herself. Nothing so sacred but they will make it a butt of their miserable sarcasm! They sneer at the saints, worshipping heathen gods and heroes instead; they think more of old pagan learning, I warrant me, than of Holy Writ!"

"Your reverence is labouring under excitement," returned the steward, quietly; "it is not so bad, surely. I have been told that these men only scoff at what has grown bad within the Church; they would wish to reform that; and surely it were no bad thing if they succeeded! There are others besides the humanists who see infirmity and failings everywhere in the Church, and are not afraid of putting their fingers to the sores. Has not Doctor Sebastian Brandt of Strassburg written and published a book called the *Ship of Fools*, dealing of these very things, and do not the people delight in the poem?"

"He is a fool who wrote the *Ship of Fools!*" cried the exasperated monk.

"Is he?" retorted the steward, getting angry in his turn; "then I suppose you would call his Holiness the Pope a fool for taking the part of the famous Reuchlin in his quarrel with the Dominicans of Cologne? I was delighted to find they had to pay the costs; it served them right, them and their leader, Jacob von Hogstraten, that fiend of an inquisitor! What crime had the venerable Reuchlin committed by his endeavouring to defend true learning against those cowls who are as ignorant as they are cruel, whose studies are directed to meat and drink chiefly? He has held up the torch of knowledge, illumining the haunt of the hooded owls; and they resent it, stretching forth their claws, and would fain kill him if they could."

"Avaunt, madman!" ejaculated the monk, now quite beside himself with wrath, "lest you experience the power of their claws yourself!"

He shook his fist with impotent rage, rousing the merriment of both steward and falconer, and quitted the scene utterly discomfited.

. . . .

The Elector Archbishop Albrecht, with his grand

steward and privy councillor Eitelwolf von Stein, was holding consultation in a superb apartment, not over large, but a very haunt of art and luxury. The floor was covered with a carpet, the softest and most perfect production of the Brabant looms. On the high-backed chairs of carved oak the electoral scutcheon was blazing in fields of gold. Low couches of deep red velvet stood about the room. The wainscoted ceiling showed the richest arabesque, a silver chandelier being suspended from the centre, the six arms of which were wrought into lilies, each holding a taper. Valuable paintings adorned the walls, a large picture representing the destruction of Troy nearly filling one side of the room opposite the entrance; to the right of it appeared a Venus, rich and radiant; to the left two smaller pieces, the one showing Orpheus in Hades, the other a vine-wreathed Bacchus. One of the window recesses held a chess-board of ebony inlaid with mother-of-pearl, the other a crystal vase filled with primroses and violets, the early gift of spring.

"I have much to ask of you," said the Elector to his councillor, when seated. "Let us begin by hearing your report concerning our recently instituted court of law. I entertain great hopes of the new appointment, the administration of justice being at its lowest ebb throughout the empire, arbitrariness often taking the place of right. There is room for improvement, indeed. John de Lune, the new judge, has been in office for some time now; is he likely to justify our hopes?"

"We could not have found a more able magistrate; none of his colleagues, though they are all men of intelligence, is equal to him in quickness of perception and uprightness of judgment, his integrity being beyond all praise. But he says the court is simply overwhelmed with lawsuits, which shows that a great want has been met, and that the people are thereby benefited."

"The matter has my sincerest wishes," remarked Albrecht; " may it prove a bright example for all Germany! But further—what of our new market regulations, and how have the people taken to them?"

Eitelwolf reported: "The inhabitants of Mainz are delighted that the butchers have been obliged to form a guild, like other trades, meeting in a common market; it is a great safeguard against unfair dealings, since the butchers are under obligation now to have a proper supply, to sell by weight, and keep their prices within the prescribed limits."

The Elector felt flattered by the evident success of his administrative arrangements, and said with satisfaction: "I am truly glad to meet the people's wants and wishes. I trust the Lord will at all times enlighten my understanding, that I may fulfil the duties of my august calling according to His will and to the well-being of our land! One thing more—what about the appointments of our court and the list of retainers?"

"The household and retinue are nearly complete. I made out seven commissions the day before yesterday, gaining an addition of sixty-eight horse."

"How is that?" inquired the Elector.

"Three of these last-installed knights are bound to furnish and accoutre twelve troopers each, which they are willing to do; each of the others providing eight."

"Well, let us hope we shall never need them—not for feud or warfare, that is. I am ambitious rather of being a prince of peace, and rule my people in happiness

Yet one thing more; how is it that mine eyes have not beheld Hutten these two days?"

Eitelwolf's features clouded. "The poor young knight is weakened by sickness. I watch him anxiously. It would be grievous to see him die, for I love him as a son, and great hopes for our country would be buried with him."

"He must not die!" said the Elector, "indeed he must not. He is not fit to think of Italy for a while; he shall go to Ems at our expense, and draw new health from its waters."

"God bless your grace!" exclaimed Eitelwolf warmly. "But I had almost forgotten a matter of importance, a letter, that is, which a messenger brought me late last night; it is from Reuchlin at Stuttgart."

"From our Reuchlin?" echoed Albrecht, with brightening eyes. "Tell me; I am glad at all times to hear of the bold champion for light and truth; the land is full of his fame, and people are in arms for or against him everywhere—tell me how it goes with him."

"He has had to battle through fresh trouble," reported the councillor, "for the Dominicans of Cologne, whom the Bishop of Spires had sentenced to silence with costs, have again broken the peace, appealing to various universities for support. And indeed they are upheld by four of our colleges, whose verdict they have published triumphantly, putting Reuchlin to the fear that the curse of heresy will yet be flung at him, if only after his death. He has called upon his Holiness, therefore——"

"He has done well," interrupted the Elector, greatly interested. "Leo the Tenth is a man of clear judgment, and he, too, loves the light. I can see how it ended."

"Yes, yes," rejoined Eitelwolf approvingly, "the Lord be praised, it came to a happy issue. Reuchlin, to be sure, was not left to speak for himself, since besides five bishops, thirteen abbots and fifty-three free cities, even the Emperor, testified to his pious course, the Duke of Bavaria and the Markgrave of Baden doing the same. In the face of such an array the Pope could not well condemn him, at the same time not daring to condemn the Dominicans either, since Hogstraten, the Inquisitor of Cologne, threatened with a revolt of the powerful order. Reuchlin would have expected a solemn acquittal by his Holiness; still he is amply compensated for any disappointment in this respect by the hearty sympathy of his many friends and adherents."

"Ourselves among the number!" cried the Elector enthusiastically. "Write and tell him so this very day, dear Eitelwolf; tell him that the Martinsburg at Mainz shall be open to receive and shelter him whenever he may need it. And this reminds me, Hutten has shown me lately a Latin poem of his entitled 'Reuchlin's Triumph.' That shall be printed at once now, that all the world may read it."

But Eitelwolf looked doubtful. "I, too, know the poem," he said; "it breathes fire and brimstone, after the fashion of our young friend. It would seem prudent to delay publishing it, lest premature triumph cheat Reuchlin out of the fulness of victory."

"You judge wisely," assented the Archbishop, after a pause. "Impart your opinion to friend Hutten."

CHAPTER IV.

THE ARCHBISHOP IN DIFFICULTY.

On a hot day in August, A.D. 1516, two courtiers holding earnest conversation went to and fro in the long dusky colonnade of the Martinsburg.

"You enjoy more of his grace's confidence than I," said the one, Burgrave Conrad von Echtingen; "can you tell me what is the matter with him? He has come back from Halle in the worst of tempers, and scarcely looked at the pomp of welcome with which this faithful town of Mainz greeted his return. He snubbed me out of my wits almost this morning when I solicited his attention to business."

Dr. Stromer, physician in ordinary to the Elector, stopped short at this question, looking about him cautiously to ascertain that no listeners were near, and then made answer: "There has been quite a combination of troubles overshadowing his grace's serener prospects. To begin with, the death of his chief councillor, Eitelwolf von Stein, has grieved him greatly, and although some months have passed the sense of loss continues. He really loved the noble knight, besides holding him in high esteem for his wisdom. But his mind is vexed with matters of other kind. Scarcely a day at Halle was free of annoyance. His very entry, usually an occasion of rejoicings, was made unpleasant, the people actually fixing upon the time to execute a Jew right in front of the palace windows. True, the delinquent stood accused, amongst other crimes, of having conspired against the Archbishop's life. It was an ugly beginning. And when his grace came to inquire into financial matters, courage almost forsook him: the coffers were simply empty. You know that things were not much better here at Mainz when he first entered upon his reign, but there was a chance of redress by means of a tax. He would fain have laid the archbishopric of Magdeburg under similar contribution, had the states of the province not put in an effectual bar. That sort of thing is not known here in the Electorate. It was vain that he summoned the ungracious representatives to reason with them by the mouth of his high steward, Count Stolberg, urging the fact that it was the late Archbishop who had contracted so alarming a debt; but though the prelates and the aristocracy were willing enough, the towns proved refractory, and no grant was made. This rebuff greatly nettled his grace's sensibility, casting quite a gloom upon his mind, and he was glad to leave Halle for his brighter dominions as soon as the most pressing business had been despatched. So he returned to Mainz, coming, forsooth, upon similar annoyance. His vice-regent has appeared before the Chapter, deprecating the miserable state of the finances; none of the public creditors receive interest, he says; the revenues seemed to go nowhere; debts were increasing, and unless the High Chapter came to the rescue the archiepiscopal Electorate was in imminent danger. The Markgrave of Baden alone has a claim of fifteen thousand gulden."

"Well, between ourselves," interposed the Burgrave, "I cannot but view most anxiously the Elector's taste for art and fancies of other kind; look at the immense cost of his courtly splendour, when there is but debt and debt around him! There ought to be but one law paramount—the law of saving and restraint."

"You are right, Burgrave," replied the physician. "I, too, stand aghast at the tremendous waste which has been going on ever since the Elector's accession. However, he himself seems to have perceived it at last, hence his moody irritability. But hush—here he comes!"

The two courtiers retired speedily, anxious to avoid a meeting.

Accompanied by a canon and a Dominican prior the Archbishop came slowly up the colonnade, leading the way presently to his cabinet. His forehead was clouded; the eyes, at other times so full of brightness, were overcast with trouble; his very step had lost in firmness; his voice, too, lacked fulness of sound.

"Tell me what to do," he said gloomily, having sunk into a chair. "The waters are closing over my head. How much did you say was the full extent of our debts?"

"If we include the thirty thousand gulden due to those Fuggers alone, the bankers of Augsburg, it is no less than eighty-six thousand gulden, so please your grace," said the canon, almost under his breath.

Albrecht groaned, passing a jewelled hand through his hair. "Those Fuggers, indeed! How *are* they to be satisfied? Their clamouring for payment is insupportable. They add interest upon interest; it is a crushing burden. Tell me what to do!"

The canon looked diffidently into vacancy.

"I wish I could advise your electoral grace to any purpose," he said, after a while. "What is to be done, indeed? To levy fresh taxes when the old ones are still to be enforced is impossible. If you order the cutting of timber in the Spessart, it might bring in a few thousand gulden, but what of that? Unless we hit upon resources more productive than this, we might as well——"

He hesitated; there was a pause of painful silence, broken at last by the prior, who had held his peace so far.

"I have thought of an expedient that might obviate all difficulty," he said, "if so be that it would suit your electoral grace."

"Speak without 'ifs'!" cried Albrecht, almost rudely.

The prior half closed his eyes till they all but vanished in the fat folds of his visage, and continued blandly—

"Your grace no doubt is aware that his Holiness, for the finishing of St. Peter's and other pious purposes, has proclaimed a general indulgence. If you could farm a part of this revenue for the Holy Father, say within your own diocese, your troubles would soon be ended."

The Archbishop stared at his tempter with the strangest mixture of greed and wrath, almost unseating the worthy prior. After a while he said:—

"I am indeed aware of this new device, but never dreamt of participating in a work which may bring gains to the Pope, if little honour, and must be displeasing to God; for the sellers of indulgences, whatever their traffic may be worth, seem to consider themselves licensed for all manner of mischief. The princes disapprove of their subjects being robbed, on the plea that these doings are sanctioned by the Pope; and even the common people here and there suspect that such a work can scarcely be done in the service of God. Some of the clergy even have been moved to discountenance it in the pulpit, perceiving it to be full of abuse. Would you indeed counsel us to assist the Pope in a matter which might be productive of plenty of money and plenty of disgrace withal?"

The prior shook his bald head. "I pray your electoral highness to forgive my dissenting entirely. We all know that there is nothing so holy but it is open to abuse, and abuse does not lessen holiness. Would you doubt forgiveness of sin because some brazen-faced monks, by way of filling their coffers, assure the believing people that the groschens they part with for release from temporal punishment are the key also to Paradise, and a means of saving them from the pains of hell?"

"I quite agree with the prior," broke in the canon. "And I pray your electoral grace to lay hold of this expedient when aught else seems to fail."

The Elector jumped from his seat, overthrowing the chair in his excitement. His flushed face and trembling features betokened the conflict in his mind. His clear understanding saw through the traffic of indulgence; he abhorred it as an insult to the Church itself, and, moreover, he could not but think of his friends among the humanists. What would *they* say, if one of these days the news should be whispered: Archbishop

Albrecht himself has soiled his hands with the despicable traffic ? Would he not have to hide himself in utter shame ? Would they not turn their backs upon him from the moment that he lowered himself to the depth contemplated by the prior ? But, after all, was not his distress a more urgent consideration than all this ? Was it not ever present, like some terrible spectre, chasing away aught else that might be a warning in temptation ? Conflicting thoughts ran high in his soul, causing him an agony of doubt. He broke forth at last with a "Get ye gone, both of you ! This evening you may return, prior, and hear my mind."

The two men took their leave with an obsequious bow, and Albrecht was alone.

He sat down upon a couch, supporting his head with his hand. He had longed to be alone, but, no sooner left to himself, he wished the prior back that he might share his misery, and help him to wind his way out of this dilemma.

He could not rest. He rang for his valet, and received him with such a volley of abuse that the poor fellow stood rooted to the ground. He had carried out his master's injunctions carefully as ever; this very morning he had received marks of the Archbishop's favour—what had happened, that all at once he should be found fault with as an awkward, good-for-nothing menial ?

"Why do you keep standing here with this fool's face of yours ?" cried the irritated hierarch, utterly dumbfounding the startled servant. "Retire !"

Again the Archbishop was left to his thoughts. The air about him grew more and more oppressive. He opened a casement, thirsting for the cool breezes of heaven ; but they had fled the place, the atmosphere was sultry and pregnant with thunder. His eye for a moment rested on the town, the high roofs of which seemed burnished with a deep red glow.

His hand gave a sudden wrench at the bell. The valet reappeared.

"Have the white barb saddled and brought round at once!" Within a quarter of an hour the Elector dashed through the town gate, turning his horse's head to the forest beyond.

The poor steed was no better off than the valet had been; there was no pleasing his unreasonable rider. Slackening in pace, the cruel spur would lacerate his flanks; quickening to a gallop, there was pull upon pull at the mouth; the willing creature could nowise be in harmony with so capricious a master. That master, indeed, continued in the worst of moods. Everything about him seemed to add to his annoyance; the glowing sun, the toiling reapers in the harvest-field, singing as though they were light-hearted, the little birds hopping from branch to branch heedless of care—was no one miserable but he, the Archbishop? Must they needs all conspire to shoot arrows at his despair?

Deep into the forest he rode, not looking whither, and when a low clap of thunder roused him at last he knew not where he was. This was more than he could brook; an unfortunate keeper, whose hut happened to be near, had to bear the brunt of his anger, as though he were committing a great crime by inhabiting a cottage so far away from the purlieus of the town.

Guided on his way the Elector returned to the city; the bells of churches and chapels were ringing evensong; the threatening storm, too, came nearer and nearer. He rode at a full gallop, but decision as to his course of action had not come to him in the wood.

When he entered his palace-yard dinner had been kept waiting for half an hour already—a fresh grievance, for the epicure desired his food cooked to a nicety. He dined by himself to-day, company was hateful. Having arrived at the third course the sound of horses' hoofs broke upon his ear.

He stepped to the window. "Who has business here, this time of day?" he murmured, little pleased. "Good heavens, the Markgrave of Baden's own livery! What can he be wanting?"

There was no more dining; the Archbishop walked the room impatiently, guessing but too well the import of this embassy. Nor was he mistaken; the Markgrave's message was to the effect that the loan in question must be repaid within a month.

That settled matters; the Archbishop arrived at his conclusion. The Dominican prior was sent for

"I have carefully weighed this question," said his grace, when the monk appeared; "I have decided to follow your advice. I dislike it cordially, but necessity is hard upon me."

The prior bent low, to hide the satisfaction gleaming from his eyes. 'Your grace has chosen the good part," he said; "you will yet thank your faithful servant for his helpful counsel. Let it not trouble your conscience, for in this case your conscience is not with you, but at Rome. It is not you who have set going the sale of indulgences—it is the Pope's doing; and if there is any responsibility of wrong connected with the business, it is not you who are accountable for it, but he whose invention it is.".

The Elector gave a long wistful glance into the evil countenance of the monk, but holding out his hand presently he said: "Thank you! Early to-morrow I will despatch a messenger to Rome; he shall fetch me the Pope's sanction for farming part of the revenues accruing from the sale of indulgences. I have little doubt but that his Holiness will be agreeable, for he has reason to oblige the Primate of all Germany. But I doubt me where I shall find the right man for the work. Sit down, and advise me in this matter also. Is there none among your friars who might be recommended for the business? I say *your* friars, for it appears to me that your order chiefly cultivates the ready tongue, which is more useful with the common people than all manner of learning."

The prior seemed lost in thought, replying after a while, "Well, there are several amongst us whom I could propose to your electoral grace, and, indeed, one man would scarcely suffice if the Pope allowed you a tolerable domain. To begin with, there is Iodocus Lorcher, doctor of church law in this very place; next I might mention George Behaim, dean of St. Laurence's at Nürnberg; John Neubar, also, vicar at Würzburg, is likely to be useful. But greatly do I lament that a fourth I could mention is quite beyond the reach of your grace. He could do more than all the three put together; if we had him there would be a speedy influx of gold filling your coffers."

"Who is this paragon?" queried the Archbishop, wondering.

"A brother of ours, Tetzel by name," said the prior.

"Ha! I know him!" ejaculated Albrecht. "You are right, there is none like him for harvesting. I

TETZEL.
From G. Hechtius' Vita J. Tetzeli.

remember his success at Görlitz in 1506; I was a student at Frankfort at the time. He had been gleaning in the neighbourhood for six weeks, and was going to betake himself to another field of labour, when the magistrates of the town begged him to assist them in raising the means for replacing the worn-out shingle roof of their church with one of copper. Mind you, he had had the best of the land already, and yet he managed an after-gleaning of forty-five thousand rix-dollars in about three weeks! Yes, he would seem the man for our purpose. You say he is beyond our reach. Where is he?"

"Where he would rather not be," said the prior, shrugging his shoulders. "Locked up at Leipzig, I am sorry to say."

"In prison! What has he done to be there?"

The prior would rather not have explained, but the Elector desiring information, he gave it. "Brother Tetzel was at Innsbruck some two years since, and found himself in a sorry plight; his life, indeed, was not worth a day's purchase. The people had dragged him to the river-side, and were going to throw him over the bridge, tied up in a sack; the Emperor's letter of grace arrived at the very nick of time."

"Then Tetzel had forgotten the seventh commandment?" inquired the Archbishop.

"It is a weak point with him," owned the prior.

"But how could Maximilian care to save him?"

"Tetzel owes that to the intervention of his own Elector, Frederick of Saxony; the Emperor commuted the sentence to prison for life. It is sad indeed that the man who might still be doing great things for the Church should be shut up in a dungeon of the Dominicans at Leipzig, dead, to all intents and purposes."

"Dead! no, we will resuscitate him!" cried the Archbishop excitedly. "I am in good favour with the Emperor; it is but a few days ago that he offered me the regency during his probable absence from the empire. He will not deny me the culprit's pardon; and our dilemma will be solved."

The prior's countenance radiated as he left the Elector's apartment.

The following morning a man-at-arms dashed from the courtyard of the Martinsburg, followed by a couple of grooms with sumpter horses. A long journey lay before him; he was intrusted with a mission from the Archbishop Elector of Mainz to the Pope at Rome, praying for an assignment of part of the proposed indulgence, that he might farm its revenues for his holiness.

About a month later a lonely pilgrim turned his back upon the town of Leipzig; his face, too, was directed to the city of the seven hills. It was Brother Tetzel, freed from prison at the intercession of the Elector Primate. He was on his way to the Pope to kneel for forgiveness. But his appearance was not that of a man who had suffered want in prison; a Dominican dungeon would seem to offer consolation to unlucky inmates— his face was round, his gait that of a hopeful man. He knew what the Pope owed him, he trusted to his merits as a trafficker of indulgences, which would outweigh at Rome any knowledge of his crimes.

Nor was he mistaken; his reception proving favourable beyond expectation. The convict-pilgrim recrossed the Alps carrying his head proudly; for not only had he received papal absolution, but had been found worthy of the dignity of Inquisitor Apostolic for Germany.

CHAPTER V.

FALLING AWAY.

"WHAT wool-gathering have you been after, Balthasar? The bread is heavy, and burned to a cinder!"

Master Riedinger, the peace-loving, good-natured man, was really vexed with the youth who had served for seven years in his bakehouse, who had been apprenticed with him as a boy, and had grown both into the business and into his master's confidence. And Balthasar was indeed worthy of all trust; he thoroughly understood the baking, and was faithful to the core of his honest heart. One need but look at him to make sure that one liked him, with his healthy, pleasant countenance, and those blue eyes of his, which never dreamt of harm. Yet dreams had come to him lately; he had blundered once or twice when he ought to have been wide awake. The truth was that of an evening, when he had retired to his little room, he would sit by his window peering across the narrow yard to another casement, longingly hopeful to see his heart's desire. And if she did appear, the lovely creature, his eye grew sad with the sorrow within. How near him she dwelt—the fairest of maidens, Margaret, his master's child—and yet how far!

It had not been so always. She used to look upon him kindly, not loth to accept his willing service, nor did she withdraw her girlish hand when he took it at times to wish her a happy day. She was his child-queen from the first, and the parents did not object that their little girl should haunt the bakeroom with a friendly interest. Master Riedinger, especially, would entertain worthy hopes: "If this Balthasar will stay with us, and be as a son to me, I shall say nothing against it."

But these early dreams somehow would not come true. Margaret was no child now, and her womanly beauty grew more brilliant day by day. Mistress Ursula, her mother, saw it, and was filled with thoughts of pride. "Your Margaret is the handsomest girl in the town," people would say; of course she believed it, and her vanity grew in proportion. "She is too good for that Balthasar," she decided presently; "a better one than he shall have her."

Indeed, Margaret Riedinger could not cross the streets now without drawing all eyes after her, those of men especially, who were simply fascinated. And if a stranger chanced to behold her, he would scarcely believe that she was but a baker's daughter of Mainz. Her beauty had something astonishingly commanding; there was an elegance of bearing about her as though she came of an ancestry of kings—and how lovely was her face, with those deep blue eyes and long silken lashes! These eyes could speak, and one could look through them into a depth of slumbering passion. Her forehead was high and thoughtful; her blonde hair silken and wavy—the whole creature a very vision of beauty; no wonder she drew all eyes! She was tall beyond her kind, but that added only to the majesty of her perfection. She was an adept too in the art of dress; she knew what suited her, and understood how to clothe her charms. There was that in her beauty which might be a good man's delight, and was sure to be a weak man's perdition.

Did she know what people thought and said of her prospects? If she did not find it out for herself, her mother did, and Mistress Ursula was not one to hide her foolish hopes.

Margaret, therefore, began to withdraw her favours from Balthasar, taking the barest notice of his existence. But the less he occupied her attention, the more need she seemed to find to show herself at the sitting-room windows, which commanded the street; there were flowers to be tended, and, that excuse failing, she drew her distaff to the casement.

Balthasar saw it all, and it cut him to the heart; he was not ashamed of tears even on his lonely pillow. Yet he hoped against hope till that happened which put out the last faint gleam, and he knew that all was at an end.

Let us cast a look through the lozenge-paned window and the flowering geraniums behind. There is a round table in the midst of the spacious apartment, and Margaret, with folded hands, standing like one in a trance; it is but a red velvet casket which so moves her, a-glitter with trinkets and costly gems. The sparkling things seem to have called up a kindred gleam in her eyes, yet two large tears trickled down her face. Her father had just declared that not with a finger should she touch that jewellery. He could not imagine, he said, what the Elector could be thinking of; he, Master Riedinger, was not aware of having done anything particular that need be rewarded with such marks of favour. It almost looked as if that lurked behind which he would not soil his lips by even naming.

Margaret held her peace, and secretly wished her mother were at home, who was absent on a visit to a sick sister.

Mistress Ursula, however, returned the following day, her daughter losing no time in telling her the wonderful news.

And now the worthy master had the worst of it, his wife declaring, unhesitatingly, that he had better look after his loaves only, that being about all his understanding seemed fit for. It was a pity he did not see the honour intended for his child. His electoral grace was known to have an eye for merit, and a heart for the recompensing of virtue according to its own deserts. Men differed in gifts: some were clever, some were rich, others had the power of wielding blows; but if a girl had a pretty face, well, that was *her* gift—why should she be barred from her rightful reward?

The honest master did not quite follow the logic of this reasoning, he even ventured to express decided doubts; it seemed a great deal more plain, he argued, that an electoral present and his daughter's beauty were not things that should have any common relation, nor could he understand that a pretty face could possibly be a virtue that needed reward. But he had a ducking for his pains, and fairly ran for shelter—his wife's volubility, when roused, being a very waterspout of feminine ire.

He took refuge in the bakehouse. Balthasar was there. It must have been the feeling of some common grief which made him speak kindly to the youth, turning to him unconsciously with the helpless hope that the stalwart young man might yet be the warder-off of pitiful ruin.

Balthasar, in sooth, was grateful for the master's kindness, but his sorrow was none the less poignant, for he knew what had passed in the dwelling-room, and knew now that Margaret for him was lost; for the mistress was master in the house whenever opinions differed, the youth was aware of that. The desire came upon him to warn the poor master, begging him to have an eye to his only child, for those who aspired high might come to fall; but he refrained, pressing his lips together closely.

It was some days after this that in the hush of the evening there was a knock at Master Riedinger's door, and, the women responding, there appeared the muffled figure of a man, for it poured with rain; but the hiding cloak could not hide the majestic portliness of his bearing. He was followed by one more humble in appearance, carrying some closely covered object.

"All blessing to you," said the former with a deep, melodious voice, divesting himself of his mantle—it was Albrecht himself, the Archbishop Elector.

Margaret, who had been sitting by the window, blushed scarlet, feeling spell-bound and unable to move. Was it terror or delight stealing through her every fibre? She dared not breathe.

Mistress Ursula, who had been busy peeling turnips, recovered first. "Maria Joseph! His grace the

Elector!" she cried, and bustling up from her household concerns, wiping her hands on her apron, she dropped courtesy upon courtesy. "What honour!" she gasped, "what undeserved favour! Who are we that your electoral highness should grace our humble abode! Alack-a-day! we have not even thanked your highness for the jewellery sent to our Margaret; but it is not my fault—holy Joseph, no! My husband would have none of it; he is clever enough to bake his bread, and there has been some talk already of his being made master of the guild, but——"

"Never mind, my good woman," interrupted his grace, "I have not come to upbraid you. My little present was meant to please this child of yours, of whose beauty and virtue we have heard. It is meet for the violet to bloom in the shade, but the queenly rose is fit for the sunlight. Where high-born damsels vie for the palm, there I should like to see the maiden Margaret; and the prize of beauty would be hers, I ween."

Mistress Ursula stood open-mouthed; the Elector's language soared above her brain. "I am a humble woman," she stammered; "I do not quite take in your gracious meaning."

"Then let me speak plain," said the Archbishop, smiling benignly. "There will be a tournament at our court, which will be attended by many knights and high-born ladies. I should like your daughter to be of the number, and, to make sure of your consent, I have brought the invitation in person."

The foolish mother fairly rubbed her eyes for gratitude; it was too touching, she thought, and said so, forgetful of all pretence at decorum. Her noble visitor, however, took no umbrage whatever, for he knew now that he had not called in vain.

"But we have only plain worsted clothing," continued Ursula, somewhat embarrassed; "what will she look like, by the side of their silks and satins?"

"Have no fear, good woman," returned the Elector; "we ourselves have thought of this." At a sign from his lord the servant now stepped forward, and from the covering folds of his cloak he produced a parcel, which contained nothing less than a dress of rose-coloured silk trimmed with the daintiest of Brabant laces and a profusion of pearls.

Mistress Ursula was dumb with delight, a gentle sob by the window breaking upon her silence.

The Elector turned towards Margaret with his most winning countenance: "Shall I have the pleasure, then, honoured maiden, of witnessing your triumph?"

Again Margaret blushed scarlet, a great wave of anticipating joys rushing through her being, and falling to her knees she said softly, "I am not worthy of the honour!"

The Elector took the girl's small, delicately-shaped hand, holding it a while within his own; raising her presently, his left hand rested on her waving hair as he said, "We knew we should find thee a good child!" And turning to the mother with a kindly remark he took his leave.

There was silence in the room for several minutes; then Margaret hastened away and returned with a lighted lamp.

They had not half seen the splendour in the deepening twilight. And now they stood, mother and daughter, scarcely venturing to touch the courtly dress with a finger. Did they understand the price to be paid for it? Their eyes were aglow with eager delight. Vanity at present was uppermost.

Mistress Ursula at last lifted the finery with the tip of her fingers. "Hold still, child," she said; "let us see how it suits you."

And suit it did, fitting her shape as though made for her. The mother could not cease for pride, turning the girl about and about, as though she had never seen her. Could so splendid a creature indeed be Margaret Riedinger, the baker's daughter of Mainz? Did she not look like a maiden of high degree, a princess at least? The foolish mother's heart leapt for joy; impatiently she wished her husband home, who was at a meeting of the guild.

He returned presently, standing transfixed in the doorway, bolt upright with surprise. "God's thunder!" he exclaimed, rubbing his eyes, "what has happened? Is this our Margaret, or——"

"Who else should it be?" cried Mistress Ursula impatiently. "Of course it is our Margaret! I hope you are ashamed of yourself now for having spoken as you did concerning our gracious Elector. He has just been here—his very own self—with one of his chamberlains, to invite our child to the tournament, providing her with a dress, moreover. There, look—isn't she a beauty to be proud of? He is not far wrong if he thinks her worthy to sit among the noble ladies of his court, for that is what he means her to do. I told you he had an eye for merit—he knows what is beautiful, he does; the baker's child of Mainz will not disgrace him."

The master scarcely knew whether he was in his right mind. What was this he heard? The Elector had been in his dwelling-room, with a chamberlain? Invited his daughter to attend the tournament, and brought her a dress? Perhaps, after all, he had wronged the great lord with his suspicions!

He said something to this effect, smoothing away the last obstacle in the path of his daughter; both Margaret and her mother revelled in expectant bliss.

. . . . .

After a while it was noised abroad that a baker's daughter of Mainz had found favour in high quarters; she has been invited to court, and takes her place among the ladies of birth and rank. And she likes it so much that she has no desire to return to her humble home. Her father, when his eyes were opened, tried to resist it, calling things by ugly names; but the mother viewed them differently, whereupon he subsided into mournful silence.

One dark evening the house door of Master Riedinger opened softly; a young man came forth with knapsack and travelling staff. Having crossed the street he turned with a last wistful look upon the window whence the lamplight followed him as a parting benediction. "Fare thee well, thou spot of my fondest dreams," he said, "of my deepest sorrow!" And with a last sigh he grasped his staff, turning his back upon the "golden city" with a manly resolution.

CHAPTER VI.

BOUND FOR MAINZ.

ONE hot afternoon in July, 1517, a lonely traveller sat in his room at the "Red Cock" of Spires, on the Rhine; he had his wallet before him, which seemed to hold more books than travelling comforts, and having found at last what he looked for, he sat down by the table.

It was a poverty-stricken figure, most insignificant in appearance; he seemed about fifty, his face was pale and furrowed, his eyes deep set, but capable of a wondrous light when he raised them. The narrow, bloodless lips were firmly closed, a smile of exquisite sarcasm flitting about them. There was nothing striking about this traveller at first sight; but the landlord evidently was of different opinion, seeing that he always received the stranger's orders standing humbly by the door.

And the man, in truth, belied his appearance. That insignificant body held one of the greatest minds of the age. It was Desiderius Erasmus.

Erasmus and Reuchlin were, as Ulrich von Hutten said, the two eyes of Germany, her morning stars ushering in a new day. They were not the sun themselves, but heralds they were, announcing the sun about to rise. Among the men who had taken up the great conflict against darkness and superstition, against spiritual slavery and sacerdotal deceit; who did their utmost to quit the quagmires of a stagnating period for heights where the breath of heaven might blow, and were anxious to draw men after them into a new liberty of mind, Erasmus and Reuchlin took a leading position. When the Middle Ages had outlived themselves and died, the school of the humanists turned to the long-lost waters of classic learning, hoping to quench their own thirst thereby, and that of the people. Reuchlin was a Hebrew scholar, and Erasmus famous for his knowledge of Greek.

He had now come from Bâle, where he had the New Testament printed in the original, and was returning to Brussels, at the court of which town he had found an honourable retreat.

Being startled from his meditation by an unexpected knock at the door, he looked up from his book; a youthful knight had entered with beaming face, and now caught hold of his hand, exclaiming: "God greet you, reverend father! How glad I am to have tracked you at last!"

Erasmus, no less delighted, rose to his feet, holding out both hands to the visitor. "Hutten, my own Hutten, my soul rejoices at thy sight! Be welcome, thou brave one; let me look into thine eyes, thou great one, crowned as thou art by the Emperor himself with the laureate's diadem! I am indeed proud of thee, Ulrich mine; thou art an honour to all of us, and thy name will be cherished by future generations. I owe thee special thanks, moreover, for having acted as my physician extraordinary, quite restoring me to bodily health."

Hutten looked at his learned friend amazed, not understanding his meaning.

Erasmus continued with a smile: "I was ill, thou must know, suffering of a troublesome boil, which Esculapius could neither get to break nor disperse, when I came across the *Epistolæ Obscurorum Virorum*, that masterpiece of wit which has done more to hold up the 'darklings' in their true light, than all the books since gone forth against them from the humanists' camp. And as the whole of Europe burst into laughter at these wonderful letters, I needs must laugh too, and so heartily did I laugh that, behold, my boil has burst. That is why I call thee my physician extraordinary!"

It was Hutten's turn now to laugh. "Has that report come to your ears even?" he cried. "Everybody will have it it is I who wrote those letters; yet such is not the case."

"Don't pretend to deceive thine own master!" said Erasmus, with playful seriousness. "As if I did not know thy pen; and I admire thee for that masterpiece. It was a delicious thought to let those owls of monks confess their secret thoughts to one another in a series of fictitious letters, showing to all the world the depth of their ignorance and of their lazy, immoral lives."

Hutten looked at his master with a smile of intelligence. "I know," he said; "and if you like I will tell you all about it. I will not deny that I had a hand in the making of that little book, but only here and there; most of it is due to Crotus Rubianus and Eobanus Hesse. A few others too had a finger in the pie."

ERASMUS.

"Well," said Erasmus, rubbing his hands for sheer delight, "be that as it may, the little book rejoiced my soul, and, as I tell thee, my boil could not stand it. But sit down now and let me hear how you fared. I know nothing of your doings since you went to Bologna to study the laws."

Hutten sat down on a low seat by his master, and, half emptying a jug of beer which the latter hospitably had filled for him, he began his report.

"I have spent a year at the Italian university, but when the hot season came upon us, I packed up my traps and recrossed the Alps. I had set my face towards Augsburg. And there a surprise was in store for me of which I never dreamt; friend Conrad Peutinger was at the bottom of it. In her withdrawing chamber the lovely Constance, his own fair daughter, made a wreath of laurel. Little thinking what might be its object, I watched the pretty white hands, admiring how deftly they proceeded. The following day I was sent for to the Emperor's presence. A brilliant assembly had gathered around him; all eyes turned upon me, and at Maximilian's desire the maiden Constance crowned me poet with that self-same laurel crown. I was as in a dream, scarcely hearing the Emperor's most kind and flattering words; only this I remember, or something to this effect, with which he concluded: 'Because you, Ulrich von Hutten, have added the nobility of learning to that of your birth, we have considered you worthy to receive a mark of our approval. It is our imperial desire that you should be honoured with the laurel and the golden ring; we name you poet and orator, and hold you entitled to teach the art of poetry and rhetoric at any of our universities, bestowing upon you moreover all its privileges, honours, and favours, enjoyed by other crowned poets and orators, according to usage and right. And, in order to give you a more special mark of our favour, we grant you the protection of our imperial person and of this holy realm; you shall be justiciable henceforth to no judge but the Emperor alone.'"

"You happy mortal!" cried Erasmus, with hearty sympathy, again pressing Hutten's hand. "And what are your further plans now?"

Hutten hesitated, playing with his sword-hilt, but saying presently: "Friend Peutinger rather pressed me to remain at court and bask in the sunshine of imperial favour, but I could not make up my mind."

"Why not?" returned Erasmus quickly. "The poet should be where the prince is, for both are rulers of men."

"No doubt you are right, honoured master," rejoined Hutten, "and indeed it was my intention to attach myself to court; not the Emperor's however—gratitude would seem to call me elsewhere."

"Ah, I guess your meaning," broke in Erasmus; "it is Mainz which draws you. Archbishop Albrecht has a claim on your gratitude, I own. I also propose taking Mainz on my way, so we can continue our road together."

Hutten moved on his chair, embarrassed. "You interrupted what I was going to say, much honoured father. I have become doubtful concerning my original intention. I seem to have lost confidence in his grace of Mainz. Indeed, I could hardly believe my ears when I heard that Archbishop Albrecht has succumbed to temptation; that he has lowered himself to the position of the Pope's accomplice in this vile matter of indulgences; that he has not been ashamed to use his influence for getting out of prison that scoundrel Tetzel, starting him afresh with his diabolical money-chest. This news has cast a great gloom over my otherwise happy days. How is it possible that Albrecht, a man of high-mindedness and intellect, the lover of art and letters, can stoop to soiling his hands with the abominable traffic, the invention of miserable priestcraft? How is it possible, I ask——"

"Stop, stop!" cried Erasmus. "The excitement of youth should not run away with you; you must judge of things more calmly. Archbishop Albrecht is still with us, and there is no reason why you should lose confidence in him. You should have seen how he laughed at the letters of the 'darklings'! He was delighted, he said, that the hooded owls were drawn to the light for once; and he who had written the book was worth his weight in gold."

"Then I don't understand him!" cried Hutten. "How is it, I pray you?"

"Well," said Erasmus, taking off his little cap and wiping his forehead, for the day was hot and the room low-ceiled and stuffy, "to tell the plain truth, he saw no other way out of his difficulty. You know what a weight of debt there is upon him; he vainly tried all other resources, and nothing seemed left at last but this one expedient—he farms part of the revenues for the Pope. It did cost him a hard struggle with conscience, but he yielded, leaving all responsibility with him who set going this work of indulgence. Matters would scarcely have been much better if he had *not* yielded; for then the Archbishops of Treves and

Cologne would have snatched at the gain, and Albrecht would only have been a loser of what, situated as he is, he cannot afford to lose. He has been successful so far, for Tetzel understands his business; the Archbishop has already been enabled to pay off the Fuggers, which is a good thing, for his liabilities to that banking concern were immense."

Hutten looked bewildered. "Am I so young or so innocent," he murmured, "that I am unable to perceive the force of such reasoning?"

"Yes, you are young," said Erasmus, laying a fatherly hand upon his shoulder. "Youth would push ahead where old age treads circumspectly. As a whirlwind you would burst upon the worm-eaten structure; and you might succeed in laying low what no doubt ought to be laid low. But what will you give instead? The building up is not so easy—what of the building up? Things need time; good things especially are slow of growth. The Archbishop judges rightly, perhaps, in thinking that the people cannot be brought from darkness into light all at once, that the stronghold of superstition must be undermined by degrees, and that we are not powerful enough as yet for the work we would do. Those who would fight for light and liberty must first join their efforts, must use their own eyes to the light, as it were, before they will shower a blessing upon the people—which might prove a curse if it comes before they are ready to receive it. Therefore, I say, Archbishop Albrecht is still as one of ourselves, and you may trust him; see if he does not receive you with open arms. Go, therefore, and help him as you may be able, that he shall remain true to our cause and true to his own better self."

"I will," said Hutten, with earnest resolve. "If you think so, I may give over my doubts; and indeed I can always leave him again, should I find him faithless to the flag we hold aloft unflinchingly. Yet I cannot go to Mainz at once and in your company; I long to see my father's house again; and I long for the quiet of Burg Steckelberg for another reason, intending to finish some work there, of which I hope you may hear before long."

"May I not hear about it now?" said Erasmus, smiling, and not without curiosity.

"I ask your leave, much honoured father, for keeping my own counsel yet a while," returned Hutten. "I trust it will not be long! Meantime fare you well!"

The two men shook hands and parted, each zealous and well-meaning in his own way; but the true light was hidden.

CHAPTER VII.

DOMINICAN AND AUGUSTINIAN.

"BAD tidings I bring you, as bad as the weather ushering in this month of November!" With these words the prior, whose acquaintance we have made in a former chapter, entered the chamber where the Elector Archbishop, sitting by the side of Margaret Riedinger, enjoyed an early meal. "Evil tidings, so please your grace, from Saxony!"

The Elector, who had liked his wine and his oysters, did not like a disagreeable announcement. Handsome Margaret, too, annoyed at interruption, treated the new-comer to such a look of anger that the features of her brilliant face quite suffered in consequence. She saw fit to bear the prior a general grudge, not approving of his advancement in the Archbishop's confidence, which he abused, she thought, almost venturing to put himself between Albrecht and her, his chosen companion.

"What has happened?" inquired the Elector, putting back the disordered hair from his forehead.

"Tetzel has come to grief!" said the prior.

"Oh no, not ill, surely!" exclaimed the Elector.

"No, not ill," echoed the prior.

"Not dead either! That would be all too soon, for, much as he has enabled me to satisfy those Fuggers and the Markgrave of Baden—nay, many another creditor besides—I could ill miss it if the trafficker stopped sending gold to our treasury."

The prior shook his head. "His life is safe enough, but his traffic, I fear me, may come to an untimely end."

"And why so?" queried Albrecht, anxiously.

"There has appeared one stronger than he, likely to stop his proceedings."

The Elector's eyes opened wider and wider, yet not understanding, he said impatiently, "Speak plain, and tell me what it is."

And the prior, coming a step closer, told what he knew. "Tetzel, going about the country, came to the neighbourhood of Wittenberg, where an Augustinian took sore umbrage at his doings, so much so that he dared refuse absolution to any person coming to him with an indulgence given by Tetzel, whom he called ugly and wicked names. And more than this, he has put up ninety-five theses at the Schlosskirche of Wittenberg, concerning the traffic of indulgences, intending to make it a subject of open disputation. These theses are even now running through the country like wildfire; they seem the one subject of conversation everywhere. A pedlar coming from Nürnberg has just told me, and is astonished that we at Mainz should still be ignorant of the event. He says that everywhere, on the high roads even, people are hotly discussing the Wittenberg theses."

"Is that all?" said Albrecht, resettling himself on

his comfortable couch. "Are these your evil tidings? Am I to be frightened with mere monkish palaver?" And he smiled superciliously.

But the prior looked serious, raising a fat finger of warning. "Take it not lightly, most noble Elector! They are but theses stuck to a church door—yes, but if even before the intended disputation they have flown through the length and breadth of the land as on the wings of a storm-swept commotion, gaining people's attention everywhere, that is more than monkish palaver, as you please to call it."

The Elector waved a careless hand. "A storm raises dust, we know, but the commotion will subside. It is not for the first time that monks have thought to shake the foundations of the earth."

"But this Augustinian is reported to be a man of clear understanding, having a tongue, they say, afraid of no man," continued the prior.

Albrecht laughed aloud. "As if Tetzel had not a tongue of his own! It will do him good to learn to hold it; indeed, I shall thank the Augustinian if he will teach him this lesson, for Tetzel has often annoyed me by the impudent way with which he carries on his business, even daring to flourish about the archiepiscopal name, to the great detriment of our honour. If wherever he goes he sets up a hullabaloo of fancy stalls, merry-go-rounds, lottery shops, with a menagerie of animals, and rope-dancing besides, this we might excuse; he understands his business, and is clever at attracting the people. But the sahmeless falsehoods of his preaching, his saying he would not change with St. Peter himself, and that by means of his letters of indulgence he passed more souls into heaven than the chief of the apostles; his telling the people the Lord had delegated all His power to the Pope, reserving nothing for Himself until the day of judgment, his daring inventions concerning the papal cross of indulgence, from which he said living blood had flown, being the blood of Christ Himself—all this has greatly moved my resentment. I have heard, too, that Tetzel and his band spend part of their daily gains holding unpermissible carousings at night. I have sent an attorney of the Fuggers after him, requesting Tetzel to give up the keys of his money-chests; but the rascal knew how to indemnify himself. The accounts show plainly that he requires no less than eighty gulden per month for himself, ten for his servant, apart from what he charges for their own maintenance and the keep of three horses. And there is no saying what he may not embezzle and purloin besides! I have long been desirous of reprimanding him for these grievous faults; if this Augustinian has forestalled me, well, I cannot be angry. Tetzel will learn to act with more prudence."

"It is too late to think of improvement," remarked the prior. "He will have to retire altogether; the people, I hear, turn against him everywhere, and pelt him with mud instead of giving their groschens."

The Elector frowned. "Do not exaggerate, prior. You repeat from hearsay, and we know how news is added to from mouth to mouth."

"If I have said more than is true," replied the prior, "I shall be glad to correct myself."

A door was being opened; a chamberlain coming forward announced an Augustinian monk just arrived with a message to his electoral highness.

"An Augustinian?" repeated Albrecht quickly. "And whence is he?"

"From Wittenberg, your grace!" said the chamberlain. There was a pause of speechless surprise, broken by the Elector.

"Let him enter!" said he.

A young, healthy-looking monk, barefooted and black-gowned, appeared on the threshold, humbly crossing his hands and bending his head with a "Praised be Jesus Christ!"

"Now and evermore, amen!" responded the Archbishop. "What is thy message? Say on."

"I bear a letter to your electoral grace, indited by brother Martin, Professor at the University of Wittenberg, and Doctor of Holy Writ."

And from within the folds of his garment he produced a scroll, handing it reverentially to the Elector.

The latter, opening it at once, glanced through it quickly, dismissing the monk with a wave of the hand; the prior, too, who would fain have remained, received leave to retire; Margaret, on the contrary, though about to rise, was invited to remain.

"Sit still," he said, addressing his fair companion when they were left alone, "thou shalt hear what brother Martin has to say to the Archbishop, for thou art the sharer of my every secret; what I would not tell my closest friend, I would not hide from thee, for part of myself thou art, and the sunshine of my life."

He drew her close, and she listened to him in silent rapture.

"This is the letter," he continued, after a while; "it is written in Latin, but I will translate it for thee as best I can.

"'Grace and mercy from God, with all my soul, Most Reverend Father in the Lord, most serene Elector! I intreat your highness most graciously to bear with me, that I, the lowest and least of men, should dare to think of, nay, write a letter to your reverence. The Lord Jesus is my witness that I am not unmindful of my own lowliness, wherefore I have long delayed this writing which I am now emboldened to undertake. I am chiefly moved thereto by the faithful service of which I own myself debtor to your electoral grace, most reverend father in God. May your reverence therefore look graciously upon me, who am but dust and ashes, listening to my desire according to your episcopal forbearance.

"'The Pope's indulgence for the building of St. Peter's at Rome is being hawked about the land under your electoral grace's own name and title. And it is not so much the great to-do of the traffickers I would rebuke, as the false meaning which the poor simple people everywhere put upon it, and take to themselves. It is this which hurts and grieves me, that the misguided folk accept and believe that on buying letters of indulgence they insure their own salvation; likewise also that souls straightway get out of purgatory when money for them is laid into the chest; again, that this same indulgence be of such virtue, that there is no sin so great but that it can be remitted and forgiven through it; further, that men by this indulgence are freed from all punishment and guilt. Woe is me, this is the way to bring poor souls under your care and diocese not to life but to death! It is a great and growing responsibility for your reverence, who will have to render account for all these souls. Therefore I could no longer be silent, for man is not assured of his salvation by a bishop's will or work, but the apostle enjoins us at all times to work out our own salvation with fear and trembling. Even the just will hardly live, for narrow is the way which leadeth unto life, and the Lord hath shown us again and again how hard it is to be saved.

"'How then dare they render the people falsely secure and fearless, by giving them worthless fables and untrue promises of an indulgence which cannot help their souls, nor cause that any man be justified and saved, but only can take away such outward and present punishment which, according to the Church's institution, might be put upon the sinner? Moreover the works of godliness and charity, which are far better than indulgences, are not preached half so diligently nor with a like show, indeed, they are quite driven into a corner, and nothing but indulgences is praised and promised, whereas it should be a bishop's one and greatest aim to have the gospel preached to the people, and to teach them the love of Christ. Nor hath Christ anywhere commanded indulgences, but the gospel only.

"'What danger, therefore, and terror are awaiting that bishop who has brought nothing among the people but indulgences with a great cry, and is more anxious about it than about the gospel! Will not Christ say to him: Woe unto you who strain at a gnat and swallow a camel! Nor is this all, most reverend father in God, but the instruction of commission, which pretends to have gone forth under your name (no doubt without your will and knowledge), announces as chiefest grace this priceless gift, whereby man be reconciled to God and all punishment of purgatory remitted; also that repentance is not needed by him who buys a letter of indulgence.

"'How then can I otherwise, reverend Bishop and most serene Elector, than conjure your reverence by the Lord Jesus Christ to have a fatherly care concerning this matter, and put down this same writ of instruction, commanding the preachers of indulgence some other fashion and form of preaching, lest one should arise in these times with books, to gainsay them and their writ to the great dishonour of your highness; which I should truly be sorry for, but fear me it must come to pass, unless the matter be speedily amended. Let this my faithful service be accepted in a worthy, princely, and episcopal manner, that is, most graciously, for I have shown this with a true heart, entirely mindful of your reverence; for I too am a sheep of your flock. The Lord Jesus keep and preserve your reverence now and evermore. Amen.'"

The Archbishop dropped the letter, and sat still a while. Turning to Margaret, he asked her presently, "What thinkest thou of this missive, my child?"

Margaret answered somewhat diffidently: "It seems to me this is not the way in which a mendicant friar should address the Archbishop."

Albrecht smiled disdainfully, but said: "This brother Martin is right, nevertheless; I look at his letter from a different point of view. He is clear-headed, and not wanting in courage to speak the truth. I rather like him for that. Nor are his objurgations as bad as I expected. I thought he would condemn the sale of indulgences altogether, but it is against the abuses only he has raised his voice."

"And what do you think of doing?" cried Margaret. "Will you send him a reply?"

The Archbishop laughed. "No," said he; "let the

friars fight it out amongst themselves. Brother Tetzel will kick against brother Martin; and if brother Martin by way of rejoinder finds means to trip him up, it will teach Tetzel a lesson, as I said, and we shall hear no more about it."

"But those theses?" continued Margaret. "You have not even looked at that copy which the prior left on the table!"

The Elector waved his hand. "Ninety-five theses, and expect me to read them? No. The letter was long enough; it must have contained everything that could be said in any number of theses."

"But the people are reported to think much of them everywhere!" urged Margaret.

The Elector grew impatient. "Has the prior put thee up to warn me? He is a cowardly fool. I tell thee these things are best left alone; they will be forgotten before a month is out—I know that! And now come, let us have a canter, the morning promises fair."

Within a quarter of an hour the stately pair rode from the Martinsburg. The Elector Archbishop by the side of his radiant companion could not be expected to trouble himself long about the worries of his high calling, debts and theses included.

· · · · · ·

Albrecht, however, was wrong in his prognostication. The matter at issue was no mere monkish palaver; it spread in widening circles, dividing the world ere long into opposing camps. As a spark amid dry tinder, the theses of Wittenberg did the work, the bursting flame testifying to their importance. That monk had dared to put into words what was moving in the hearts of thousands—unconsciously perhaps, needing his touch only to rise as a great tide of conviction. Impotent was Tetzel's revenge—his burning of Luther's theses at Jüterbogk, and publishing counter-theses in their stead. If the latter met with a like fate at Wittenberg, it was without Luther's knowledge; and a new set of opposition theses, which Tetzel devised for himself, with the assistance of a certain rector named Wimpina, intending thereby to gain his degree as doctor of divinity, proved the death light of his earthly fame.

Higher and higher rose the waves, more and more voices giving their assent to the monk of Wittenberg. Nor did Luther remain on his first position; step by step he advanced in the knowledge of truth, and before long he denounced the Pope's indulgence altogether, as entirely at variance with the teaching of Holy Writ.

The Roman owls were heard, hooting ominously; a Sylvester Prierias, the Pope's minister of the palace, a Jacob von Hogstraten, Inquisitor at Cologne, a John Eck, vice-chancellor of the university of Ingolstadt, raised their hue and cry, thinking thereby to annihilate the heretical monk; but one and all retired from the scene, leaving their feathers behind them. Indeed, their opposition only served to advance Luther with the people at large, thus assisting the spreading of truth against their will.

As for Archbishop Albrecht, the march of events rather went beyond him. In his heart he was inclined to patronise Luther, for, together with his friends the humanists, he chuckled over the thought that the Pope for once should be humbled by a bold-faced monk. The Primate of Germany was jealous of the Roman see; indeed, he was the avowed protector of Ulrich von

Hutten, although the latter had lately published a book wielding an unmistakable blow against popedom. But that Luther should have laid low the power of indulgence, spoiling entirely that fruitful source of revenue, did not suit the Elector's need; his cupidity was stronger than his half-hearted inclination towards truth.

But he was obliged to keep his counsel; opinion amongst the humanists ran high; he did not like to go against it. He felt his hands bound, secretly chafing at times against brother Martin's open action. If that Augustinian could not hold his peace, why of all things must the traffic of indulgences be the mark of his attack? There were worse sores than this in the Church, the Archbishop thought, and for all he cared the monk might fight them.

Yet, nevertheless, alarmingly empty as the coffers were growing, Margaret Riedinger was clothed in jewels upon jewels, and never a desire of hers remained unsatisfied. Nor must the electoral table suffer restraint; and the magnificent hierarch did not dream of denying himself the purchase of any treasure of art, any costly gem that moved his fancy. He saw well enough the drift of his habits, but as for modifying them or curbing his passions, it was beyond his will.

Meanwhile Luther, having learned that the Emperor also looked askance at the Wittenberg movement, had addressed a humble letter to the Pope to justify his position. His enemies, hearing this, did their utmost in calumny, anxious the Pope should cite the heretic before his judgment-seat. And they succeeded. In the month of August, 1518, a papal brief was issued, requiring Luther to appear at Rome within sixty days upon pain of the ban, unless he saw fit to recant.

Luther's friends took alarm, conjuring him not to comply. He himself saw that a journey to Rome under the circumstances would end for him on the pyre or within prison walls; he was grateful, therefore, that his Elector, at the intercession of the Wittenberg university, protested against the papal rescript. Before, however, the Elector's messenger could reach Rome, opinion there had changed. The German business should be settled on German soil; it was referred to the Diet of Augsburg.

The friends of Luther were relieved of their worst fears, but thought it advisable to procure for their Doctor a safe-conduct from the Emperor; they had heard it whispered that Cajetan, the papal legate who was to try brother Martin, was empowered to carry him off as a prisoner to Rome, should he refuse to recant.

On foot, after the fashion of the apostles, Luther, trusting in his God, set out upon his way; it was on the 27th of September, 1518; and having preached the gospel at various places, having stopped also at Nürnberg to receive at the hands of his friend Link a new cowl for the threadbare old one, he on the 7th of October entered the town of Augsburg.

CHAPTER VIII.

THE CARDINAL'S HAT.

THE bow-windows of the Chapter room at Mainz gleamed brightly into the night. At an unusual hour the High Chapter had been called to deliberation.

"I crave pardon of the reverend brethren," began the Provost of the cathedral, "to have invited their attendance so late in the day; but important news require immediate consultation. It is deeply to be regretted that the matter was not heard of at Mainz at an earlier period, before his electoral grace, the Archbishop, quitted our midst. Now, when he is already at Augsburg, an abbot of the Franciscans brings me certain information that a peculiar distinction is about to be conferred on him. It has been decided at Rome to add the cardinal's hat to .his archiepiscopal and electoral honours."

A low murmur went round the Chapter, each looking at the other with questioning eyes.

The Provost continued: "If I understand you aright, you all share my opinion, that this new honour is nowise to our advantage, for there lurks mischief behind. The hat will be a pressing burden upon us all. It is clear that Rome intends it as a snare, and that what liberty and independence still is ours is to be taken from us. Every German Chapter must resist it, if a German, a non-Italian, is thought worthy of the cardinalship; for the scarlet hat is only a means by which Rome claims leave to meddle with our affairs, and to subjugate the German Church entirely. If any of you hold different opinions, let them speak."

Not a voice was heard.

"Then the reverend Chapter are unanimously with me?" continued the Provost. "If so, attest it with an amen."

"Amen!" echoed from mouth to mouth. A smile of satisfaction hovered on the lips of the Provost.

After a short pause he went on: "There is yet time for action; let us improve it by sending a courier to Augsburg: he may not be too late for acquainting the Archbishop with our earnest prayer that his grace might refuse the honour which is likely to prove detrimental to the Church over which he reigns. If the reverend Chapter agree with me, attest it."

"Amen!" went round the room. The youngest member present received orders forthwith to put into writing the resolution arrived at, in order that a messenger might be despatched early the following morning.

The missive being made out and accredited with the great seal of the Chapter, the prebends bent their heads to a silent paternoster, and the meeting rose.

The following morning—it was towards the end of July, 1518—a man-at-arms rode at a quick trot from the town gate of Mainz, taking the high road in the direction of Augsburg. He had been enjoined the greatest possible speed, nor did he save his horse. But the sun rose high, burning pitilessly upon his cuirass, and before the evening sank he fain turned to a village inn for rest. Accommodation there was not for sickening travellers; he felt scarcely fit in the morning to mount his horse, and reaching a country town in the afternoon, was obliged to give in. It took three days before some helpful Esculapius set him on the road again. The lost time could hardly be made good; he rode apace, and saw afar the church steeples of Augsburg.

Solemnly the bells did peal, the country folk in Sunday best arrived from miles around, the streets were thronged, all the world seemed bound for the cathedral. Making his way through the crowd, the messenger happened to catch the words "cardinal's hat." He stopped short. Information was readily forthcoming. Too late—yes, he arrived but in time to see the last of the procession entering the sacred pile.

He threw the bridle to some loiterer, and himself entered the cathedral.

Splendid indeed was the spectacle before him. Enthroned beneath a canopy of red velvet, to the right of the high altar, appeared the venerable figure of Emperor Maximilian, gorgeously arrayed in a gold-broidered mantle. Opposite, and sitting between the two cardinals, Mathias and Cajetan, the Elector Archbishop of Mainz had a prominent place. Behind him the lords of the Diet, the Electors of the Palatinate and Saxony, the Dukes of Brunswick and Bavaria, the Markgraves Casimir, Frederick and John Albrecht of Brandenburg, the Archbishop of Bremen, the Bishops of Bamberg, Eichstädt, Regensburg, Augsburg, and Salzburg.

The choir burst forth with *Veni, sancte spiritus*, whereupon the Pope's legate, Thomas de Vio (commonly called Cajetan [1]), took his position on the steps of the altar, before which the chancellor of Archbishop Albrecht now read with a loud voice the papal bull of installation. This done, two priests, stepping up to Albrecht, hung upon his shoulders the purple cloak and led him to the altar, that from the mouth of the Pope's ambassador he should receive the cardinalate. With well-worded flattery the legate dwelt on Albrecht's personal claims which had moved his Holiness to admit him to the purple. A man of such superior eminence would no doubt prove the Pope's able coadjutor in Germany.

Albrecht, having yielded his solemn oath kneeling before the altar, received on his brow the cardinal's hat, acolytes filling the place with incense, which clothed him in a mysterious veil.

Again the organ joined in with a jubilant anthem, high mass was celebrated by the legate, and the *Te Deum* sung. Such was the course of the solemnity by which Albrecht was invested with the cardinalate. He left the cathedral by the side of the Emperor, followed by princes, prelates, and nobles of high degree.

Returning to his quarters, he found the Chapter's missive lying on his table.

"Too late!" he said with a smile, having glanced at its import. "But you need not have troubled, my friends; there is no fear that the cardinal's hat will turn me into a slave of Rome. I am a German prelate,

---

[1] From his birthplace, Cajeta, which name he adopted in accordance with a fashion prevalent in those times. For his zeal in defending the papal pretensions, he was promoted to the Archbishopric of Cajeta, whence he was raised to the archiepiscopal see of Palermo.

and mean to keep a German heart even beneath the purple. Didst thou mean to catch me, Leo, with the high honour thou gavest me, free of payment, to the surprise of all? if so, thou wilt have to be taught that the Primate of Germany is strong enough to burst the fetter when it becomes irksome. I understand thee well enough; I know why thou hast chosen a German for the purple: thou seest the need in Germany of props of thy power, for the country is full of complaint against the Roman see. Thou wilt be surprised, Leo, to see thy legate return with a long list of grievances made out by the Diet of Augsburg against thee and thy rule. Germany means to free herself of thy leading-strings. A strange spirit seems moving in the land, the birth-throes of new things are upon us—"

He stopped, losing himself in thought, and murmuring after a while: "If thou didst choose me to fight thy battles against my own people, thou art mistaken! Ulrich von Hutten, the bold champion now afield against thy tyranny, is *my* retainer. Didst thou think I would snatch the pen from his hand, as soon as I was crowned with the purple hat? No, indeed! write away Ulrich, fight away—and if the people join thee, calling out at large: 'We will not have this man across the Alps there, to reign over us,' well—well— Why *should* the Church have but one ruler? Suppose we had a German Church with a German Pope!"

Again the Cardinal fell to thinking, and a sudden glow diffusing his face betokened the emotion within.

His contemplation was interrupted, steps resounding in the ante-hall. The velvet curtain was lifted to admit Ulrich von Hutten and Dr. Stromer, Albrecht's physician, the two having followed their master to Augsburg.

Reverence, if not awe, held them standing by the door, awaiting permission to approach.

The Cardinal looked up surprised. "What is the meaning of this strange deportment? Is friendship not strong enough to lift you above the ceremonies of etiquette?"

"We have come to pay our respects to your eminence," said the physician solemnly.

Albrecht winced. "Ah!" he said, "has the purple frightened you away from me—is it likely to part old friends?" A frown overcast his features. "If so, the hat is a burden already. I do not hold myself the Pope's debtor for this honour. Since I am a cardinal, I will be one, but a *German* cardinal. Let Leo be sure of this! . . . Step closer, my friends, and sit ye down by me as ye are wont."

Obeying eagerly, both shook hands with the Cardinal, and composed themselves by his side on one of the luxurious settees.

Hutten having regained his confidence, said warmly: "I *am* glad, your eminence—"

"Spare thyself the trouble of this title!" interrupted Albrecht impatiently. "For thee I am the Elector, as before."

Flushing up with joy, Hutten repeated: "I *am* glad, and grateful besides to your electoral grace for the grand and honourable sentiment just expressed. You have taken a load from my soul. I entertained the worst fears when I learned the Pope's intention of crowning you with the purple. If you are the Pope's servant, Ulrich von Hutten can no longer be yours."

Albrecht gave a smile of intelligence. "I see, Ulrich! Thou hast thrown the gauntlet to papacy; it scarcely suits thee that thy avowed patron should suddenly find himself wearing the Pope's livery. But be of good cheer; I continue Albrecht of Brandenburg, and thy friend. Only be advised, and let not thy pen run away with thee, for fear of exposing me imprudently."

Hutten thanked his gracious master with a warm grasp of hands, Dr. Stromer adding, equally pleased: "This Hutten of ours is an impulsive fellow, but I, in duty bound, am guided by prudence. I will have an eye to him, and lower the hot-blooded temperament, if need be."

Albrecht laughed gaily. "Happy is the man who is blest with such a physician; even though he be Elector of Mainz, he is beholden to his art!"

An attendant meanwhile had placed three tankards of Cyprus wine before them; the fiery influence of which beverage, adding to the charms of friendly intercourse, differences of rank were entirely forgotten, the time passing pleasantly in merry chat.

CHAPTER IX.

THE "HERETIC" AT THE BAR.

The Diet had a lengthy session, for much business was on hand. Maximilian was anxious to make the best of the short span of life yet granted to him; he really had the welfare of his people at heart. And the world was full of the news that the Emperor was about to die: for had there not been a great solar eclipse on the 7th of July, true to the very hour predicted by George Tanstetter, the famous astronomer of Vienna, and what else should it mean? The people believed it, and the Emperor believed it, so much so that he had his coffin made, and carried it about with him. In the face of this coffin now he kept the princes and prelates sitting, autumn surprising them at their unfinished task.

"What has happened, Ulrich mine?" inquired Albrecht one afternoon in October, as the latter in unceremonious excitement entered the electoral presence.

"Great things have happened!" cried Hutten breathlessly, "great things indeed, while your grace was away on the Emperor's hunt. I have seen Doctor Martin, ay, and heard him!"

The Elector smiled ironically. "Is this your wonderful news? Has the legate cast him in irons?"

"Do not speak banteringly of the monk, I pray you!" cried Hutten, still more excited. "Had you heard him as I have, in sooth you would think differently of him. The very fact that he has come at all gained him my heart. He has courage, that barefooted friar, and I love courageous men. You know yourself that I rather looked down upon him before; I took him for a dreamer, filling men's ears with idle words; when I had hoped he would enter our ranks and assist us to wield the sword of sarcasm against the 'darklings' of miserable renown. But he is for going in another direction than we humanists, he is for attacking the root at once. And surely I own him better and greater than ourselves! I have seen him to-day, and have heard him with mine own ears. Indeed, one has but to look into those deep dark eyes of his, to see that he is no ordinary man; there is a power in those eyes, to which one cannot but yield oneself prisoner. Twice already he had appeared before the legate, and given a fine proof of his courage. The legate had asked of him to retract his ninety-five theses, and in future to hold his peace; whereupon Luther declared his readiness to do so from the moment they convicted him of error by Holy Writ. The legate made answer with scornful pride: 'Avaunt! barefooted monkling! Thinkest thou I have crossed the Alps to dispute with a mere German friar? It is the Pope's gracious desire that I should bring thee back to the fold; but thy Bible lore we want not. The holy fathers and the teaching of the Church are proof against the notions of a foolish dreamer!' Cajetan imagined it needed but the word from a cardinal's lips to overawe the poor monk entirely. But he found himself mistaken: the

German friar held his own before the Italian grandee, so much so that his eminence grew tired, and put him off for another day. This morning, then, he appeared a third time before the legate's judgment-seat, which by-the-by seems a bad means, if the Pope intends to solve matters in peace. For Thomas de Vio is proud and overbearing; even at the Diet he claims precedence of German Electors, and is not satisfied with two guards of honour at his gates, but needs must have four. Nothing is good enough for the Italian among us German barbarians, and entering his chamber is like dropping into a lady's bower. I am glad that the vain-glorious fool was so grandly defeated."

"What, Hutten! The Cardinal Legate defeated?" exclaimed the Elector greatly interested. "You don't mean that the monk had the best of it?"

"Let me report to your grace," said Hutten, and continued: "The false Italian, not being generally trusted, Doctor Martin's friends saw to safe company. Two councillors of Electoral Saxony, Von Feilitsch and Dr. Rühel by name, Councillor Langemantel and Canon Adelmann of Augsburg, were with him, besides Dr. Staupitz, the Augustinian Vicar-General, not mentioning three imperial councillors and several others. Myself was among the number, for I desired to hear the monk's defence. We were ushered into a chamber hung with rose-coloured silk, and beheld the proud legate sitting as a king on a throne of purple and gold amid a splendid retinue and a whole tribe of Dominicans. Coldly he looked down upon the humble monk, who, barefooted, approached his greatness. Brother Martin knelt, doing reverence to the prelate, awaiting permission to rise. 'Art come to thy senses, friar?' demanded the scornful legate. 'Let us have the last of it, and recant.' Luther rose to the full of his figure, his dark eyes alight with a wondrous fire, a holy courage surely, and with a brave voice he made answer: 'Once more I repeat it: I hold myself in readiness for public disputation, and I will submit to the universities of Basel, Freiburg, Louvain and Paris, Here is my defence! Seeing that word of mouth avails nothing before your eminence, I have put to paper what I have to say.' The legate took the writing ungraciously, barely glancing at it. 'Empty words,' he said, and threw it down contemptuously. Brother Martin was about to appeal against such abuse, but Cajetan took the word out of his mouth, peremptorily commanding him to retract. You should have seen Luther meeting thunder with thunder in the righteousness of his cause! He quite forgot he was addressing a cardinal, turning to him as to an ordinary mortal. 'Ask of me what you will,' he cried, 'and you shall have it, but not this! not this! I stand on the Scriptures, and I cannot retract.' All the company present were moved; all eyes watched the legate who sat trembling, with blanched lips and quivering features, silent a while, as though he were gathering strength for a final onslaught. And then he burst forth forgetful of all dignity : 'Begone, and let me see thy face no more, unless thou art prepared to retract! And ye others, all of you who stand by the heretic, are in danger of the ban; every place which yields him shelter does so under pain of the interdict! It is the Pope's will and pleasure!' Each and all must have felt his wrath; but calmly, in the power of noble consciousness, Luther once more faced the legate with a look only, and the latter dropped his eye! Brother Martin turned and left his presence."

Albrecht listened with a sensation hardly understood by himself, Hutten's enthusiastic account carried him along.

Again he felt himself face to face with the Wittenberg monk. There was something in his heart siding with the bold spirit who dared oppose the Pope's very envoy; and yet was he not the same who had also dared to stop the influx to his money-chest? The Archbishop kept his thoughts to himself. There was an embarrassing silence; he would have liked Hutten to continue, but the latter was evidently waiting for something to be said. Albrecht after a while remarked evasively: "I understand thy admiration, Ulrich! This brother Martin is not unlike thyself in fearless courage; that is what gains him thy heart."

Hutten glowed with genuine enthusiasm. "Mine own Elector!" he cried, "great deeds are never done where people walk circumspectly. Look at Erasmus, that quiet hero, always considering; what has he achieved? A fortress must be stormed, you see! nor is it foolhardiness which moves this Luther; it is the holy daring of trust in God, the stronger for his humility. If you could but see him face to face, and hear his voice! Shall I bring him to you?"

The Elector stepped back, saying coldly: "This is going too far, Ulrich, for friendship even! My time and thoughts are taken up with other things."

Hutten's face fell. There was no more to be said, and taking his leave presently, he went his way to the Carmelites, with whom Luther had taken up his abode. "I pity thee, Albrecht," he murmured, walking along.

"I am but a knight-errant, but I would not change with thee, for I may speak and act as the heart prompts me; thou art driven into a corner against thyself."

The following morning, just as his grace of Mainz was about to have a canter in company with Hutten, the Cardinal Legate appeared at the door.

"I consider it fortunate not to have missed your eminence," began the Italian eagerly, "for I have called on most serious business."

Albrecht desired Hutten to have the horses taken away, and re-entered the house with his visitor.

Cajetan was no sooner seated than he plunged into the matter. "This mendicant is of tougher metal than I thought. So far from giving in, he is now writing a letter, I understand, appealing 'from the badly-instructed to the better-to-be-instructed Pope.' This is beyond endurance!"

"Well," said Albrecht, "the monk must have fair play; you did not allow him to speak his mind, I hear."

Cajetan frowned and gave a searching glance into the Elector's countenance. "What is this you say? I did not let him speak his mind! Far too graciously I listened to the German blockhead, who dared address me as though I were his equal. I think you must have heard him roar even at this distance, when, looking at me with those queer eyes of his, he tried to advance some of his strange doctrines."

Albrecht smiled imperceptibly. He personally disliked the legate, and felt highly tickled at the proud Italian's discomfiture. "Yes," he responded; "but methinks your voice overtopped his. You seem to have thundered him into silence; may I ask—did you succeed in refuting him?"

The legate looked daggers. "How am I to understand your eminence's question? I have come to consult you as to the best mode of dealing with the heretic; it almost looks as though you meant to take his part."

"Imagine no such thing," returned Albrecht coldly. "I can have nothing in common with this mendicant friar!"

"Neither do you seem to have anything against him!" continued the legate, with emphasis. "Is it wise to look carelessly at so dangerous a matter—you of all men, who have suffered so greatly from the effect of his theses? You have little choice, I ween, but to assist me in getting rid of the heretic."

"What!" exclaimed Albrecht, "are you meditating aught against his life?"

Coldly, but with a hiss, Cajetan made answer: "I am the servant of my master. The servant has no will of his own, but does as his master would have him."

"I understand your eminence," said Albrecht, with distant haughtiness. "But there are other masters besides him whom you serve. Be warned, lest you should make an enemy of the one while doing the business of the other. Maximilian is emperor here. He will not break his word, nor suffer another to break it with impunity."

The legate bit his lips. He knew he had stepped on dangerous ground, and somewhat changed his position. "The Pope's power is like the sun, we know, leaving the imperial dignity to shine as the moon. You agree with me, surely. Where the Pope commands the Emperor must yield, inasmuch as the Church is above the kingdoms of this world; and whenever the Church is endangered, the Vicar of Christ must hold his own."

"And do you fear a mere mendicant can do aught against the Church? Stronger than the walls of Jericho I deem her structure; the blast of a monk will not lay it low."

"This is utter carelessness!" cried Cajetan; "nay, wilful blindness, not to see so great a danger! There is but one way; we must stamp it out ere it strikes deeper root; when the storm-bird has disappeared, the storm too will yield."

With growing eloquence the legate hoped to gain the Elector to his views. But Albrecht, whatever his faults, had a German heart, turning with loathing from the crooked ways of the Italian. He had no love for Luther, the rather that his cupidity bore him a grudge; but he spoke a manly word to hold him safe from the assassin's dagger.

Whether he succeeded in convincing the legate of the wickedness of his intention, he knew not, for with ambiguous speeches and burning with inward emotion, the Italian Cardinal left his German peer.

Several days after this, towards nightfall, two men in silence, and choosing by-ways, rode towards the cloister of the Carmelite friars, which was situated in the outskirts of the town of Augsburg. Stopping at a wicket gate leading into the monastery gardens, they dismounted. "Bide here with the horses," said the one, not raising his voice above a whisper; and, disappearing within the cloister precincts, he made for a side door connecting the abbot's cell with the garden.

He had wrapped his mantle about him, for the night was blustering; fitful blasts shook the leafless tree-tops, rain fell in heavy showers, the weathercocks groaned in their sockets, while an owl kept moaning in dismal loneliness.

The man stood waiting; a quarter of an hour had passed, he was growing impatient, and creeping stealthily along the building he searched the windows anxiously. "Has Langemantel failed his promise? Or could Luther be raising objections? He has a brave courage, but defiance would be his ruin! He little knows what an Italian is capable of—how should he in his German simplicity? He trusts the imperial promise, he little thinks—"

The man stopped in his soliloquy, steps approached, and a cautious voice called: "Hutten!"

Turning quickly, the latter perceived two figures. "Is it yourself, brother Martin? The Lord be praised! for indeed to-morrow's morning would scarcely have found you alive."

"God greet you, noble knight, and reward you for this act of generous risk. I have more friends than I wot of!" a deep voice responded.

The two men shook hands, each seeking the other's eyes, darkness interfering. Hutten was the first to speak: "It is not long that I have come to your side, brother Martin," he said, deeply moved; "I was hostile, not understanding you. Brother Martin, thou art greater than I! I put down my pen in thy presence, but if ever thou needest a sword to defend thee—call me!"

"My thanks to you, noble knight!" replied Luther warmly. "The word of God is powerful, and sharper than any two-edged sword; earthly weapon will not be needed, I deem."

Luther's companion prevented further discourse, urging the advisability of immediate action. Brother Martin, yielding, turned at once, following his two friends through the garden to the wicket gate.

"Thou art sure of the way, I hope?" inquired Langemantel of the attendant, who had stood patiently by the horses' heads, in spite of the pouring rain.

"Sir," replied the man, almost hurt, "have I not served the town these twenty years, and do you doubt my knowing the way?"

"Well then, be mounted, and God speed your journey! But can you ride, brother Martin, without boot or spur?"

"Have no fear, sir councillor," answered Luther; "my feet have seen harder work than this."

"May He protect thee whose servant thou art!" cried Hutten, in the warmth of his feeling.

The clasping hands unloosened. Hutten and the councillor stood listening till the last faint sound of the horses' hoofs had died away in the distance.

CHAPTER X.

CHANGES.

THE monasterial halls of St. Maurice's at Halle, one day towards the close of the year 1519, were startled out of their customary quiet, agitation and tumult filling the cloister. The monks forgot their religious duties, no *horæ* resounded, no priest took his place by the altar to read the mass—and yet the prior thought not of reproof, the rather that he shared the general excitement, feeling quite unable to have a watchful eye to the rules of the convent.

And, alas! what was the use of rules, since it had happened now, the dreaded calamity? Cardinal Albrecht, who for some time had been holding court at Halle, had given orders that within three days St. Maurice's must be cleared of the Augustinians, in order to make room for the Dominicans, who had been obliged to quit their own monastery.

The noise in cells and cross-walks swelled louder and louder, till the outside people heard it, forcing an entrance into the cloister.

The passion-moved monks quite forgot the reverence due to their spiritual head, upbraiding him disrespectfully, so that the Cardinal at last had to interfere by means of his officials, at the same time despatching his chancellor, Dr. Turk, who now entered the cell of the prior for the further discussing of matters.

With gloomy, hostile countenance the superior received the Cardinal's messenger, barely nodding the head in answer to his deferential greeting.

But Chancellor Turk was a man of business, whose imperturbation and tenacity soon got the better of the awkwardness of his position, and he quietly addressed the prior.

"I am sent hither by his eminence the Cardinal, who has been moved to most just resentment by the spirit of uproar abroad within the monastery; he requests you forthwith to make use of your authority that the cloister be evacuated without delay. For such is his will and pleasure."

"And why should it be his will and pleasure?" retorted the prior, aggrieved. "What crime has been brought home to the monastery of St. Maurice, that such an outrage should be our share?"

Unmoved the chancellor made answer: "It behoves not the subject to inquire into reasons when the ruler has spoken. Yet I will meet your desire and appease your resentment by explaining the Archbishop's intention. It is no new plan he is carrying into effect, seeing that his predecessor, Archbishop Ernest, had thought of it before him. There are no less than eleven cloisters in this small town of Halle, and what is their usefulness? You observe the *horæ*, you read the mass, and that is about all. But this occupation does not require so great a number of monks; the spiritual estate nowise gains by being over-stocked, the rather that it is greatly endangered by idleness and sloth. Do not interrupt me, reverend father! I have satisfied myself of the state of things within our holy houses; I could mention worse frailty. Great is the ignorance among our monks and their dislike to all learned occupation; about as great is their propensity to luxurious living, including all manner of infamous and profligate practice. His eminence has decided therefore to lessen the number of cloisters in this place, to draw together their possessions, which shall form the basis of a new collegiate foundation, to which pious and capable monks only will be admitted, who shall cultivate learning, more especially theology."

"And with us you make the beginning?" returned the prior, scarcely able to speak for indignation. "Does his eminence consider the monks of St. Maurice's the most profligate of them all?"

"Not so!" rejoined the chancellor. "We desire to make no distinction of badness. It is the rich possessions of St. Maurice's which make it advisable that it should go first. Cloister Neuwerk will follow next; not that it is to be abolished, but it shall yield the spiritual jurisdiction to the new foundation."

"Indeed!" groaned the prior. "Oh, it is a perilous game his eminence has ventured upon! To touch time-honoured institutions in these days, when the Wittenberg commotion is endangering the very pillars of our existence. My grey hairs will descend with sorrow to the grave, for I see destruction bearing down our strongholds met by dissolution within and without. Alas! if those who should be as the watchmen of Zion help digging the grave for papal supremacy! Have you no eyes for the Wittenberg heresy, flourishing in this very town of Halle? I conjure you, sir, to turn the Cardinal's mind, if this indeed be possible! His intention may be good, but the end will be misery and ruin. Would I could move him to quit the counsel of the ungodly, and sit not in the seat of the scornful. I mean the humanists, who, with their heathen learning, introduce heathen freedom of thought, preparing a way for the Wittenberg seducer. Tell him this as the dying bequest of one who is nigh the end of his course, and dares speak his mind all the more boldly: he wields the temporal sword aright, I say; not in vain is he a prince of the house of Brandenburg, but the hierarch's staff is powerless in his hand; he will fail entirely unless he listens to advice. Is it not he who, if unwillingly, has stirred up the fire which is ablaze in the Church—will he stand by, nor help in stamping it out? But no! such is his dire infatuation, that, far from attempting the putting out, he yields fuel upon fuel. Woe is me, I see the end! I shall be gone, but you remember my words when the fulfilment is upon you. Ah me, how great will be the fall!"

The grey-haired man spoke tremblingly with burning eyes and uplifted hand; as a prophet he appeared, foretelling a destruction he knew must come.

The chancellor felt a creeping horror at the picture unrolled, but he could not be angry with the man who raised such dire complaints against the Primate. He stood meditatively, and then, taking the prior's hand, he said soothingly: "Your eyes have grown dim, your spirit is weary with age. Courage and hope are not the old man's portion, who lives in the past, who cannot keep up with the active present, who looks misgivingly into the future. The self-same things show a different face to me. My heart as yet is proof to such fears as yours. I do perceive that we are in a state of dissolution and ferment; the country is in travail—a new birth is upon us, but it will come, it will be given. And firm as a rock stands the Church amid this turmoil; for is it not written that the gates of hell shall not prevail against it? See if it does not come forth victorious from the dread conflict. Be comforted then, reverend father, and depart in peace. But have a care first that your monks subside. Farewell!"

The chancellor took his leave hastily, as though fearful of another outburst.

With a quick pace he returned to the Moritzburg, where the Cardinal was holding court.

In the ante-room of the archiepiscopal closet he met with three members of the town council, who on important business were about to be admitted to the Elector's presence. The chancellor joined them, well aware that the ruler would be glad of his attendance.

The magistrates bowed, awaiting permission to speak; it having been given, the spokesman raised a solemn voice: "The worshipful council of this town of Halle has been honoured with your eminence's request, understanding from the same that a new collegiate foundation is to be added to the churches and cloisters of this place. And, albeit the council is fully desirous in all things to oblige your eminence, we cannot join in such a plan, since of churches we have more than enough, and our prayer would rather be for well-fitted teachers and preachers, who will give us the Word of God pure and unalloyed. In order to acquaint your eminence that such is the council's well-considered resolution, we have been sent to crave this present hearing."

The Cardinal listened with increasing amazement, but, conquering his rising temper, he made answer calmly: "The worshipful council of Halle has returned a decision the like of which we did certainly not anticipate. We believe, however, that our intention has been misunderstood, which is no other than by means of a new foundation to bring new life into the monasterial stagnation of the town; by a drawing together of the several convents we mean to lessen the number of monks, and replace the worthless cowls by a new generation of educated ecclesiastics. We leave you, dear Turk, to tell these gentlemen more about it."

And saying so, the Cardinal raised the audience, to seek solace in the society of Margaret Riedinger, who would expect his visit about this time of day.

For another hour the magistrates and the chancellor remained closeted, and when they left their countenance looked satisfied and their mind was changed. The clever official had succeeded in convincing the fathers of the town of the great benefit that must accrue from the archiepiscopal intentions, so much so that they went their way, prepared to move in council that the Cardinal's plan should be favoured and his grace subsidised by a grant of eight thousand rix dollars.

Not a little elated was Albrecht on learning that the council had fallen in with his views, and forthwith gave direction to his architects to set about the work.

To the south of the Moritzburg, on an eminence by the side of the river Saale, a busy scene presently met the eye, in spite of the advancing season. A number of workmen were engaged laying low the pride of the ancient cloister of the Dominicans, pulling down its walls; for on that site the new foundation should lift its head, taking a foremost rank in all the diocese. Of the old church the basement only would remain, on which a great cathedral should arise, a worthy monument of the Elector Primate's magnificence. Much time was lost in preliminary preparations, carting away of rubbish and the like, winter supervening, so that the Cardinal could not await the solemnity of laying the foundation stone; matters of far-reaching importance peremptorily demanding his presence at Mainz. The aged Emperor Maximilian had departed this life in January of that year, 1519; who should be his successor had for a long time claimed the careful attention of the Electors. And to Elector Albrecht, the Lord High Chancellor of the realm, all eyes had turned now, awaiting his powerful influence in the matter.

How will the dice be cast? Will Albrecht show himself a man of German worth? will he resist the gold of France? For with enticing sums the French king was trying to gain Albrecht's voice for himself; Francis could pay, and meant to pay, high for the imperial crown. It was a sore temptation to the poor Archbishop, whose money distress was an ever-threatening spectre, and was again looming on his horizon at the present juncture. But the prior of St. Maurice's had been right: he of the princely house of Brandenburg was not likely to disgrace the electoral hat, whatever might be his bearing as a ruler of the Church; Germany owed it to him chiefly, and to his powerful speech before the election, that in Charles V. of Spain, the grandson of Maximilian, a German ruler was raised to the imperial throne, and the realm was saved the disgrace of becoming a mere appendage of France.

Great were the rejoicings throughout the empire when the result of the election at Frankfort had become known, and with happy hopes the people looked for the advance of the youthful Emperor, who, on account of troubles in Spain and Brabant, kept the German people in expectation for thirteen months. On the 23rd of October, 1520, only, he arrived for his solemn coronation at Aix-la-Chapelle. Sublime and dazzling was the splendour of the ceremony, the trustful people believing that so much glory must needs argue a time of resurrection for the land; that beneath the blissful rule of the new monarch, mercy and truth should meet together, righteousness and peace would be kissing each other, that the religious troubles too should be guided to a haven of heaven-sent rest. Even Luther looked hopefully to the new Emperor, who had agreed to a special promise, as a part of the solemn compact, "that everything hitherto attempted by the Roman Imperial crown to the detriment of the German Church should be done away with." In his heart's trust the Wittenberg reformer directed a letter to Charles V., in which he said: "And seeing that all my endeavours hitherto have proved fruitless, I have now thought well of calling upon your Imperial Majesty, if so be that the Lord will do the work by you, it being His work, not mine. I therefore kneel to your Imperial Majesty, in humble loyalty, praying your Majesty, not to save me, but to take the cause of Divine faith beneath the shelter of your wing, granting to myself no further protection than may come to me from the setting forth and vindicating of my teaching; am I found to be a godless man and a heretic? then I ask no protection. But this I ask, that neither truth nor error be judged unheard."

Will Charles, then, justify the great hopes built upon him? There is German blood in his veins, his house and lineage are German. But what of his heart? What augurs it that he understands not the German tongue? Take up thy hopes, O people, for he who is thy ruler understands not when thou speakest!

CHAPTER XI.

THE HORIZON OVERCAST.

In one of the numerous luxuriously fitted withdrawing-rooms of the Vatican sat his Holiness, Pope Leo X., with his secretary Bembo playing at chess. Carelessly the well-formed, almost womanishly beautiful hand of the "Supreme Head of the Church" moved the ivory figures, and his eye, which at times could be sparkling and fiery enough, followed the game languidly, the heat being such that even the white airy dressing-gown was oppressive, great drops gathering on the exalted forehead. He liked to spend a pleasant hour at the chessboard whenever the rule and guidance of the great Church left him at leisure, and he had gathered about him a shining circle of artists and men of letters—he who was the friend and patron of the Muses, whom his princely father, Lorenzo de Medici, had trained to the enjoyment and appreciation of all that was beautiful, who on the papal throne had become the centre of the intellectual life of all Italy.

On the present occasion, then, the Holy Father was absent-minded. The secretary, in spite of all manner of leniency, had checkmated him once already, and was in a fair way of doing so a second time, when a chamberlain, stepping softly, announced Doctor Eck, Vice-chancellor of the University of Ingolstadt, who had just arrived from Germany.

The Pope overthrew the chess-men, exclaiming disgustedly: "Can this barbarous nation not leave me in peace? Germany and Italy never yet yoked pleasantly together, but I especially have little cause to look with a friendly eye upon this people. They are an ill-bred, stiff-necked race, with minds full of cobwebs and dreams. What is it that has brought this German doctor across the Alps? Let us hope that the religious peace which our nuncio, Carl von Miltitz, so warily has worked for is now concluded, and that the Wittenberg brawler has been silenced. It was an ill-advised plan of ours to send Cardinal Cajetan as our legate to Augsburg, for the proud, vain-glorious man has only added fuel to the fire, which we hoped he would be able to subdue. Far better pleased were we with the results of our chamberlain Von Miltitz; he seems to understand the art of muzzling the German bear. But this visit bodes little good. Doctor Eck is an unpleasant man, full of spite and malice. Leave us, Bembo, and admit the German Mercury."

The secretary disappeared, and within a few moments a gaunt, evil-visaged figure with an ill-shaped nose entered the apartment, paying the usual knee tribute to the Holy Father, and stooping for the inevitable kiss of the slipper, adding courtesy by word of mouth which amounted to a long-winded speech.

"What is the German news?" interrupted the Pope presently. "Let us hope you are no unwelcome messenger."

Doctor Eck's ungainly mouth broke into a deplorable grin, and he shrugged his shoulders. "I pray your Holiness not to vent displeasure upon the bearer, if his news is not what he himself would desire! It was but a rotten peace which your Holiness's chamberlain arrived at with Luther, for the villain has broken it."

The Pope's foot stamped the ground. "Woe to him! What has he been doing?"

"I had invited his friend and confederate, Doctor Karlstadt to Leipzig," reported Eck, "in order to hold a disputation with him, when Luther needs must meddle too, making it a hard day's work for me."

The Pope gave a searching glance at his visitor. "Who told you to hold a disputation—with his friend too, above all men? Of course he would meddle; it is you who tempted him to break the peace!"

Doctor Eck felt losing ground at this unexpected turn, but showed no dismay, continuing quietly, "I was obliged to have a trial of strength with Karlstadt, who had cast a slur upon my honour. I little dreamed that Luther would join in the matter, which was no concern of his."

The Pope shook his head impatiently. "You have shown little wisdom," he said; "your untoward zeal deserves our displeasure. Yet proceed with your report."

"As for Karlstadt, I soon got the better of him," continued Doctor Eck, "for his voice is poor and his tongue not a glib one. Luther, however, proved troublesome, especially when he turned the disputation to the all-important question of the Pope's supremacy. With a bold forehead the monk maintained that popery was but

LEO THE TENTH.

of human invention, and that the Bishop of Rome, just like any other mortal, was capable of error. And when I wrathfully reminded him that Christ Himself had appointed the spiritual power of the Pope, since it is written: 'Thou art Peter, and upon this rock I will build My Church,' he turned these words to quite another meaning. I appealed to the authority of the œcumenical councils, whereupon he burst upon me as one demented, crying, 'And I say the holy councils themselves are liable to err!' There was a desperate uproar at this unheard-of statement, Duke George of Saxony crying, horror-struck, 'The devil defend us!' All present, in fact, were shocked at the presumptuous heresy of these words, by which Luther, having broken with the Pope, broke with the councils also, and with all Church authority, taking his stand on the Scripture alone, which he dares expound to his own liking. I regret to say the disputation ended sadly."

"And you came forth from the tournament a conquered hero?" queried the Pope, sarcastically.

Eck gave a look of disdainful conceit. "No!" he cried. "Much praise was awarded me by those who understand; they yielded me the palm."

"Indeed!" returned his Holiness, drily. "I fear, then, that those who understand Luther believed the victory with him."

"I cannot but own that," said Eck, somewhat crestfallen; "but for this very reason I have crossed the Alps to kneel to your Holiness, hoping that a word from your throne will be sufficient to annihilate the crown he imagines he took away from the disputation at Leipzig, and that the heretic shall yet meet with his reward. Far too leniently your apostolic forbearance has dealt with the wretch hitherto. Far better would it have been if Cardinal Cajetan, instead of pretending to hear his defence at Augsburg, had brought him a prisoner to Rome, for impunity has only added to his brazen-faced courage; he has kindled anew the fire which we hoped had been got the better of, and by all manner of writings he vilifies the sacredness of the see, resuscitating those very heresies for which John Huss was brought to the stake. No wonder that the Hussites venture forth from their hiding-places, claiming him as their own, since they think he is the swan of which Huss is said to have prophesied when overtaken by his fate."

The Pope's patience was at an end; he rose from his chair abruptly, upsetting the elegant chessboard, and the ivory figures rolled hither and thither about the apartment. Doctor Eck stooped officiously to pick up the king and queen, the bishops and the wandering pawns, Leo the while standing by the window in discouraged soliloquy: "Oh, these Germans, these Germans!" he groaned. "Would I had the power to punish the cursed race! May the Lord and His saints prevail with the new Emperor, that perchance he will lend me his arm for the rooting up of those devil-sown weeds of heresy!" And turning again to Eck, who by this time had succeeded in re-establishing the chessmen in their places, he said, "Let a council of orthodox theologians be called together, who with your assistance shall inquire into the matter and pass judgment."

"The Lord reward your Holiness for such wisdom!" ejaculated Eck, his eyes afire with revenge. "If I may offer my humble advice, no time should be lost, for day by day infatuation swells the number of those who join the prophet of Satan; more especially since Luther's

Elector, Frederick the Wise, openly patronised the heretic, protecting the evil cause effectively during his regency of the empire. Matters have come to a desperate state in Germany; wherever three men are together in conversation, you may be sure that two of them are for Luther and one only for the Pope. Franz von Sickingen, also, that unruly champion who is day and night in the stirrup, creating quite a distemper in the empire, has announced himself as a friend of Luther, another well-known knight having followed his example, of whose doings I would fain report more to your Holiness."

"Who is that?" asked Leo, with growing impatience. "When shall I hear the last of these German barbarians? Who is this new disturber of our peace?"

"It is Ulrich von Hutten, holy father!" replied Doctor Eck.

"What!" exclaimed the Pope, "this promising youth whose genius we remember having noticed with much delight when he paid his respects to our court—has he too forsaken us for the enemy's camp? Is it possible that he has turned traitor—so noble and so brave?"

Eck gave an envious grin. "Yes, he is a genius, and great things might be expected of him, had he not turned his back upon the Church. But as it is, his pen is a dangerous weapon. Pamphlet upon pamphlet goes forth from his hand, pouring sarcasm upon all things holy, more especially upon the papal see. I will not offend your Holiness by quoting the wicked things which have been hatched by that man's prolific brain; but three of his publications must be brought to your notice, that you may understand the peril which threatens from that quarter, and that you may not hesitate giving over this dangerous youth to a like damnation with the Wittenberg heretic. Your Holiness may remember that a certain Laurentius Valla wrote a book which was condemned by the papal courts and numbered among prohibited writings. That book maintains it is an untruth that the Emperor Constantine, retiring to the East, delegated, not only Rome and Italy, but the whole of Western Europe, to the Bishop of Rome. Its denial was intended as a great blow in the face of papal supremacy. And this book, in spite of all prohibition, has been published afresh by Hutten."

"The miscreant!" cried Leo, hotly. "Is he possessed?"

"Not a doubt of it," returned Eck. "But there is worse impudence behind. He has actually dared to dedicate that book *to the Pope's Holiness!* With biting taunt, he says in the preface he felt sure Pope Leo would thank him for resuscitating this hidden treasure, since he, the builder-up of peace at Rome and elsewhere, had thrown wide the doors to justice, truth, and liberty; that all manner of knowledge could come forth now from its hiding-place, that the important discovery of the late Laurentius Valla too might walk the daylight, since intellect sat on the see. Other Popes had forbidden the book, fearing the truth, but Leo X. would welcome it, being a lover of truth. Bad Popes had been glad to believe the myth of Constantine's gift, because it attributed to them a power which in reality they had not; but Leo, being a good Pope, would yield of his own accord what otherwise must be taken from him by force. Again, he says in his preface that the falsehood of that myth was so stupid that its inventors could have intended it to be received by the Germans only, of whom the Italians believed that they were without brains. If the papists had meant it for other nations, they would have set about it much more cunningly. But for this very reason the unmasking of the fraud fitly came from Germany, if as a proof only that the Germans had brains after all."

"Stop, stop!" cried the Pope, with barely suppressed emotion, his voice trembling with ire. "Is it possible, is it conceivable, that such language be addressed to the holy see?"

But pitilessly Eck continued: "It is not all. Hutten has dared worse; he has sent to Archduke Ferdinand, the brother of the newly-elected Emperor, a certain writ which he calls an old parchment provided with new stings. That parchment is nothing else than the old apology in behalf of the Emperor Henry IV., who, barefoot and in the penitential sackcloth, was for three days kept standing by Pope Gregory in the courtyard of Canossa. He has called up this recollection of past insult in order to rouse the German people against the Roman see. And yet this is not all, but the more he writes the more monstrous becomes his contumely. He has sent forth a third publication, entitled the *Trias Romana*, in which he reaches the very climax of impudence. I have brought a copy of it with me, that your Holiness may see it for yourself. Let me give a specimen of it: 'Three things are murdered at Rome—the good conscience, true piety, and the sanctity of the oath. Three things are a laughing-stock at Rome—the virtue of our fathers, the priesthood of St. Peter, and the great judgment day. Three things are set store by at Rome—beautiful women, fine horses, and papal bulls. Three things are general at Rome—lust of the eye, the pride of life, and lust of the flesh. Three things are venal at Rome—pretty girls, ecclesiastical benefices, and the grace of God. Three things might better Rome—if the German princes would rise in opposition, if the German people were goaded to despair, or if the Turks would invade the Pope's domain. Three things might be a thorough cure of all evils—doing away with Romish superstition, giving up all Romish benefices, and entirely overthrowing the papal see—'"

"Hold thy tongue!" cried Leo, forgetful of all dignity. "We have heard enough, and more than enough!"

"And yet I must crave permission to add one thing more," said the relentless Eck. "What would the holy father say if he knew under whose patronage these things have been published?"

The Pope stared at his interlocutor helplessly. "Say what you have to say," he panted after a while.

Eck continuing, with a sneer:

"Hutten's patron is no other than he whom your Holiness honoured with the cardinal's hat but a year ago—to whom you sent the rare distinction of the golden rose but lately."

'Albrecht of Mainz!" groaned Leo, raising both hands in unfeigned horror. "It is not possible! Albrecht is an honest man!"

"An honest German—yes!" interposed Eck, with nice distinction.

The Pope sank into his chair, gasping for breath, and folding his hands upon his bosom.

"We must act!" he exclaimed after a while. "Leave

us, dear Eck. We are beholden to your fidelity, on which we built as on a rock. Though you are German yourself, your heart is Romish, and we trust you. Go now, and consider who may be fit to sit in judgment on those heretics. Hutten, however, must be dealt with less harshly than Luther, for Albrecht's sake, without whom we cannot do, and whose opposition we would rather not rouse."

He waved his hand, and Doctor Eck, greatly elated at the result of the interview, left the papal presence.

CHAPTER XII.

FRIENDSHIP PARTED.

ONE bright morning in August, 1520, a knightly figure might be seen riding from the gates of Brussels. It was Ulrich von Hutten, who had travelled to the court of that city, a gift of a hundred florins having been granted for this journey by the Elector of Mainz. Archduke Ferdinand, who was at Brussels awaiting the arrival of his brother, the new German Emperor, on his way now from Spain, had received Hutten graciously, taking quite an interest in his plans for the liberation of Germany from the Romish yoke. He also would have liked to prolong his stay until the Emperor's coming, having found friends moreover who shared his fondest hopes. But of enemies too there seemed no lack. Not that the generous Hutten, too great-souled himself to suspect meanness, discovered any of the designs against his person, nor did he readily accept the warnings of others; again and again the necessity of flight had to be urged upon him before he saddled his horse and took to the road.

He was on his way to Louvain, to his friend Erasmus, who lived there.

In the vicinity of that town, at a spot where his path was closed in on both sides with high banks, he was startled by the sudden appearance of a man, who jumped aside dismayed, pressing close against the hedge, evidently hoping the rider would pass on. He wore the habit of a monk.

Hutten fixed him with his eyes, recognition making the blood boil in his veins. He had met with his mortal enemy, Jacob von Hogstraten, the inquisitor of Cologne, the chief of the " darklings " who had embittered the days of the noble Reuchlin, who would have taken his life had he been able. Hutten hated this agent of the powers of darkness from the bottom of his true heart, having sent him word at various times to beware of ever meeting at arm's length with Hutten, else the world might have to mourn the loss of an inquisitor. Now they had met, Hogstraten finding himself face to face with Hutten, and with no means of escape.

The knight's hand grasped his sword, his voice sounding as a trumpet of the great reckoning day as he cried, "Well met, thou fiend! Death itself is too good for thee, thou who hatest righteousness and killest the truth!"

The bared sword glittered cold in the sunlight.

In abject fear the inquisitor sank to the ground, quaking on his knees as he begged for life. It was a despicable sight.

For a moment the sword hung suspended, then it flashed through the air—not to be buried in the heart of the monk, but to return to the scabbard. "No!" cried Hutten, "my honest blade shall not be soiled with blood such as thine; but know that other swords will find a way to thy infamous heart. Thou shalt not escape!"

And, spurring his horse, he rode away.

For a moment the inquisitor was stunned, but recovering his fright his eyes filled with a fiendish hatred, and shaking his fist after the departing knight he hissed between his teeth, "Go thy way, fool; thou shalt not rejoice in safety much longer!"

For a short time only Hutten remained with his fatherly friend Erasmus, proceeding on his journey.

Arrived at Aix-la-Chapelle, he put up at an inn. In the public room a lonely stranger was taking a meal. At Hutten's entrance he put down his knife, rising with an exclamation, "Is it you, most noble knight?"

Hutten recognised a travelling merchant of his acquaintance, shaking hands with him heartily.

"What are your news?" he inquired after a while.

"There are all sorts of news," replied the traveller. "Going about from place to place one learns a good deal. One thing I heard quite lately which you will be sorry for; you can scarcely be aware of it yet, to judge from the serenity of your brow."

"What is it?" cried Hutten, concerned.

"Bad news from Rome; the Pope has put Luther under the ban."

Hutten flushed, and grew deathly pale. "Lord in heaven," he cried, "is it possible? Shall the light go out again in darkness? Shall the evil one carry the day? Ah, poor Germany, put on thy sackcloth and bury thy hopes! How bright seemed the dawn; but the sun has not power to carry us through!"

The knight sat down as one in a dream, hiding his face in his hands.

The merchant looked as though he had more to say, but he refrained, fearful of adding to Hutten's distress.

ULRICH VON HUTTEN.
From a portrait in the Moll Collection in the British Museum.

Yet was it right to keep silence? Did he not owe it to the brave champion to warn him? Coming up to him closely, he laid a timid hand on his shoulder, saying with honest kindliness: "Dear sir, I have further news, and it grieves me to tell it. The measure is not full as yet, and over your own head the sword hangs suspended."

The knight looked up, scarcely understanding, and the other continued: "The Pope's wrath is upon yourself also; the Elector of Mainz, your friend and patron, has received a writ which might well set you thinking, since it does not stop short of prison chains."

Hutten started, rising to his full height. Fear and weakness had left him, his dark eyes burning with a beautiful fire. "I thank thee, Leo!" he cried, with a voice of thunder; "from my heart I thank thee, that thou hast thought me worthy to be the good man's, the great man's, fellow in danger! Whet the dagger, thou murderer with the triple crown, plunge it in Luther's breast, in Hutten's breast! Thou mayest kill us, and yet not kill; the seed has been sown, it will bear fruit; posterity shall reap, and our children will rise in judgment! But thou hast not caught me yet, Leo; thou shalt hear of Hutten before thou hast him. I will work while it is day, and if thou must have my life, I will sell it dearly!"

He called for his horse, and paid for the meal he had not touched.

"What are you about?" cried the merchant anxiously.

"To ride straightway upon Mainz!" said Hutten, girding his loins.

"That means riding straight to destruction!"

"No!" retorted Hutten, almost passionately. "Albrecht as yet is my friend; to him I go. I will hear what he has to say; I will look into his face, and see if he can, if he dares, play false to his friend!"

Vainly the merchant urged prudence; Hutten had made up his mind, and within half an hour he rode apace on the high road towards Mainz. At Coblentz he came to a dead halt; if his own strength would have lasted, that of his horse was at an end.

He fretted at the delay, but it enabled him to gather particulars. It was true, then,—the Pope had asked of several German princes, but more especially of the Archbishop of Mainz, that Hutten should be taken and sent a prisoner to Rome. Even the new Emperor, though he had not yet set foot into his realm, had been urged by his Holiness to spare no means for the seizure of the culprit.

Hutten chafed, but when he was on the road again it was not towards Mainz that his face was set. He longed for quiet, for stillness within and without; he must collect his thoughts, must see his way, before he would meet his fate.

On the boundary line dividing Franconia and Hesse, between the Spessart and the Vogelsberg and the Rhön, where the Kinzig and the Salza wind their picturesque course, Burg Steckelberg raised her turreted front—the ancient castle of the knightly family of Hutten. Thither Ulrich directed his horse's head; he longed to see father and mother again, and would rest a while in their love.

In a village by the roadside he took opportunity to

indite a letter to his friend Wolfgang Capito, who had lately entered Albrecht's service as court chaplain, and had been appointed his privy councillor besides. This is what he wrote:—

"MY DEAREST CAPITO,
"The fire has begun to burn, and I marvel if it is not to be put out with my blood. But I think my courage is yet greater than mine enemies' power. Let me be up and doing then; the time of waiting is at an end. I will know leniency no more, freely will I speak, for I perceive the Romish lions are athirst for my blood. Yet before they taste it they shall hear the utmost I have to say of them in this world. I retire for a while to Steckelberg, then I shall come to Mainz and face the Cardinal. Fare thee well! If there be any letters for me, take them till I require them at thy hand. For ever thine,
"HUTTEN."

And on he went, being clasped presently to the heart of his parents. His mother shed many a tear, and would not hear of her Ulrich's intended departure; Steckelberg was the only place, she averred, where his enemies would not dare to touch him. But the father gloried in his son, and agreed with him that it was the right thing, and worthy of their unspotted name, that he should go like a man and show himself to his Elector. So once more he saddled his horse, and set out upon the journey, of which he knew not how it would end.

The people of Mainz looked at him as though he were an apparition as he entered the gates of their town. Still more startled was the doorkeeper who admitted him to the Martinsburg; his friend Capito paling, with tears in his eyes, as he wrung his hand.

"Nothing but difficulty and trouble lies before you, my Ulrich," said Capito, when the first excitement was over. "The Cardinal is taciturn and morose; an ominous silence has spread her wings over the palace; all the household go on tiptoe, none dares speak his thoughts. I myself have seen the letter which the Cardinal has received from the Pope, and which says, that his Holiness has learned, to his deepest mortification, that a certain Ulrich von Hutten had published pamphlets and books full of insult and invective against the holy see; and upon inquiry it had become apparent that this same Ulrich enjoyed the patronage of the Archbishop of Mainz—to wit, that the notorious books had been printed in that town. And although it was scarcely conceivable that the Archbishop had been ignorant of this, yet he, the Pope, felt unwilling to suspect a prince to whom he had given so many proofs of his personal favour—the golden rose in particular; he preferred the alternative that those things had escaped the archiepiscopal knowledge. But, all the more, the Pope must expect of the Cardinal that he would speedily suppress the daring spirit who had ventured to cast opprobrium upon the see, and that the blasphemer would meet with just retribution."

"And what was the Cardinal's answer?" asked Hutten, with beating heart.

Capito hesitated.

"Tell me, tell me all, whatever it be!" urged Hutten.

"Alas, that I must say it!" replied the chaplain. "I

myself have been obliged to put on paper what the Elector dictated to me; it was a hard day's work, believe me, and he, too, thought it so. I saw that plainly. But he sent his excuses to the Pope, regretting that his Holiness should have been annoyed by books printed at Mainz. He, the Archbishop, greatly taken up with other things, had not paid much attention; but that, in obedience to the supreme Head of the Church, he would do away with the offence."

Hutten paced the room, beginning to give vent to his feelings, but Capito interrupted: "Judge calmly, Ulrich mine! Do you not know our Elector? and that, with all his lovable qualities, his is not a high and lofty nature? He is full of benignity, ay, of generosity too, but he cannot stand in the storm. His intellect is clear and far-seeing, but his will needs marrow, and his heart is weak. I understand him thoroughly in this present case, for I have looked into his soul. Many a one has been surprised all along that the Cardinal should befriend a man, retaining him at his court, whose pen had attacked the Roman see, waging war with papacy for life or death. But I think I know what moved Albrecht's heart. It was his secret delight to watch you wielding blow upon blow against the Romish tyrant, and his thought was this: whatever in this feud will be snatched from the Roman Pontiff will fall to the share of the German Primate. If Hutten's pen and Sickingen's sword will help the nation to cast off the Italian yoke, the German Church will need a head at home, and its Bishop will rank next after the Bishop of Rome. It was this expectation which caused the Elector to be your friend, making you welcome at Mainz; he had accepted the thought that

Germany should be free of the foreign yoke, that her Church even should break the bond. But you went further; papacy itself you would destroy, pulling down the stronghold of the lying spirit. And now the Romish lion has perceived your aim, setting up a roar which is heard even at Mainz. Elector Albrecht has not the courage to withstand the lion, and, fearful lest he rouse him further, he has disowned his friend."

Hutten listened with deepest emotion, vainly trying to master his grief, which kept welling up to the brim even of tears. "Oh, how art thou fallen from heaven, thou brightest star! Yea, put not your confidence in princes! O Albrecht, on whom I rested my trust entirely, how great were thy thoughts, how generous thy intention, how noble thy bearing! But thou art fallen from thy height, grovelling before him who is in power, and sacrificing thy friend! .... My soul is full of sadness, my spirit has lost her strength. Is it true, then, that I am become a stranger where I had a home—shall I leave this place where for three years I loved and was loved? Not that I grieve leaving court. I have long hated this luxurious living, this pampering of the body by day and night, this excess of pleasure, this life of sycophants and miserable toadies; but woe is me, it is hard to leave a friend! .... Where is he?" he asked abruptly, turning to Capito, who stood by the window lost in thought.

"Here he is—just riding from the courtyard," replied the chaplain, starting from his reverie.

Hutten flew to the casement, and beheld the last of the Elector, as by the side of fair Margaret he cantered away. A proud smile rose to the lips of the knight, and he refrained not from giving expression to harsh truth.

Capito laid a hand on his shoulder: "Be not carried too far, Ulrich; the feeling of being wronged makes thee unjust. Can you not see deeper? The Elector would rather not meet thee, since rupture is inevitable; he would shorten the pain both to you and to himself. Moreover, he feels he is giving you the opportunity of escape."

But Hutten seemed heedless. Hotly flashed his eye, his lips trembled, and hoarsely he spoke: "Friendship is easily parted; the love of woman—of that woman—holds him in bonds. Go thy way, then, follow the way of the flesh—*I* know the path which lies before me. Albrecht is bound for Rome, Hutten for Wittenberg!"

CHAPTER XIII.

FIRE FOR FIRE.

AUTUMN advanced. The last of the shrivelled leaves had fallen to the ground, the breath of early frosts having killed every vestige of vegetation. The world had put on the garb of mourning, dreaming only of past delight; death was doing its work in nature.

But another messenger of death sped through the land. From across the Alps he had come, his voice was even now resounding in Germany: "He must die, the faithless son who has dared rise in judgment against the Mother Church!"

Burning with revenge, Doctor Eck, together with the legates Aleander and Caraccioli, had returned from Italy, bearing the ban bull, and therewith the Pope's reply in answer to the cry of conscience which had appealed to him on behalf of the Gospel. From all the pulpits this bull should be made public, that Germany should know the fate in store for him to whom half the people had begun to look as to a prophet sent from God; his writings, the writ ran, must be destroyed with fire, and his mouth be silenced for ever.

On a cold cheerless day in November, a great concourse

of people was gathering on the market-place at Mainz. A pyre had been erected, and was even now surrounded by a guard of thronging monks and servants wearing the electoral livery. "They mean to burn Luther," said the people: "let us go and see it!"

Beneath the Fisher-gate two horsemen met.

"God greet you, noble knight of Veltheim!" cried the one. "Let us proceed together, for methinks we are on the self-same errand."

"My thanks to you, sir of Steineck," returned the other. "Whence come you?"

"From Cologne, turning neither right nor left."

"From Cologne, you say! Is it true, then, what has been noised abroad—that the writings of Luther have been burned there by permission of the young Emperor himself?"

"True indeed! I saw it with mine own eyes, sad at heart that this should be the fate of a man whom I believed a messenger of God, sent to destroy the works of darkness."

"And has the Emperor actually allowed it?"

"Ay, more than allowed! It was by his order, they say. The twenty-year-old monarch is led entirely by priests and Spanish grandees, all of whom see in our Luther a very personification of the evil one. The pyre has been lit at Louvain, and Mainz is about to witness a like spectacle, I hear."

"Alas! alas! If the Pope has gained the Emperor to his side, the light must go out in darkness, and our hopes of liberty are over! I entertained better expectations of our new Emperor; and in sooth I had not believed that the Elector of Mainz would permit such disgraceful proceedings within his own town."

"Ah, but Albrecht, too, has turned against the truth, fearing the Pope and the Emperor; he has actually parted with Hutten, whom he always befriended. Let us drop this topic—I never trusted the cardinal's hat! But as for our Luther, his courage remains unshaken, and his own Elector holds him safe."

"So I hear. Can you tell me more about it?"

"I can give you certain information; I have it from Spalatin, the Saxon court chaplain. It appears that Doctor Eck, feeling himself propped up by two legates, addressed insolent demands to the Elector of Saxony, requesting his assistance for the carrying out of the papal bull. That he should order Luther's writings to be burned, and send him a prisoner to Rome, unless he preferred passing sentence on him himself. Whereupon the Elector, having taken counsel with Erasmus, informed the Romish would-be murderers that it was not his business to judge or condemn what Luther had done or not done, nor to decide whether his teaching were Christian truth or otherwise; that learned theologians and dignitaries of the Church must sift this matter. He vastly regretted that such had not done their duty hitherto, the rather that they had condemned Luther unheard. How could it be expected of him who desired to rule righteously to be guilty of a like injustice! If by proper trial Luther, through his own writings, could be proved in the wrong, he, the Elector, would know his duty and would see to the maintenance of justice, without being counselled thereto by messengers of his Holiness."

"That was a brave word, well befitting him whom his people call the Wise! I would fain take it as a good omen that the great cause will be brought to a glorious end. Burn away, then, ye Rome-servers, burn Luther's writings—he is secure from your grasp. Elector Frederick will hold him safe."

The two knights meanwhile were riding within the town, making their way through the thronging populace towards the market-place. They arrived just in time to witness the solemn procession as it left the cathedral for the place of judgment. It was headed by a division of the Archbishop's body-guard, which was followed by a long train of monks intoning lugubriously Psalm xciv.: "O Lord God, to whom vengeance belongeth; O God, to whom vengeance belongeth, show Thyself!" The monotonous chanting rose on the dismal November air, the wind, as it were, snatching up the sounds, blowing them hither and thither, as though nature must rise in protest against man's evil blindness. The monks were succeeded by the Chapter in full force, Aleander, the Pope's legate, bringing up the rear— he being on horseback and surrounded by a troop of halberdiers in black slouched hats and brimstone-coloured cloaks, evidently intended to strike terror into the people, by reminding them of the inevitable fate in store for heretics. For behind them on a hurdle, dragged by two muffled henchmen, lay a great bundle of printed matter, closely tied up and bearing the superscription: "Depart from me, ye cursed, into everlasting fire, prepared for the devil and his angels!" The dreadful procession closed with the hangman's company of men with blackened faces and armed with fire-hooks.

A great silence had fallen on the people; but when the pile was about to be lit a deep murmur arose, rolling onward as a gathering wave and breaking into a great cry: "Stamp out their fire! down with the monks!" Even the legate's name resounded again and again in threatening tones.

There was a general commotion. The people were pressing round the doomed books, effectually inclosing the hangman and his helpers, rendering them altogether powerless; and gibes were heard: "Why don't you set fire to the books? they are waiting patiently!"

The legate, indeed, awaited the fire impatiently, and forcing his horse among the people, he held forth, threatening them one and all with the Pope's displeasure. But a stone flew against his hat, another hit the horse, mud was being thrown profusely, and speeches hurled at him nowise redounding to his honour.

The legate was in a critical position, the Chapter hopeless of results, when suddenly the mob dispersed. Matters had been watched from the Martinsburg; a division of the Elector's men-at-arms with drawn swords came bursting upon the scene, clearing the place in a moment. The pious intent experienced no further hindrance, and the writings of Luther, the heretic, could be burned.

.   .   .   .

As at Cologne, Louvain, and Mainz, the fire flared up wherever the Pope's cohort was strong enough to keep down the people and carry out the pontifical command.

But in his cell at Wittenberg sat he who was the object of all this impotent rage. Very calmly he took the Pope's decree; his hopes could rest on God, to whom he looked with a good conscience, ever meeting his anxious friends with the assurance: "If God be for me, who can be against me? If Christ be on my side, antichrist can have no part in me."

A great change was passing within him. Sitting

in his cell, he wrote as for very life. Not long, and two further pamphlets shot, meteor like, through the world, reaching Rome and bursting over the palace of him with the triple crown. The one was addressed: "To the Christian Nobility of the German Nation," the second dealt of "The Babylonian Captivity of the Church."

A great step had been taken by the Reformer; these pamphlets form an era in his history. Up to the present time he had still hesitated to break with the Church openly and entirely, he had still acknowledged the supremacy of the Pope; but now, the Church herself having thrust him out, he had burst the last bond in his heart which held him prisoner to Rome. "Since they drove me out of the old house," he wrote, "which is eaten to pieces by the worms of error and superstition, I will raise up a new structure, in which the light of truth shall dwell. I have called to thee, Vicar of Christ, but thou wouldst not hear! I have interceded with thee to free the building of the gnawing worms, but thou wouldst not. Let responsibility be on thy head, if there be schism now, and struggle, and fight. I call God to witness, I have not wished it. But thou, Leo, hast driven me to this step. Let happen then what must be done!"

On the 10th of December, 1520, early in the morning a great throng of people—students and citizens—pressed round the University of Wittenberg. The faces of all were aglow with excitement; some, however, were scarcely free of apprehension; there was news posted up at the blackboard this morning which one must read with one's own eyes to believe them true. He was going to do it, the undaunted monk—he was going to declare before all the world what he had shown in his recent writings; he meant to testify to it by an unmistakable, if figurative, act: he was going to break now with the Pope solemnly and for ever—would meet his enemies with a just retribution—he would burn the Pope's bull, together with the decretals, this very day.

From the university the people streamed to the Augustinian cloister, watching its exit expectingly. The day was intensely cold, the frozen snow creaked like dry sand beneath the footsteps of the hurrying people; but no one thought of cold, the excitement of the moment ran as fire through their veins.

And as the watchman of the tower sang out the ninth hour, the convent gate opened, Doctor Martin appearing with a solemn countenance, his flashing eyes seeking heaven; and then with a loud voice he called out to the people, "In the Name of God!"

A long procession of students and professors followed him through the Elsterthor of Wittenberg to a free space beyond, where a large pile had been erected.

The people gathered in a great circle, looking on breathlessly. One of the graduates stepped forward, torch in hand; tongues of fire leapt from the pile, and a black column of smoke rose athwart the shining day.

Now Doctor Martin himself came forth, lifting a bundle of considerable size, and saying with far-sounding voice: "Inasmuch as thou hast afflicted the Holy One of God, eternal fire destroy thee!"

The bundle of scrolls flew into the flames—the bridge between the monk and the Pope was broken for ever, the chains of Roman tyranny were burst.

A deep silence had settled on the crowd. The people

perceived the import of that great moment, colouring the history of future ages; but in another moment the jubilant hymn, "We praise Thee, O God!" burst from a thousand hearts.

The fire did its work, diligently stirred by the students, who, when Luther and the professors had retired, found further fuel in the writings of Eck, Hogstraten, and other papists, which at their hands shared the fate of the bull.

And the smoke of the great fire at Wittenberg was felt at Rome. The Pope gasped for breath. His throne shook to its foundation; half the world seemed ready to hurl him from his seat.

CHAPTER XIV.

WORMS.

PROUDLY and luxuriously nestling on the song-famed Rhine, a very gem of the sunny Palatinate, rose the free town of Worms, of venerable antiquity and clothed with a halo of poetic fancy. A chosen residence of kings as early as the days of Chlodwig, the place was a favourite with Charlemagne for the gathering of princes and people, a favourite also with later German rulers whenever returning summer invited them to the banks of the vine-clad stream.

Charles V., too, fixed upon Worms for his first meeting with the Diet of his imperial realm.

The month of November, 1520, witnessed a great scene at the so-called Bishop's Seat: the hall of the ancient building was being prepared for the reception of the Diet. Workmen of all manner of handicraft were in requisition; there was gilding, painting, tapestry-hanging—hands innumerable plying their art with ceaseless industry, for the Emperor, already at Mainz, had announced his coming before the month was out.

And a grand entrance he made, with his Spanish

Netherlandish train of courtiers, the members of the Diet gathering speedily about him—three temporal and three spiritual Electors, no less than four-and-twenty reigning dukes, eleven markgraves and landgraves, seven sovereign princes, thirty archbishops, bishops and abbots innumerable, two papal legates, five ambassadors—from England, France, Bohemia, Hungary, and Venice respectively—fifty counts of the empire, a goodly show of knights and nobles of lesser degree, besides the deputed senators of various towns.

Important questions required to be settled; all the world looked to this Diet, watching the first public act of the young Emperor. Will he be equal to his high vocation? Will he show a German heart for his German realm, he of whose sway the vast empire was but as a province? Will his be the eye and the hand of the circumspect ruler, since, after all, he was but a youth of twenty summers? He had entered upon his reign under circumstances of peculiar difficulty; the times had outlived themselves, so to speak, things required a general recasting, the country was in a state of seething solution, in birth-labour of new things at hand. Would the Emperor be equal to it all? was his the strong hand to guide the disentangling threads? People knew not, but hoped. Complaints were rife on all sides, the country was overwhelmed with grievances calling aloud for redress. The exchequer was in all but hopeless condition, the army entirely disorganised, the Turks an ever-present danger on the eastern frontier. And what dissension, what constant rupture between the imperial Estates! The Electors ever anxious to set their prerogatives over against the Emperor of their choice; the princes quarrelling with the nobility and the townships; the peasantry bearing a lifelong grudge to nobleman and priest alike. And now, over and above these social evils, the misery of schism lowered on the horizon, the worst of contention, breaking up the land into two great camps, Protestantism meeting Papacy face to face. To steer the vessel clear of rock and shallow, to lead the country to its haven of peace at such a time, required a man of men, a prince gifted with heavenly wisdom. Would Charles prove himself the true guide of his people?

Among the manifold questions awaiting the consideration of the Diet, the matter of religion, if last, was not least. The Emperor, indeed, believed not in its importance; he had been brought up to outward mechanical form of worship, and had no possible understanding for the deep sacred conviction coming from the heart of Luther, and pulsating throughout the new-born movement for the purification of Christian faith. The monk of Wittenberg was but a dreamer, he thought, who would stand abashed before the tribunal of the Diet; the august company of so many lords, spiritual and temporal, would impress him with his own nothingness, and he would straightway recant. The young monarch expressed this view to some of the princes in private conversation; but the better instructed among them reserved their decided doubt.

It was early in February, 1521. An oriel window of the episcopal palace showed a bright glow long after the rest of the building had yielded to the silence of night. It was the room of the papal legates whence that light proceeded. They were sitting up in earnest consultation.

"Matters are taking a most critical turn," said Aleander, with an anxious look; "we may expect a hard battle yet. I could never have believed that the Emperor himself would add to our difficulty, for both at Aix-la-Chapelle and at Cologne he seemed quite at one with our way of thinking. How are we to explain it to his Holiness, that the Imperial Diet is careful of justice even for a heretic under the ban! No doubt the Pope would think by this time that Luther is safe in some prison, if not safe in another world; and here they are actually treating with him, ready to hear his defence, though long condemned by the Pope's own bull—actually promising him a safe-conduct for his journey! Is this not casting a slur upon the holy father's authority, endangered as it is by the heretic's far-spreading influence? I fear me the Pope's wrath will turn upon us, his ambassadors, if we cannot bring matters to a different issue. He will scarcely believe us that we have done our best to influence the Emperor."

"I quite share your apprehension," replied his joint legate, Caraccioli; "and let me tell you I had a private audience of the Emperor. I did my utmost in persuasion, assuring him that he need not keep his promise of the safe-conduct; his word to a heretic could nowise be binding, the rather that it was a work of high merit to free the world of heresy, no matter by what means."

"Have you ventured to say this?" returned Aleander. "And what answer did he give you?"

Caraccioli smiled grimly. "Charles is a German after all—these people have wooden hearts, and consciences as tough as shoe-leather. The Spanish crown has not rendered him more tractable. He turned upon me wrathfully, saying he desired not to be considered of a likeness with Emperor Sigismund, whose name for all ages to come was marred by his broken word, inasmuch as he permitted Huss to be dragged to the stake in spite of his imperial promise of a safe-conduct. There is no playing with Charles as regards this matter, I plainly saw; so I did my best to allay his anger, lest he should turn against us altogether. For the present we seem to have no choice but to acquiesce. Some dagger may find the way to the heretic's heart, in spite of the safe-conduct. Nevertheless, I am greatly troubled; matters seem to take a most unexpected turn. We have come hither to work for the unity of the German princes in opposing this heretic; and now the princes themselves come forward with all manner of grievance against the see itself, stirring up enmity between the Emperor and the Pope. Some of these princes are powerful enough, and I find that each of them has prepared his own special charge; even George of Saxony, whom I believed one of the truest sons of the Church, has resolved his ducal complaints under twelve different heads. I hear that no less than a hundred and one causes of complaint have been made out by the princes themselves. It will require our most careful manipulation lest these alleged grievances, apart from their taking up the best of the time, should turn the Estates in favour of the heretic, as seemingly of a like mind with themselves, and not to be blamed, therefore, for what he calls his preaching of the gospel."

"You greatly alarm me!" exclaimed Aleander. "I know nothing of these complaints you speak of. What are they?"

"The German princes consider themselves overtaxed by the Roman see. Whatever grudge they bear each other, they seem unanimous in this," returned Caraccioli testily. "There is but one cry among them concerning the Pope's extortion, as they call it; they accuse him of violation of right, and all manner of abuse."

"But I should like to know the particulars," persisted Aleander.

"It is scarcely possible to recount them all," replied Caraccioli; "one of their greatest objections seems to be this, that the Pope sometimes grants benefices to men nowise fitted for the Church—bakers, donkey-drivers, and grooms even having been invested, they say; which persons, knowing their own ignorance, put out their livings to curates upon a miserable stipend. Another matter of complaint, it appears, is this, that the Pope allows Germany to be overrun with sellers of indulgences, whereby the pockets of the poor fools are sadly drained."

Aleander's well-fed countenance fell. "The German princes are not far wrong," he said; "but on no account must they be allowed to be in the right!"

"The very opinion I would hold," assented Caraccioli, "but the worst is this, they have concocted an address to the Emperor, entitled, 'The Great Need of Reform,' which need they sustain with these words: 'Whereas, poor Christian souls are brought to great danger for the offence permitted at Rome, and the German nation thereby is impoverished; we consider it needful that a general amendment and reformation be advised, in order to prevent the further ruin of this people. With all diligence and earnestness we beseech your Imperial Majesty graciously to grant us redress.'"

Aleander stared aghast, lifting up both hands, as though to ward off the prayed-for reformation. "Alas for our hopes," he cried, "if the Emperor be weak enough to lend a willing ear! Is not this preparing the way for Luther and his heresy?"

"No doubt!" rejoined Caraccioli; "but it must not be. We must do all in our power to gain the Emperor. I rest not much confidence in Glapio, his father-confessor; I would rather try to work upon His Majesty by means of Cardinal Albrecht. As Elector of Mainz he is a very prop of the imperial throne, and he is devoted to Charles. I little doubt but we may gain him; for Luther's preaching against the indulgences has harmed him grievously. It is for his own benefit clearly that Luther should be tried and condemned before the Estates find a hearing for their grievances, which perchance they may retract altogether if we succeed in our endeavour."

Aleander seized his colleague by the arm, "Let me deal with the Cardinal," he cried, "for I believe I have power with him!"

Caraccioli assented, advising great prudence, however.

Early on the following morning, while Albrecht was yet breakfasting, Aleander attempted his mission. The wily legate did his utmost to gain the Elector to his views; but it was not so easy; for Albrecht secretly approved of the defeat which the Diet seemed likely to inflict upon his Holiness. If but recently he had assured the Pope of his true allegiance, to the parting even with his friend and retainer Hutten, that was a concession to necessity, and not of his choice. He lent but half an ear now to Aleander's proposals. But when the Italian touched upon the indulgences as forming part of the intended complaints, the Elector winced, becoming more tractable as the legate continued; ending with a promise, at last, that his influence with the Emperor should be for the remanding of the said grievances.

The legate triumphed, and, parting from the Elector, he hurried back to his colleague to impart him the news.

But more promising news than this even arrived that very day from Rome, elating the papal envoys not a little. A new ban had been prepared against Luther, and if the former had been conditional—allowing a sixty days' respite that he might retract—the latter anathematised him absolutely, giving over him and his followers to eternal damnation, and pronouncing the interdict upon any place which had accepted the heretical doctrines. Together with this bull arrived a papal writ to the Emperor, enjoining him not for a moment longer to tolerate the spread of heresy. And there was that in the Pope's letter which highly gratified the legates. "For now we have a hold on him," said Aleander, " if he proves unyielding. Great is the Pope's wisdom in having thought of this bait; there is little doubt but that the fish will bite. The papal brief tying his hands with regard to the Spanish Inquisition has always annoyed him; he will be glad to hear, therefore, that the Pope is willing to rescind that restriction, if he, the Emperor, will do his duty in Germany as regards the suppression of heresy. What think you, sir brother, had now be our best line of action? Strike the iron while it is hot, I ween! Let us announce the bull to the Diet at once."

Caraccioli agreed, and the following morning, it being

the 13th of February and Ash-Wednesday, the papal legate, Aleander, having donned his full splendour, appeared before the assembled Estates, requesting a hearing in the name of his Holiness, the supreme head of Christendom.

The matter in hand was broken off immediately, the august assembly preparing itself to listen attentively to whatever the purple-clothed messenger was about to deliver.

With great assumption of dignity the legate first read the papal bull, following it up with a powerful discourse. Eloquently and cleverly he put forward the alleged heresies, showing how they were detrimental to God in heaven, to angels and saints, endangering the Church, the holy father, his Imperial Majesty, and all worldly rule. If a Huss had been burned, and burned justly, for his teaching, surely this Luther had deserved a tenfold death, for he had outdone all heresy hitherto heard of in the Church; for had he not declared the Pope to be antichrist, and impugned not only the council of Constance, but all councils, arrogating to himself a better understanding of Holy Writ? Therefore the heretic was barred of all further hearing, seeing that the Pope had passed judgment already; and he prayed his Imperial Majesty graciously to desist from the intention of citing Luther to Worms, granting rather an immediate effect to the papal bull.

The legate's rhetorical display, occupying three hours, left its unmistakable impression upon the Diet. With growing interest the assembly had listened to his evolutions, and many a one who had hitherto looked carelessly upon Luther began to entertain misgivings lest he should prove the dangerous corrupter of mankind, the child of hell, as shown forth by the bull. His friends and patrons even felt overwhelmed with the accusation.

As for the Emperor, the spark had caught, the legate's speech had done its work; the papal envoys saw it, and failed not to improve the occasion. Effecting an entrance into the Imperial closet the following morning, they were lucky in hitting upon an hour when interruption by Glapio, the monarch's confessor, was not to be feared, whose jealousy both the Italians instinctively dreaded.

They remained closeted with Charles for two hours, and upon leaving their countenances betrayed satisfaction.

The very next day an Imperial edict was laid before the Diet, according to which, Luther, as a convicted and already condemned heretic, should have no further hearing, but should, after the burning of his books, be taken prisoner and await the due course of the law.

A bomb-shell suddenly bursting in their midst could not have surprised the Diet more than the reading of this edict; a great tumult arose, disclosing much difference of opinion. The Emperor felt nettled, nowise composing himself when it became apparent that the Estates required time for consideration.

The legates lost no opportunity to work upon the Emperor. Dr. Eck, too, at that time at Ingolstadt, wrote a letter which concluded with these words: "May it please your Imperial Majesty to throw your authority into the balance. Charlemagne of old forced the necks of refractory Saxons under the yoke of faith; let it not be said that at the time of the greater

Charles, Luther the Saxon caused men to fall from the faith."

Charles did his utmost that his will should be law, but the Diet proved stubborn, its majority eventually agreeing that at all events Luther must appear at Worms, not for further disputation, but for retracting the worst of his errors, perchance ; in which case they would treat with him concerning the rest of his teaching.

The fury of the legates knew no bounds. What could they expect, if the Estates claimed the right of distinction concerning the heretic's tenets? If he retracted some, they had said, they would treat with him concerning the others. And supposing these "others" were found to agree with their own complaints against the see? What then? what then? A vista opened before the eyes of the purple-robed dignitaries which seemed ready to confound their hopes.

They turned for counsel to the Elector Archbishop of Mainz, whose vote, they knew, had been with the minority. He received them graciously, for he too had experienced the full effect of the legate's speech, fairly shaking him out of the carelessness with which he had hitherto saved himself the trouble to examine the importance of Luther's influence.

"We will not hide from your electoral eminence," said Aleander, with a wily show of confidence, "that his Holiness the Pope was greatly incensed on learning that Hutten, of baneful memory, actually stood in your service, publishing his wicked writings in the daylight of your cognisance. Since then the Pope's anger has been allayed, seeing that you have withdrawn your friendship from Hutten; but his Holiness continues apprehensive, aware that your electoral grace has not done so of your own free will, but in obedience only to the papal command. If your grace, however, is desirous of regaining the Pope's full confidence, this present crisis would seem to be your opportunity. If the news be heard of at Rome that Cardinal Albrecht of Mainz has been chiefly instrumental in silencing Luther, your former friendship for Hutten will not be remembered against you, and you may bask in the fulness of papal favour."

The Cardinal continued in silence, lost in thought; conflicting desires passed through his mind. At last he said: "I will do what I can. It is plain that neither of the papal bulls have produced the impression they should. Luther himself laughs at them, and the people at large are not overawed by them. These bulls need the additional influence of some greater terror; where the Pope's arm is not sufficient, the Emperor must come to the rescue. If Luther does not retract, we must have him put under the ban of the Empire. This will put an end to his laughing, for then he will be given over to death."

The legates were deeply sensitive of the Elector's home-thrust concerning their master, but they swallowed their vexation for the sake of the new prospect of the heretic's ultimate discomfiture.

One fine morning early in March, half Worms had gathered on the market-place. The news had transpired that an imperial herald was being despatched to fetch the bold monk who had dared to defy the Pope, and who no doubt would have courage also to stand up for the truth before the Emperor and his Diet.

And as the bells of the ancient town struck the ninth hour, the imposing figure of Caspar Sturm, on his well-accoutred charger, and followed by a man-at-arms, appeared upon the scene. The Imperial eagle blazed from his chest, and his right hand carried the herald's staff. His eye flashed proudly, as though he felt the grand import of his mission, and the citizens with loud acclamation wished him a happy despatch.

CHAPTER XV.

HE CANNOT OTHERWISE.

SPLENDID and imposing had been the scene when the most powerful of rulers, on whose realm the sun never set, made his entry into Worms with all the grandeur of his Spanish-Netherlandish retinue; but when on the 16th of April, 1521, a bare-footed Augustinian entered the precincts of the venerable city, that was greater still. Not one of all the thousands gathered there from all parts of the vast empire had ever seen a like arrival.

The whole journey of Doctor Martin, from the first outset of his leaving Wittenberg, could be compared to a king's procession through his land. From far and near the people flocked together to see the man who to some appeared a very angel from heaven, to others a messenger of hell. Old men came tottering, mothers brought their babes, and those who could not get near enough envied the more fortunate who saw the great man face to face, and perchance had the happiness of pressing his hand. If he preached anywhere—and he did so on several occasions—the church could not hold the thronging congregation, men stopping without listened through door and window to his far-sounding voice.

He had been seriously cautioned against this journey, his anxious friends conjuring him to desist from what they believed would bring him to the stake. And when, having started, he was taken ill suddenly at Eisenach, his "beloved town," they saw in this delay a heaven-sent sign confirming their apprehensions. Luther, however, had set his face bravely towards Worms, and having recovered from his indisposition, he went his way fearless of man. Yet danger, so his friends assured him, lay waiting on all sides; the papists, they said, were on the watch for him everywhere, his death being desired at Rome. Still Luther made answer: "To Worms I have been called, to Worms I will go, were the town as full of devils as there are tiles upon the roofs of its houses. For *He* lives and rules who saved the three in the fiery furnace. And if He will not save me, it will be the worse for this head of mine, if you mean to uphold it against Christ Himself, who was laid low in grievous and ignominious death. Look to me for aught, but not that I should either take flight or retract. Take flight I will not, and retract I dare not. The Lord Jesus be my strength!"

On the 14th of April he arrived at Oppenheim, a small town on the Rhine, where he made halt. There came to him a messenger, despatched by Franz von Sickingen, the noble knight, delivering an urgent request that Luther should not proceed to Worms, but come to Castle Ebernburg instead: the Emperor's confessor, Glapio, and the Imperial chamberlain, Paul von Amsdorf, had arrived there, the message ran, and were anxious to come to an understanding with Luther.

"What!" said Doctor Martin, "am I called to Castle Ebernburg? Is this a snare, perchance, to detain me beyond the time of the safe-conduct, of which but three days now remain! If it is Glapio who desires my presence there, Cardinal Albrecht has a hand in it, for he and the Emperor's confessor have been friends of late, I hear!"

"Yet you are mistaken, reverend doctor," replied the messenger, who was no other than Martin Bucer, the theologian. "Am I not sent to you by the noble Sickingen? You have no truer friend than he and the brave Ulrich von Hutten, who at present also is seeking shelter at the 'harbour of righteousness,' as the Ebernburg has justly been designated. Believe me, you are called thither in honest friendship."

One of Luther's companions, Dr. Jerome Schurf, now joined with the messenger in pressing the invitation; but before Doctor Martin was ready with his answer, a stranger, who had come up to the little party unnoticed, took the word: "I crave your pardon, sirs, for offering advice, but there is error on both sides; I would fain tell you the truth, having left Worms but shortly. Father Glapio has no worse intent than to waylay you, good doctor, that perchance you might retract before seeing the steeples of Worms, or else return whence you came. For it is a fact that some at Worms are afraid of your coming, well knowing that your fearless confession will enlist the masses on the side of the Gospel, and thereby bring trouble to Emperor and Pope alike."

When Luther heard this, he turned to Bucer, saying:

"Take my greeting to the noble Sickingen, not forgetting brave Hutten; tell them not to trouble about me, for Luther must go his appointed way, and the Lord of Hosts is his shield."

Within an hour the little procession was again on the road, the Imperial herald with his man-at-arms heading the party; behind him, on an open car, sat Luther, still wearing the Augustinian dress, and accompanied by his friend Nicholas von Amsdorf, together with a Swedish nobleman, Peter Slawen by name. The rear was brought up by Justus Jonas, the Wittenberg preacher, and Dr. Jerome Schurf, Luther's legal adviser, both on horseback.

As the steeples of Worms grew upon the horizon, a noble train came meeting the travellers. The colours of Electoral Saxony could easily be distinguished, and there were happy acclamations on both sides. It was the retinue of Frederick the Wise and some other Saxon nobles, whose hearts prompted them to make him welcome who was about to make a stand for the truth, and to grace his entry into Worms. Presently more knights appeared, being of the followers of Ludwig, the Elector Palatine, the procession swelling as it went along. Luther's friends gathered about him.

The nearer they came to the town, the slower they could advance for the great concourse of people, and reaching the town gate, the clocks chiming the ninth hour of morning, it was scarcely possible to make way. The whole of Worms had left breakfast untasted, anxious to see him of whom Huss had prophesied a hundred years before. All the windows, the very roofs even, were thronged with expectant faces; had it been an emperor's triumphant entry, the people could not have cried, Hail! Hail! more eagerly.

Luther was glad, and breathed more freely when he gained his quarters at the Hospitallers of St. John. But little peace at first did he find, for all day long counts and prelates, doctors and senators, succeeded each other, anxious to see the famous monk and hear him speak. And though many came but for curiosity, Luther yet felt able to thank his God, when midnight at last brought quiet to his chamber, that the Gospel was already becoming a power in the land. He had satisfied himself also that the stranger at Oppenheim had spoken the truth : the papists dreaded his coming, lest there should be a tumult.

The following morning, when Luther, with his friends Amsdorf and Schurf, was sitting down to breakfast, the door opened, admitting Ulrich von Pappenheim, Hereditary Marshal of the Empire, in full dress, come to cite Luther in the name of Charles the Emperor to the bar of the Diet for the fourth hour of the afternoon.

"They are in a hurry to have done with me," said Luther, smiling, when the marshal had withdrawn. "But I thank God that the hour has come. I am of good cheer, for I know that the power of God will be strong in my weakness. Let us turn to breakfast now, blessing the Lord for His every mercy."

The day passed quickly, Doctor Martin again being sought by those who were anxious to show their sympathy; and Luther felt almost overpowered with so much kindness, for he longed to be alone with his God, to whom at all times he could speak as a man to his friend. He was able to retire at last, and seek strength in prayer before setting out for the great confession

And those who remained in the outer room heard him wrestling with God, even as he wrestled who was called Israel, having prevailed—heard his, "I will not let Thee go except Thou bless me!" And Luther received the answer of faith: his God, he knew now, would grant him power and victory.

At the appointed time the marshal reappeared, to usher the monk into the hall of the Diet.

There was a great light in Martin Luther's eyes, and solemnly he said: "In the Name of God!"

They went into the street, but it was quite hopeless to advance, for head to head stood the people. There was nothing left but to re-enter the building, and seek to gain the house of assembly by the back yards and gardens. But even there numbers followed him with silent gaze, men baring their heads.

Luther and his guide entered the ante-hall of the Diet, finding it partially filled with armed men and patricians of Worms.

For two hours he was kept waiting. Did those in power intend him to understand the Diet had more important business to engage its attention than the fancies of a mere monk?

Twilight deepened, torches were lit in the gloomy chamber.

As he stood waiting, an old, bearded, weather-beaten soldier coming up behind him, laid a hand upon his shoulder, saying with cordial kindliness: "Little monk, little monk, thou art about to make a stand, the like of which is unknown to me and many a brave soldier in hottest battle. But if thou art sure of thy faith, go forward in the name of God, and be of good cheer—He will not forsake thee."

"Is it you, dear Frundsberg?" returned Luther, clasping the honest captain by the hand. "I owe you thanks for a timely word. We are soldiers both of us, both ready to fight; you will know then that victory is of the Lord; in Him do I repose my trust!"

At last the door was thrown open, the light of a thousand tapers streamed into the half-lit lobby, quivering on expectant faces. The marshal giving the sign, Luther together with his counsel entered the spacious hall.

For a moment he seemed dazzled by the unaccustomed scene. What a difference between their grandeur and his cloister-like lowliness! Nor could he at first suppress the feeling that he knew little of the ways of the great ones upon earth, a stranger to their very mode of speech.

In the centre of the vast dome, upon a throne of gold beneath a purple canopy, sat the German Emperor of "sacred majesty," with crown and sceptre and ermine cloak, resplendent with jewels, which, catching and reflecting the rays of light, surrounded him with an almost fairy-like halo. To his right and left appeared the Electors, spiritual and temporal, blazing with the emblems of their dignity. The eyes of all dwelt upon Luther—Frederick of Saxony, and Ludwig Count Palatine, looking upon him with sympathy and almost fatherly encouragement; Elector Archbishop Richard of Treves viewing him with a glance of supreme dispassion; Joachim of Brandenburg and Herman of Cologne scarcely veiling their inimical feelings, while Albrecht, the Elector of Mainz, gazed upon him which was a curious mixture of interest, pride and aversion: this then was he who had caused him trouble and vexation, whom he now saw face to face. Albrecht's eye met the Emperor's, who from his throne with curling lip looked down upon the humble figure of the pale-faced monk, saying, as though he were thinking aloud : "*He* will not lead me to heresy ! Good heavens, what an abject creature ! Can it be he who has written those books, who has filled the realm with the sound of his voice ? "

Close beside the temporal Electors Archduke Ferdinand's chair had its place; the glory of the spiritual magnates, on the other hand, being added to by the purple splendour of the papal envoys. The eyes of both legates were filled with hatred, their trembling features betokening the excitement with which they anticipated the result of this hour.

Around and behind this centre of power sat princes and lords of the empire, rulers and dignitaries of the church, dukes, markgraves and counts on the right hand, archbishops, bishops and abbots on the left; the lesser nobility and deputies of free cities filling the ranks behind them, while the background was thronged with knights, councillors, doctors of universities and secular priests, who, having no vote, assisted as listeners only, representing the nation at large. The great hall of the Bishop's Seat had never seen so splendid, never so complete an assembly as that which is known in Protestant history as the Diet of Worms.

If Luther stood still at the entrance, it was for a moment only, till the wave of excitement had passed over the convocation; and then, preceded by the marshal and followed by Dr. Schurf, he advanced to the free space in front of the throne, where a heap of books, his own writings, lay piled on a table.

A voice rose from the multitude: "God judge thee, thou whited sepulchre!" another voice forthwith making answer: "Fear not them which kill the body, but are not able to kill the soul!"

John von Eck, Official of Electoral Treves, standing by the table, now began with low-toned voice:

"Martin Luther! His most sacred and invincible Majesty, acting upon the advice of the Imperial Estates, has called thee to appear before his presence, that thou shouldest give an answer to two questions: Firstly, dost thou acknowledge thyself to be the author of these books which have gone forth under thy name; and secondly, wilt thou retract some of the doctrines therein contained?"

Luther was about to speak, when his counsel stepped forward, saying: "Let the titles of these books be specified."

It was done, Luther thereupon giving his reply:

"All these books which have just been enumerated have been written by my hand. I acknowledge each one of them. But if I am asked either to defend or revoke them, this is a matter concerning Christian faith and the salvation of souls; concerning the Word of God also, than which there is nothing higher upon earth. It would be presumptuous and perilous to speak lightly. Without due thought upon the matter I might say less than is rightful, or more than is warranted by truth; and in either case I should be guilty of judgment; for, saith the Lord: 'Whosoever shall deny Me before men, him will I also deny before My Father which is in heaven!' Wherefore I humbly pray your Imperial Majesty to grant me time for reflection, that without prejudice to the

Word of God, or peril of my soul, I may meet this question."

He spoke under strong emotion, which some were glad to take as a sign of faint-heartedness.

A rustle went through the assembly, as of the wind lifting waves, or brushing through tree-tops. There was an exchange of opinions on all hands, which, however, varied greatly. Some attributed this evasive answer to loss of courage, shaking their heads contemptuously, while others admired the presence of mind which in the face of an unexpected question at once perceived a rightful expedient. The legates looked crestfallen.

The Emperor having consulted for a moment with the Official, the latter turned again to Luther and said:

"His Imperial Majesty might well refuse such a request as altogether unworthy of Imperial grace, but nevertheless has condescendingly resolved to grant thy desire and to expect thy answer to-morrow at this hour."

A wave of the hand, and Luther was dismissed.

He hardly knew how he came back to his lodgings, a crowd of impressions went heaving through his soul, and wearily he sank into a chair, feeling as though fortitude had left him.

But not for long. The next moment found him on his knees wrestling in prayer for the needful strength. And his prayer was that of a child, yet of a strong man of God.

On the following day, at the selfsame hour, he reappeared before the Imperial Diet. His step was firm, his walk erect ; and upon his countenance lay a light which was not of earthly kindling. When the question was repeated, his answer could be given with the assurance of a good conscience, rising from the heart, and testifying to liberty of soul.

He seemed another man. Those who heard him perceived at the very outset that he knew now exactly what to say.

His words came forth, resistless as a flowing river, his dark eyes burning with the fire of holy enthusiasm, his very figure seemingly growing with the fulness of his burden—he spoke, and they listened in breathless silence. Clearly and eloquently he passed from point to point, showing by the light of the Scriptures that he had taught nothing but what was in accordance with the Word of God.

The assembly, friend and foe, hung at his lips, his power was upon them, they could not otherwise but listen; not a sound was heard, save an occasional acclamation of admiring delight.

Not from the papists! And presently the legates were seen moving towards the Emperor, conferring with him under their breath. The Official was called to receive instruction; he was evidently intended to interrupt the speaker, when the latter, having reached his climax, came to a stop with a bow of respect to the Diet.

"Martin Luther," said the Official, somewhat roughly, "this is detaining us with needless talk. Not for disputation thou art called hither; his Majesty desires to hear nothing but a single and straightforward answer whether thou wilt retract or not."

Luther held his peace, hurt in his zeal for the truth; there was a great silence; every one present seemed to feel that an answer now would be given of great and far-reaching consequence.

Luther had recovered himself, his eyes flashed with a noble consciousness, a holy self-yielding; and resting a burning gaze upon the assembly, he opened his mouth and spoke: "Inasmuch as your Imperial Majesty and your Lordships require a straightforward answer, I will give one having neither horns nor teeth, to this effect: Unless I can be proved in the wrong by the clear evidence of Holy Writ—for I will not believe either the Pope or the Church councils alone, since it is manifest that both have erred upon several occasions, plainly contradicting themselves—I must hold myself bound by the Scriptures I have quoted, and my conscience is a prisoner to the Word of God; retract therefore I cannot, and will not, since it is a doubtful and dangerous expedient to do aught against conscience. So help me God! Amen."

Murmuring sounds arose, swelling to a tumult, voices here and there applauding the fearless confessor; and the louder these voices became, the more horrified seemed the legates: they sought the Emperor's ear, Aleander breaking into a hoarse whisper: "He has given the lie to the councils of Holy Church—that is the point. I pray your Majesty to make him repeat these words, that his adherents may take warning."

The Emperor yielded, and once more the Official put the question, Luther repeating without a moment's hesitation: "It is clearly manifest that the councils have erred upon various occasions, the Council of Constance plainly so, by deciding in the face of unmistakable passages of Holy Writ; wherefore I am constrained by the Scriptures to say that this council has been guilty of error."

"Thou art unable to prove it!" cried Eck wrathfully

But Luther dauntlessly made answer: "Yea, I will prove it in many points."

"It is enough!" thundered Charles, half rising on his throne. "Unheard-of things have come to our knowledge. Are we to understand, then, that this is thy opinion, monk, and that thou seest fit to insist upon it?"

Luther met the Emperor's indignant gaze. There was a momentary pause. Slowly he raised his right hand towards heaven, as in appeal to the King of Kings, and the memorable words resounded through the hall: "*Here I stand, I cannot otherwise. God help me! Amen.*"

The Emperor burst from his seat, there was a general rising, a passionate exchange of opinion; admiring applause on the one hand, imprecation on the other.

But he who had raised all this commotion had vanished from the scene. We find him again in his chamber, quietly refreshing himself with a draught of Eimbeck beer, which Duke Erich of Brunswick had sent him. But he was not left long to peaceful enjoyment. His abode at the Hospitallers of St. John seemed a very place of pilgrimage, admitting visitors all night long. Dukes, princes, counts, councillors, and plain citizens—all were anxious to see him and press his hand who had taken his stand upon the Gospel, who seemed above them in heavenly daring.

Meanwhile, in the Imperial closet, Albrecht, the Elector of Mainz, and the papal legates, consulted with the youthful ruler as to the course of action to be taken, the very next day revealing the conclusion arrived at in the dark of night. This is what an Imperial councillor laid before the Diet in Charles's own handwriting:

"Inasmuch as the Christian Emperors of Germany have always proven themselves brave defenders of the faith and true sons of the Church of Rome, it is our intention to save and protect everything held sacred by our predecessors, more especially the decrees of Church councils convened at Constance and elsewhere; we are firmly resolved therefore to hazard kingdoms and rulerships, yea, land and life, rather than permit the wicked designs of Luther, who presumes to know better than all other Christians, overthrowing the belief of a thousand years. Having heard his pertinacious answer yesterday, we hereby declare that we are sorry to have hitherto delayed interfering with him and his false doctrine; we command therefore that Luther be speedily returned to whence he came, but let him take care, in accordance with the safe-conduct, not to add to the commotion by fresh preaching, since we are resolved to deal with him as with an open heretic, looking to the princes of our realm to do their duty as becomes Christian rulers.

"Given with our own hand, this nineteenth of April, 1521."

This rescript did not fall short of effect; a wave of amazement and consternation passed through the assembled Diet.

"The meaning of this is that they are about to put Luther under the ban of the empire!" said Frederick of Saxony to his neighbour, Ludwig, the Elector Palatine. "I perceive the influence of the papal legates, who are anxious to turn our eyes from the many sores within the Church, that we should drop our grievances against the Roman See, and occupy our attention with Luther and his alleged heresy instead."

FREDERICK OF SAXONY.
After Albert Dürer.

"You are right," replied the Palatine. "It is greatly to be regretted that the Emperor allows himself to be the tool of the Pope's creatures, not seeing that he is caught in the Romish net. Wiser by far would it be did he urge the Pope to convoke a general council, not only for the hearing of Luther's cause, but for a beginning of that most needful reform of Church matters for which the whole of Germany is anxious, ay, more than anxious!"

The Elector of Saxony shook his head. "I see the ins and outs of the business," said he knowingly; "it is just this: the Emperor must conciliate the Pope, in order to gain him to his side, should it come to a war with France. Truly the Imperial crown will prove a heavy burden to his youthful head. For my part, I thank God, who gave me wisdom to refuse the dignity offered me at the demise of the late Emperor."

The estates meanwhile exchanged opinion upon opinion, the majority agreeing at last to solicit the Emperor for the appointment of a special committee of thoughtful men, and versed in theological matters, to whom the Lutheran cause should be referred.

Charles grew wrathful, the legates ground their teeth, but they were obliged to yield, and to witness, moreover, that Luther was honoured by the people as though he were a king. From far and near men came to consult him; the very citizens of Worms took his part, ready to fight his battle. And more than this, the Emperor one morning found a paper in his private chamber containing the words of the preacher: "Woe to thee, O land, when thy king is a child;" while the Elector of Mainz had his dwelling placarded with the information that four hundred noblemen had bound themselves to protect Luther, announcing enmity therefore to all papists, especially to his grace of Mainz; and that eight thousand fighting men were ready to strike the blow. The legates saw the prudence of holding their peace, trusting that the stiff-necked Luther himself would make further transaction, if not impossible, at any rate useless.

Nor were they deceived in their hope, for Doctor Martin remained firm; and on the 25th of April the Official of Treves announced to the Diet the contents of another Imperial rescript: Inasmuch as the heretic turned a deaf ear to all exhortation, he would be given over to the full rigour of the law. His Majesty commanded, therefore, that within twenty days he should return to Wittenberg, under the protection of the promised safe-conduct, after which time he should be dealt with according to his deserts.

The Diet listened in silence, and on the following morning Luther quietly left the town which had witnessed his greatest act of faith. It had been something to burn the bull at Wittenberg; it was another thing to confess his Lord before the great ones upon earth—needing a nobler courage and far higher trust, and both had been given him. Happy, therefore, and with renewed assurance, he went his way, careless of the Imperial ban following upon his footsteps, which Charles had extorted from the unwilling estates, after Luther's most influential friends, like him, had turned their back upon the Diet.

The bold confessor could rest his soul in twofold protection: he had received a secret message from his own Elector, who sent him word through Spalatin not to fear, should the Imperial ban be flung at him, inasmuch as he would be cared for, and a safe retreat be found for him. But, better than this, the comfort of the Holy Spirit was shed abroad in his heart—that He who had been his shield and buckler hitherto, in whose strength he had gone forth from the first, would not forsake him now, but continue with him in the battle.

CHAPTER XVI.

FRESH DIFFICULTY AND A NEW EXPEDIENT.

It was high time for the Archbishop Elector to quit Worms and to return to his own domains. He was looked for impatiently both at Mainz and Magdeburg, for those who governed in his absence hardly knew where to turn for help. Debts had increased more than ever, and no adequate resource seemed at hand. At Mainz the alarming figure of ninety thousand florins stared in the treasurer's face, matters at Magdeburg being about as bad.

The good folks at Mainz prepared a brilliant reception for the returning ruler; but their pleasure was seriously damped; each and all felt the overhanging cloud, and the Elector as soon as he was informed of the state of affairs positively took to flight.

"We long to return to Halle!" he explained to the Chapter; "we are anxious to see how the building of our new cathedral has advanced in our absence; for our heart has set great stakes upon that rising structure, which we look upon as a stronghold of the Romish faith, whence we hope to fight the creed of Wittenberg."

The Chapter looked blank, their faces lengthening at the hierarch's speedy departure.

But Albrecht's hurry slackened as soon as the "golden city" lay behind him, coming to an actual standstill at Aschaffenburg, where he possessed an inviting castle. It was a pleasant abode in the sunny season—that picturesque town, nestling on a slope of the Spessart, whence the eye overlooked the fruitful plain, the broad Rhine winding as a silver ribbon through the haze, the landscape glowing with colour and warmth. Margaret Riedinger used to say she wished she could spend her life there, for there she could breathe more freely and enjoy herself more fully than either at Mainz or Halle. And Albrecht, not loth to meet her wishes, spent many a week in the charming place, all the more willingly, as he owned forests there well stocked with deer. It was May now, and for three whole weeks he lingered in delight.

But he must delay no longer; repeated messages had arrived from Halle and Magdeburg, urging his presence. He was obliged to take his leave, Margaret being in no hurry to quit the land of milk and honey, as she called it, for the briny desert, so his grace must needs go his lonely way.

It was early in June that with a small retinue he proceeded to his eastern diocese.

If the pleasant time at Aschaffenburg had been sufficient to chase away his every vexation, the subsequent journey on horseback through tracts of beauty, when all nature was aglow with the life of returning summer, added not a little to his easy-going gladness. He felt the happiest of princes, receiving his chancellor, Doctor Turk of Halle, quite graciously, who came to meet him in an open carriage at a little distance from the town, and such were his own spirits that the chancellor's depression positively escaped his notice.

The Elector dismounted, taking his place in the vehicle.

"It is a long time since we have been favoured with your grace's presence," said the official, in a tone which covered reproof.

But the Elector did not take it as such, returning pleasantly: "The longer our absence, the greater will be our enjoyment in seeing the progress of our new cathedral church. I trust the builders have done their duty."

"They were willing to do it," said the chancellor, gloomily, "but the work has not advanced as it might have done. The body of the church, apart from the towers, is finished so far that the sacred relics could be moved thither from the private chapel; but I cannot speak of much progress besides."

The Elector raised questioning eyes. "These are no cheering news," he said; "what has retarded the work?"

The chancellor shrugged his shoulders significantly. "The men do not care to take a blessing for pay; they must live, and seek work elsewhere."

"Is that it? The old story; our want of money!" returned the Elector, heaving a sigh; a dark shadow had overcast his serenity. "I left Mainz to its own devices because they had nothing but complaints there to grace my return; we trusted for a brighter welcome to Halle and Magdeburg; and now it seems you intend singing to a similar tune! I dislike your woe-begone countenance, as though you knew not what else to advise. You *must* be able to advise! What should you say to a new tax?"

The chancellor's puny figure wriggled as though he were in a fit, his nostrils working like a rabbit's. "I would not counsel this expedient," he whimpered; "the estates are tired of taxes, the last one requiring all our efforts to push it in spite of them."

The Elector's countenance showed annoyance; he rested an absent gaze upon the landscape, and held his peace.

"I might suggest another means of help," continued the chancellor, when silence became irksome; and the Archbishop turned to him abruptly. "Those were days of blessing when Tetzel went about the land. Silver and gold flowed in torrents; it was a pleasure then to be chancellor of the archiepiscopal diocese. Cursed be he who bound our Tetzel's hand! But is he not bound himself now? Nay, Luther is dead! Who shall hinder us to re-open the traffic? Our troubles would soon be ended."

The Archbishop turned in disappointment. "If this is all your advice," he said, "it is not worth your breath! The days of that traffic are over; for, in the first place, the time is past which had been fixed by the Pope for the offering of indulgences; secondly, Tetzel is dead, without whom we could not think of re-opening the business, seeing there is not the like of him in all Christendom. And, moreover, that news seems false which says that Luther has departed this life! The rumour is abroad even now that the sparrow hath found an house where he abides his time in safety. But even if it were not so, and the outlaw had met with his fate, I should not care to meddle a second time with indulgences; the traffic has come to evil report, the people detest it and laugh at it; and among the princes of the realm too, complaints concerning it are rife, as the Diet of Worms has shown but too well. It would be foolish under these circumstances to rest our hopes once more on the sale of indulgences. However, I *have* thought of putting forward an indulgence—of another kind, that is. You know my plan of admitting the people to a sight of our relics, granting remission of sin to all such who will give a free-will offering of alms. Have you been able to find out whether this idea is likely to be favoured?"

The chancellor looked disgusted. He felt secure of the place he held in his master's regard, and made answer with a gruff boldness: "Much use that would be! We want a great deal of money, mere alms would be as a drop in the sea."

The Elector seemed nettled by this reply, wrapping the folds of silence about him. The chancellor then could but take the hint, and nothing more was said, till his grace, evidently displeased with the absence of conversation, took the lead, remarking: "Let there be an end now to disagreeable things. What news of our clergy?"

But the chancellor did not recover his equanimity so easily as all that. A flush of sarcasm lit up his features at the question. "Delightful news!" he said. "There has been a wedding to interest all the country side; Brother Bartholomew Bernhardi, the Provost of Kemberg, has taken a wife."

Albrecht gave a start, looking daggers at the chancellor. "What is this you say? And you dare make it a matter of fun, you to me, Doctor Turk! Are you so certain of our favour as all that?"

The chancellor, quite frightened, hastened to change the subject, and having succeeded in smoothing away the cloud of wrath from the Elector's brow, the current of conversation ran its even course.

"Look yonder!" said Albrecht, after a while, pointing to two figures in the distance. Both were on horseback, the one leading a heavily laden sumpter by the bridle. "Look yonder! Is it not our Schönitz?"

The chancellor put his hand across his brow, saying after a while: "I seem to recognise the merchant and his servant."

The foremost of the two, a young dapper man, somewhere about three-and-twenty, appeared to have formed an idea now as to who might be sitting in the carriage, for spurring his horse, he rode up alongside, taking off his hat reverentially. "All hail, your grace!" he cried. "I rejoice in the honour to be the first to call you welcome here."

The Elector waved his hand benignly. "Whence are you, friend Schönitz?"

"I have been to Frankfort, your grace."

"You seem to prefer the trader's life to looking after the salt-works at home."

"Well, my activity brooks not overmuch leisure. The salt-proprietorship at home scarcely fills my time, and trade is handy. Moreover, I delight in seeing something of the world, and getting to know other people."

"I fancy you found your reward; the sumpter could scarcely carry a better load."

"I am satisfied, your grace. Business prospered—

new connections have opened, I was introduced to rich people, met with unlooked-for honours, struck some good bargains, in silks especially, and a few splendid knick-knacks I bring home with me; one, particularly, which ought to be in your grace's possession; it *is* a beauty, and well worthy to be added to your collection of holy relics."

"You quite raise my curiosity!" said the Elector, with glittering eyes. "What is this treasure?"

"A casket of pure gold set with topazes and turquoises, and ornamented with representations of saints all round; it rests on four lion's paws, and its lid bears a capsula of silver and carved ivory. It is two feet long, and about a foot in height."

"Can you lay your hand on it?" inquired the Elector, turning towards the sumpter. "We should like to see it forthwith."

The chancellor cast a wrathful look upon Schönitz, anxious to ward off the tempting sight. "Why examine it now? It would only delay his grace's entry, the town being so near!" But the Elector gave no heed; as for Schönitz, he was already busy looking for the treasure among his baggage. Having disengaged it at last, he handed it into the carriage.

With speechless delight the Elector took the precious thing upon his knees, gazing upon it with the eye of a connoisseur, starting as from a trance presently. "We must have that!" he exclaimed. "Unworthy is the vessel of our collection which contains the blood of John the Baptist. This splendid casket will be far more fit to enshrine the holy relic. What is the price, dear Schönitz?"

"Twelve hundred florins Rhenisch I have paid for it

myself," replied the merchant. "But if it can be of use to your eminence, I shall be happy to part with it without gain to myself."

Again the chancellor interfered, with anxious countenance. "Your grace!" he cried, "might not the transaction wait for better times? It is but a useless bauble—and the money, the money!"

The Elector turned upon him with a frown. "It is the voice of Chancellor Turk, I hear! *You*, I dare say, can call such a beauty a bauble. Money only is delightful in your sight, for art you have no eyes, however—"

But Schönitz, aghast at the chancellor's hints, interrupted hastily: "Let your grace not be troubled about the payment. Indeed, I rather desired to offer it as a present, if I might make so bold."

The Elector looked at the merchant with unfeigned surprise. "Yours is a good, pious heart, dear Schönitz," he said, after a while. "For our own person we would not accept so valuable a present; but as you intend it for the new cathedral, and to the honour of God, it shall be received as the offering of childlike loving faith, and your reward shall be great in heaven. Put up your treasure now, and bring it to us to-morrow morning; we will receive you ourselves at the Burg!"

Beaming for joy, the merchant did as he was desired offering voluminous thanks for so much favour. He was proud of a link between him and the princely hierarch, considering his twelve hundred florins a small sacrifice for the confidence of such a magnate.

The journey proceeded without further delay, and after an hour and a half the electoral carriage passed the shingle-roofed old bridge, entering his town of

Halle. The magistrates and citizens, the corporations of salt-workers and others, the clergy and the school-children were ready to receive their ruler with solemn welcome, accompanying him amid the singing of Latin psalms to his princely dwelling at the Moritzburg.

. . . . .

The following morning the salt-spring owner and merchant of Halle, with delighted countenance, crossed the drawbridge of the episcopal palace, not disdaining to carry a covered baggage; he requested to be taken to his grace.

The great Cardinal came to his very ante-room, receiving the citizen with all manner of condescension. The precious casket being laid open to his sight, he again and again gave vent to his rapture, requesting the merchant to accompany him at once to the new cathedral; the beautiful thing should forthwith be admitted to its destined use.

Schönitz was profuse in thanks, but Albrecht interrupting him, the two left the palace.

They reached the place where the new collegiate church was rising, the cathedral itself being partly rebuilt only, the beautiful old monastery church of the Dominicans serving as a foundation; the nave was complete, the inside at least, outward adornments remaining to be seen to, and both the towers, which were planned for an unusual height, not far beyond their base as yet. Nor was the rest of the structure much advanced.

The Cardinal looked about him with evident annoyance, counting the workmen. "It is most disheartening to see the slow progress," he said, frowning. "We have centred all our hopes in this collegiate church. Heresy, like ill weeds, grows apace. That too should grow which we intend as a bulwark against it!"

And, approaching Schönitz, he continued, lowering his voice: "You are a good man, we trust you! Can you tell us why our hopes are held back so grievously?"

Schönitz averted his eyes.

"You do know the reason," continued the Cardinal. "It is money, wretched money! Look here, dear friend, could you assist us? You have so many connections, knowing rich people, as you said—do you know none who would come to the rescue with an adequate loan?"

Schönitz meditated. "I will show myself deserving of your electoral grace's confidence," he said; "I will try and procure what is wanted."

The Cardinal caught the merchant's hand. "Our thanks in advance, dear friend, our warmest thanks—we were not deceived in you! And now follow us to the holy relics."

The two men entered the church.

Again the Elector stood still, casting an inquiring look about the edifice in which all his pride had centred. What though this or that was wanting, or half finished only, he, with the eye of a lover of art, saw the perfect structure of his intention. He scarcely recognised the ancient building. Everything that could hurt the eye had been done away with, the pure Gothic forms were clothed in chastest beauty, proclaiming the true cathedral, and one fit to grace the abode of a great hierarch.

"Follow us to the relics," repeated the Archbishop.

"and behold the treasures brought together here by our predecessors and ourselves. It is indeed our pride and heart's delight. For hours we could remain here lost in the contemplation of so much beauty, and satiate our soul with the wondrous results of pious art for the worthy adornment of the sanctuary. But we will not keep the enjoyment selfishly to ourselves, it shall be an attraction to our new church, for nowhere in all Christendom is there a like collection of holy things. We have caused a catalogue to be made, giving illuminated representations of its various objects, for the better understanding of the common people; and we have ordered the relics to be divided into nine different lots according to their distinctive importance. The first order contains the relics of saints and those of the Holy Land; the second, those of the Saviour; the third, of the Virgin Mary; the fourth, of the patriarchs; the fifth, of the apostles; the sixth, of the martyrs; the seventh, of confessors; the eighth, of holy virgins; and the ninth, of elect women and widows."

With secret awe, Schönitz followed the Cardinal all round the collection, which impressed him, partly by its value as objects of art, partly by their supposed sanctity.

Shall we enter upon a description of the various relics? Here it is: let the reader see what our fathers worshipped when their very high-priests stood up, saying, "These be thy gods, O Israel!" Let him give thanks to our Father in heaven, who hath delivered us from the power of darkness, and hath translated us into the kingdom of His dear Son: in whom we have redemption through His blood, even the forgiveness of sins.

At the beginning, and, as it were, forming an introduction, were two costly objects, not exactly of ecclesiastical meaning; firstly, the consecrated golden rose which Pope Leo X. had given to the newly-appointed Cardinal; and secondly, the splendid sword with which the same Pope presented the Emperor Maximilian, and which the latter subsequently gave to Albrecht. Then there followed a whole galaxy of precious little coffins, some larger, some smaller, some containing bodies of saints, others but fragments of bones. To these were added bones, capsules, and shrines innumerable, some of gold, some of silver finely embossed, others of carved ivory, cunningly cut into representations of flowers, animals, or armorial devices The benighted visitor might imagine himself in the Holy Land almost, viewing these wonderful things; for there was earth of Damascus, taken of the self-same field of which God in the beginning took up the dust of the ground of which Adam was formed; earth also of the field of Hebron where Adam repented, and stones of Mount Sinai; there was manna, of which the Israelites did eat in the wilderness; and twigs were there of the burning bush, of the very tree even on which grew Aaron's rod that budded, and a fragment of the rod of Moses wherewith he did signs; there were bits of Mount Tabor, of Mount Olivet; leaves of a shrub in Gethsemane, by the side of which the chief priests and elders appeared with their swords and staves; sand of the valley of Jehoshaphat, of the tomb of the Virgin Mary, of Bethlehem, and what not besides.

The next order was supposed to refer to the life of our Lord exclusively, art vying with art to make it a fit abode of the holiest. Had they never heard that His true dwelling is the humble and contrite heart? Bring no more vain oblations—yet here they had set up a golden shrine with pearls and precious stones, containing the "miracle of the mass," or, to quote more fully, the "true Corpus Christi for the redemption of mankind, sacrificed to His Heavenly Father in willing death." There were pieces of the cross of Calvary in gold or silver setting; entire thorns from the crown of sorrow; shreds of the seamless coat, of the towel with which He girded Himself when washing the disciples' feet, of the only garment left Him on the cursed tree, of the purple robe when Pilate said: "Behold the man!" of the gorgeous robe with which Herod arrayed Him. Some of the myrrh there was, which, mingled with wine, they gave Him to drink. Other relics were there, referring to the miracles; some of the wine, for instance, that was made of water at the marriage of Cana, and a bit of one of the very waterpots of stone which held that water. There were crucifixes innumerable, of priceless value, and a representation of the resurrection, the treasure of treasures of the collection.

The following order was dedicated to Mary, whom they styled the "Mother of God," giving her in all manner of likeness; here also there was shrine upon shrine containing supposed relics of her who was called blessed among women; bits of her robe, of her shift, of her veil, of her girdle, of the flax which she spun, of the hair of her head; some of the very milk even of her virgin bosom, carefully kept in transparent crystal tubes.

The next order was of the patriarchs and prophets; there was a picture of the holy Joachim, father of the blessed Mary, with actual relics of his head, his ribs, etc.

A piece of the veil of the temple was shown. A silver-gilt shrine contained one of John the Baptist's fingers, another preserved some of this martyr's blood.

Here Archbishop Albrecht stopped to exchange the unworthy vessel with the precious casket he had received from Schönitz.

Then they turned to the relics of the holy apostles and evangelists, showing their images in silver or gold embossed and set with precious stones, St. Peter being prominent; the Cardinal, indeed, prided himself on possessing more precious parts of the body of him who was chief of the apostles, than could be found in any other collection of relics throughout the land.

The last three divisions referred to saints only, to martyrs, confessors, bishops, and elects of the Church.

It took a long time to see it all properly, the eye was dazzled, and the mind invited to pious enjoyment.

"Immense is the value of this sanctuary," said Schönitz at last, returning to conversation.

The Cardinal nodded, well satisfied. "I know it," he said; "the Archbishop of Magdeburg is envied by many on that account."

"But these treasures have a double value—that which is inherent in their sanctity, and that other which is of more tangible kind."

"How do you mean this?" asked the Cardinal.

The trader looked knowing. "If I lock up money in my chest, it may be a pleasure to look at; but only the miser would delight in such pleasure, and a miser is a fool. Put out your money at interest, and you double it."

"Yes, yes, but how am I to take this simile?" inquired the Cardinal, half guessing its meaning.

Schönitz came a step closer, saying in a loud whisper: "I would not keep this treasure all to myself, electoral grace, I would admit others to the sight."

"This has been done for some time," said Albrecht. "We exclude no one, and the pious may even take an indulgence if they are so minded."

"But this is not enough," urged Schönitz; "men set little store by what they get for nothing. What a man has given money for, that he will value; and the more he has paid for it, the more he will think of it! My meaning then is this: these indulgences must not be given gratuitously, and if your electoral grace would but issue new letters of indulgence, after the fashion of Tetzel, there would soon be money enough and to spare."

The Elector was silent. Again the thought was brought home to him to get rid of his difficulty by another indulgence; had not his chancellor given similar advice, urging him to re-establish the practices of Tetzel? And here was Schönitz suggesting something very like it; that he should take payment, certain sums for certain indulgence, obtainable only by a pious beholding of the saintly relics! He rather liked the proposal; it was something new, and not quite so bad as sending a Tetzel about the country, offering indulgence for money.

Should he do it? and *how* should he do it?

His thoughts reverted to Luther, who, he felt, was alive somewhere, and he saw his line of action. "Your advice is good and bad," he said to Schönitz. "That these holy relics and the indulgence obtainable thereby should bring in some money, is quite our intention; but the question is, can we so hide our object that evil tongues will not again make a butt of us and spoil our hopes? This is what we intend to publish."

And the Archbishop took a notebook from his pocket, reading: "Be it known to all men, that all such who are devoutly disposed to view these relics, offering their prayers to God, and their alms to the cathedral, shall receive unrivalled indulgence for the remission and forgiveness of all their sins in this manner: that through each part of a relic there are obtainable 4000 years, 3140 days and 800 quadragenes;[1] therefore, seeing that there are 8133 parts and 42 entire saints in our collection, a full sum may be arrived at of 39,245,120 years and 220 days, besides 6,540,000 quadragenes. Blessed are they who will assure themselves of so great a salvation! What think you, dear Schönitz, of this kind of proclamation?"

The merchant gave a nod of assent. "Your electoral grace has hit the very form; I see that my advice was bad, and might have brought good intentions to an evil end. But your grace's idea is deserving of all admiration; no one can take offence at it, nor pretend to hinder people's *free-will offerings*. With all wisdom, too, your eminence has so worded it, that no one could well suspect a hidden aim, and say that gain of money is the object. Great will be the throng of visitors anxious to avail themselves of so much grace, and alms will be given unsparingly."

The Elector was pleased with such manner of speech. There was Chancellor Turk, who had quite pooh-poohed his plan; but this merchant, on the contrary, admired it,

[1] A period of forty days.

and promised great success. "God grant it that our hopes be not deceived!" said the Cardinal presently, with an honest sigh. "Meanwhile I trust you will be mindful of your promise, dearest Schönitz, and procure us something for our most pressing need; for not before the 8th of September this year, being the day of the Virgin's nativity, shall we be sufficiently advanced to admit the people to a sight of these relics."

Schönitz repeated the assurance of his willingness to do his utmost in proving himself worthy of such high confidence, Cardinal Albrecht thereupon dismissing him with his most gracious smile.

CHAPTER XVII.

THE IDOL AT HALLE.

DREARY November once more came round. Pitiless winds rushed through the tree-tops, flapping their wings about the battlements of the Moritzburg. Showers of sleet filled the air with discomfort, the low-hanging clouds ushering in the evening before its time.

The watchmen posted about the Burg and its courtyard drew their cloaks over their heads, murmuringly looking for shelter against the ungenial elements.

From the windows of the banqueting hall streams of light flowed down upon the cheerless courtyard; strains of merry music, mixed with the sounds of carousal, falling upon the lulls of the storm.

"The company up there are having one of their fine evenings," said one of the electoral halberdiers to his comrade, the two seeking a moment's protection beneath an overhanging balcony. "One feels inclined at times to accuse Heaven of unjust dealings. Why should some few be revelling, while hundreds have but the wherewithal to starve? And the worst of it is that the revellers mostly are the bad ones, leaving the good to famish."

"Hold thy peace, Sigismund!" replied the other, in a loud whisper. "Let one of the courtiers hear this, and apply it to his grace, thou wilt be the worse for it. On the whole, thou hast spoken the truth; but after all I would except the Elector, who is a kind master to such as we. Have we not better pay than any other prince's men-at-arms? A cousin of mine is serving under the Duke of Saxony, and he told me——"

"Who has business to talk here?" interrupted a gruff voice. It was the captain of the body-guard, making his round.

The two halberdiers darted asunder, pleading the bad weather, which had driven them under common shelter; but this did not save them from severe reprimand, and they were glad to gain their respective posts.

The company in the great hall were indeed having a fine evening, according to their ideas. It was a lordly place, all arts combining to render it so—tapestry, sculpture, painting, lit up by a profusion of tapers. In the midst of this splendour a board was spread with choicest viands and abundant flowers; and, that the sense of hearing alone should not remain uncourted, his grace's orchestra did their best to amuse his guests. The Archbishop loved to display his greatness; and it tickled his pride if people averred that even the Imperial table was not more magnificently appointed than his grace's at the Moritzburg of Halle, or at the Martinsburg of Mainz.

A numerous company had assembled. At the head of the table sat the Cardinal, his chair slightly raised and bearing two scutcheons—the city arms of Mainz, being a white wheel on a red ground, and those of Halle, a crescent with two stars. To his right, decked with silks and satins broidered with pearls, the bright waving hair confined within the daintiest head-dress of purple velvet and airy plumes, sat she who gloried in swaying the great man's heart, surpassing all others in beauty, and basking in the pride of her much-envied position. The place to his left was assigned to a man who, if insignificant in appearance, was, as we know, an important personage nevertheless, the Chancellor Turk. Nearly opposite to him sat one, blue-eyed, delicately-featured, and wearing the priest's dress, who, on account of his obliging nature and loyal amiability, was almost a greater favourite with Albrecht than the chancellor, viz., the Elector's court chaplain and privy councillor, Wolfgang Fabricius Capito.

Courtiers, members of the nobility and patricians of the town made up the distinguished party, both sexes being represented. For the Cardinal, who prided himself on being a connoisseur of beauty in all her types, whether in art or nature, was not slow in appreciating feminine charms; and that beautiful women should grace his table pleased him better than filling his halls with the attractions of art. Nor did the ladies thus "honoured" despise taking their place in a circle which had not its equal among the courts of the realm, the Emperor's alone excepted. That Albrecht was a *spiritual* ruler, whom the celibacy which he professed ought to have rendered insensible to the fascinations of womanhood, was little thought of in a time when right and wrong, morality and immorality, had come to be hopelessly confused; and all being equally poor in honourable feeling concerning such things, men excused themselves with each other's precedent.

One among the guests yet remains to be named, Hans Schönitz, who had his seat among the nobility. The Elector, without exactly taking him into special employment, had somehow attached him to his person, honouring him with his confidence; and worthy Hans, anxious to repay the same, had prevailed upon a Dutch trader, and subsequently upon a Frankfort merchant, to supply his grace with a considerable sum of money. It was in acknowledgment thereof that the plain citizen was honoured with an invitation to the electoral board; but his neighbours of the country nobility did not quite relish his company. They did not know that Schönitz after all was of noble extraction; it was no fault of his that his family, a few generations previous, had relinquished the distinction.

Conversation flowed as a merry stream, and precious wine, figuratively, likewise.

Albrecht was in serenest mood, and many a pleasant banter passed between him and the fair creature at his right. Even the chancellor, usually inclined to be serious and somewhat morose, made merry to-day, enjoying the well-filled glass and delighting if the company appreciated his occasional jokes. Nor was he light-hearted without cause, for the great weight of care he had borne ever since his grace's accession concerning the electoral coffers was suddenly taken from him, inasmuch as these coffers were experiencing an unexpected influx. It had nettled his pride at first that he should have been in the wrong with his fears; for Doctor Turk was inclined to overrate his wisdom, and to distrust any expedient not originating with his own brain; but the patent fact that there was a paying off of debts now, leaving hopes even of surplus funds before long, had a wonderful influence over his feelings, smoothing away the last shade of annoyance.

The Elector, bending towards him, said with satisfaction: "We have heard that yesterday, it being the day of the Virgin's offering, there was an unusual throng of pilgrims anxious to be admitted to a sight of the holy relics. Can you tell me the amount of alms thus yielded?"

The chancellor winked knowingly. "Alms!" he said. "I ween if gold and silver be as plentiful everywhere as at present within the church of Sts. Maurice and Magdalene, it were no bad thing to continue a receiver of alms for ever. The pious pilgrims give most largely; the alms of yesterday, the treasurer tells me, amounted to upwards of seventeen hundred gulden. There seems to have been some great lord among the palmers, for five hundred florins wrapped in a linen bag were found in one of the boxes. May the Lord keep up this pious zeal but for the space of a year, and we shall be able to sing a *Te Deum!*"

"No doubt, no doubt," replied the Elector eagerly, and with flushing face, for he had not saved his wine. "The noise of our holy relics has gone abroad in the land, and the devout are coming from far and near to see what nowhere else is to be seen. But a few days ago I was pleased to notice a band of devotees whose travel-stained garments betokened their distant home; and upon inquiry we learned that they have come from Swabia, not grudging the journey."

"There are pilgrims from the Rhine, too," rejoined the chancellor, "and others from the far east of Germany; they all bless themselves at the shrines, and leave their gold behind. Nor is it surprising; how should they think lightly of the benefit, that at Halle, in Saxony, by dint of pious alms and prayer, forty thousand years of indulgence for sin are to be obtained? I hardly know much about the duration of purgatory, but methinks such a span of time is sure to cover it; poor souls therefore can be freed at Halle from all their fear."

Capito, the Elector's chaplain, listened to this conversation with eyes apparently studying the contents of his plate, giving careless answers to his neighbour, anxious to lose not a word of the chancellor's account. With difficulty he mastered his feelings, the knife and fork in his hands trembling involuntarily.

His neighbour noticing it, inquired whether he ailed anything.

"I feel grievously troubled," he replied; and perceiving that the Elector had overheard him, he prayed for permission to retire.

Albrecht, at all times kindly disposed towards his chaplain, dismissed him with a look of sympathy; and Capito hastened away, breathing more freely when the banqueting hall lay behind him. "Whither are we drifting?" he groaned. "The Elector sees nought but sunshine, careless of the clouds gathering overhead. I dare not open his eyes; rather will I attempt to act independently—perhaps I may succeed in warding off the blow! To-morrow at daybreak I will set out. I must consult with Spalatin."

He was a nobly-disposed and well-inclined man, this electoral councillor and court chaplain, Wolfgang Fabricius Capito, true-hearted and clear-headed withal, and more than half gained for the Protestant truth, but all too prudent and fearful of harming a good cause.

He thought there was no other way but that of circumspection for impressing the Cardinal with the power of the Gospel—if he were open to impression at all—the unfathomable man who seemed to have nothing but enmity for Luther, while not hindering the progress of Gospel teaching within his dominions. "He does not understand Luther!" sighed Capito.; "and the Gospel is hidden to his eye, because his heart is far from it and filled with this world's gain, delighting in honour and power, in art and sensuous enjoyment. God grant he may yet be a different man! Lord help me to prevail with him! Thine is the cause, O Lord, yet fill me with wisdom and strength to do the work!"

Capito stood by the window of his own chamber, lost in thought. The sounds of revelling, of music and table delight were heard even in his quiet retreat, not lessening his fears. "If thou but knewest, Albrecht!" he groaned, and, dressed as he was, he sought his couch.

. . . .

That same evening two citizens of Halle, the stocking-weaver, Gabriel Rennepfennig, and Jonathan Ehricht, master of the springs, were passing away the twilight hour in the taproom of the "Golden Heart," talking of this and that, the landlord going to and fro.

The room was filling with strange visitors, not to the satisfaction of the worthy citizens, he of the springs presently remarking to his friend of the stockings:

"Pilgrims upon pilgrims, having walked miles, to judge by their speech, for the worshipping of dead bones and rags, thinking to gain heaven thereby, forsooth! I call it foolery and superstitious nonsense; and his eminence can scarcely hide it that money, after all, is the object. Would our Luther were still in the land;

he would not hesitate to call things by their names; but that watchman of Sion has vanished from the wall. Perhaps the Lord will raise him up a successor; his voice has been heard far and wide, awakening many who are ready for the battle now, though the leader is gone, ready to fight against Popish fraud."

"Hush! this is not for all men's ears!" whispered Gabriel. "Over there is one watching you with widening eyes."

"Let him!" cried Jonathan, half querulously. "Surely a man may speak the truth! I call it foolery and superstition, and so it is! I pity each poor creature toiling away with the pilgrim's staff. That Luther has opened my eyes. I have read his books; and, to the face of the Romish antichrist, I believe him to be a messenger of God."

The stocking-weaver again felt anxious to warn his friend, but before he could speak the stranger of the watchful eyes, a big bulky fellow, had approached the two, crying with threatening gestures: "What disgraceful blasphemy is this? Will you stop it at once or take the consequences?"

"Indeed!" cried the salt-master, indignantly. "Who are you, to attack a citizen of Halle in his own town?"

But the stranger, little abashed, raised a fist, others of the pilgrims coming up behind him, and cries arose: "Down with him, he is a Lutheran!"

The salt-master, having strength of body and courage of mind besides, defended himself with well-aimed blows. The stocking-weaver, of more puny kind, had slunk away, but returned presently, followed by several of their fellow-citizens, who, coming to the rescue of brave Jonathan, plied their clubs as though the stranger pilgrims were so many barley sheaves. More citizens arrived, and of salt-workers not a few, and the palmers had the worst of it.

The brawl had been dragged into the street, so that even the constabulary was required to separate the combatants.

The pious pilgrims retired to more congenial quarters, and forthwith resolved to despatch a deputation accusing the citizens to the Cardinal. Their landlord, however, advised them to leave matters alone; they would do better, he said, to withdraw from the town as quietly as possible; for Halle was full of people inclined to the Lutheran teaching, and they knew their own mind. Moreover, these Lutherans were not only common citizens, but were to be found among the magistrates, and even among noble patricians. There was no saying, he added, how many secret friends of the Gospel could be found at Halle, besides those who confessed themselves as such openly.

The palmers grew frightened, wondering how such things were possible beneath the very eyes of the Cardinal, and when the morning dawned they stealthily quitted the town.

The feasting Cardinal heard of this occurrence at the time. He frowned, gave a grunt of displeasure, but saw no occasion for rising from his evening's enjoyment.

CHAPTER XVIII.

LUTHER VERSUS THE CARDINAL.

At nightfall a horseman arrived at the gates of the electoral castle at Torgau; having dismounted, he knocked for admittance somewhat impatiently, requesting to see the court chaplain of his serene highness.

He was informed that the reverend gentleman had accompanied the Elector to Altenburg, and was not expected back before the morrow.

The traveller was evidently vexed, not hiding his disappointment. Leaving his horse in the charge of a groom, he entered the castle, asking for the court chaplain's rooms; but finding them comfortless for want of a fire, he retired to an apartment in the lower regions where he could thaw his frozen limbs.

Time hung heavy on his hands. He cared not for conversation with the lackeys, but tried to amuse himself with some books of the absent chaplain's; his very thoughts, however, seemed congealed; it had been a miserable cheerless day.

The following noon the court preacher arrived, coming in advance of the Elector.

Entering his rooms, he stood still exclaiming: "Is

it yourself, Capito, dear friend ? What brings you hither ? "

"Anxiety for him I call my master," replied the other, quickly.

The friends shook hands, sitting down by the fireplace.

"This uncertain fear is killing me," said Capito. "I hardly dare to look the Cardinal in the face. Unsuspiciously and unconcerned he lives his thoughtless life, not understanding my timid hints. He cannot but have noticed that I am troubled, and indeed he has asked me several times within these last few days what is the matter with me; I cannot hide my sorrow much longer. This is what brings me hither, dear Spalatin; I have come hoping you have comforting news. Did you succeed in appeasing Luther ? "

Spalatin shrugged his shoulders. "You know Doctor Martin yourself by this time; and you know that he will do what he thinks right, and no power on earth, neither friend nor foe, will dissuade him. When I first learned that he intended a new pamphlet against the Cardinal concerning this recent matter of indulgence, which should expose his eminence to public shame, 1 wrote him a long letter praying him to desist; moreover, I have been empowered to inform him of his serene highness's opinion in the matter, which is neither more nor less than that Elector Frederick would withdraw his friendship if he dared to insult the most powerful prince of the realm, who stands high in the favour of both Emperor and Pope, the Primate of all Germany and Lord High Chancellor of the 'Holy Roman Empire of the German Nation.' In fact, our Elector sees something of a personal thrust in Luther's intended attack upon the worship of relics, since in his own cathedral at Wittenberg he preserves a number of these sacred things to which indulgence is attached, though not for money, and he cannot wean his heart from them. He has never allowed the sale of indulgences, as the Cardinal has done; but he does not see much harm in the worshipping, and he feels annoyed now that Luther should direct his shafts against both practices alike. But it was of no use my reasoning with Luther; nor had it any effect my pointing out to him that his attack upon the Cardinal would place our Elector in a most awkward position as regards his relation with the powerful representatives of the house of Brandenburg, since they would naturally suspect that Luther would do nothing without the sanction of his sovereign protector. But Doctor Martin has his own thoughts and opinions, and cares for little else. The considerations of politics are nothing to him, nor does he stop on his way for courtly reasons. What his heart and conscience prompt he will do in the face of the very devil, not to say of his Elector. And fancy now the plight he has put me in: he has sent me that very pamphlet, that I should revise it and see to the printing!"

"No!" exclaimed Capito. "No, in the name of all the saints! Is that pamphlet a fact already? I heard that he was busy writing his sermons on the Wartburg! And he has sent it to *you* actually?"

"It is our Luther!" said Spalatin, not without emotion. "He is great in all things, great also in his trust."

"But what have you done with it?" inquired Capito, excitedly.

"The only thing I could. I took it to the Elector,"

continued Spalatin. "His highness was furious, as you may imagine, calling Luther a madman. And then he charged me to inform him that he would never consent to his attacking the Cardinal, that he would consent to nothing, in fact, intended to disturb the public peace."

"The Lord be praised!" ejaculated Capito; "and blessings upon the Elector. Truly he has not been called 'the Wise' undeservedly."

"Do not rejoice too soon!" warned Spalatin. "We have not done yet. Luther of course sent a reply, and what a reply! His wrath made me tremble even at this distance. Here is his letter—listen to this: 'This of all things I will not stand. Rather will I lose thee and thy Elector and all the world. Have I withstood the Pope who made the Cardinal, and shall I be fearful of his creature? Truly this is a most righteous proceeding, not to have the public peace disturbed, but allow the Cardinal's disturbing the eternal peace of God by his wicked doings! My Spalatin! my own Elector! For the sake of Christ's little sheep, this heinous wolf must be resisted with all power, as an example to others. Thy letter cannot move me to alter a single word of what I have written, although I gave leave to Melancthon to make what alteration seemed good to him. Take warning, therefore, not to keep back the pamphlet; let him have it, that he may get it printed. I will not take thy advice, and there is an end of it.'"

Capito grew white, shaking as though seized with ague. He stared, speechless, asking after a while:

"And have you done his behest?"

Spalatin moved uneasily. "Well, no," he said,

pausing. "I have ventured to detain the manuscript. I have not given it to Melancthon."

Capito pressed his friend's hand eagerly. "This is courageous resistance, but keep to it! It must not be printed! Let Luther roar out his anger; he is a prisoner on the Wartburg, and will have to calm down. His wrath will pass away, and then he will be able to thank his friends that their prudence saved him from a hasty and dangerous act. I conjure thee, by all that is sacred, be firm, my Spalatin."

The Saxon court chaplain was glad to have found one on whom to rest half the responsibility in the matter; and he assured his friend that he would do his utmost to save the Cardinal from disgrace, thereby shielding his own master from annoyance and embarrassment.

Capito had no further occasion for continuing at Torgau. Ordering his horse round, he trotted away more light-heartedly than he had come.

The cold was intense, turning each breath into frozen moisture; the departing chaplain soon changed to a quick gallop for the warming of man and beast. Night was falling when he arrived at Eilenburg, where he put up, continuing his journey in the morning.

He had not ridden far when, reaching a cross-road, he saw another horseman approaching with a servant behind him. The stranger was dressed in a darkish grey jerkin, black leather cap, a long sword hanging from his side. The lower part of his face was hidden by a full beard, dark and curling.

Coming close, Capito perceived that he pulled up short, fixing a searching look upon the Cardinal's councillor, his lips parting as though he were about to speak. But, apparently changing his intention suddenly, he spurred his horse, turning in his seat as it bounded away with a " God speed you, reverend sir!"

Now it was for Capito to pull up short, in utter surprise moreover. Who could it be? A stranger to all appearance, but a well-known voice!

He was baffled; by the voice alone he could not make him out, and almost angrily he pulled his horse's rein. The little incident was soon forgotten, however, and towards evening he who was the Cardinal's trusted servant, and yet also Luther's secret friend, crossed the drawbridge of the Moritzburg far more hopefully than he had done on leaving the palace a few short days since.

It was about the same hour that there was a knock for admittance at the door of Nicholas von Amsdorf at Wittenberg. The worthy Professor giving leave to enter, there appeared the same tall knightly figure met by Capito on the road.

"God greet thee!" said a voice proceeding from the depth of the hiding beard. It was a well-known voice, electrifying the Professor. For a moment he too was baffled; but with a sudden start he came forward, peering close into the stranger's face, receding again as from a vision supernatural.

The stranger burst into hearty laughter. "Well, Amsdorf," he cried, "art afraid of an old friend? I am not a ghost, but my own self bodily."

"Brother Martin! is it possible? But why this mummery, and for Heaven's sake why have you left your safe retreat?"

"Hush; do not proclaim it at the top of your voice. I have come secretly, to avoid trouble to the Elector; I could not otherwise but come, for evil tidings have reached me from Wittenberg."

It was indeed brother Martin, in spite of this disguise. He felt unable to continue quietly in his "desert," news having reached him that the Wittenberg students had fallen into all sorts of pranks against the papists rousing his fears, lest what had been begun in the spirit should be in danger of ending in the flesh., Moreover, he felt anxious personally to consult with Melancthon, and to satisfy himself concerning his pamphlet against the Cardinal.

Amsdorf locked the door, Luther divesting himself of hat and sword, after which the two friends sat down to quiet conversation concerning events at Wittenberg. Luther was glad to hear that proper behaviour among the students had been restored, which information greatly assisted the return of his usual good humour; and breaking off the matter in hand, he said with a twinkle of amusement: "Do send for friend Kranach, I long to see him! You might let him know that a stranger knight, having heard of his fame, would wish to sit for his picture. Magister Philip, too, I fain would see."

A messenger was despatched, and presently the tall venerable figure of Lucas Kranach, the Wittenberg painter and magistrate, made its appearance in the ill-lit little room, politely bowing and saying: "You have desired my presence, noble knight, I shall be pleased to take your picture."

But the knight, unable to keep up his character, wrung the artist's hand with gladdening delight, quite bewildering his unsuspecting friend, till he too made the discovery that it was indeed brother Martin, and was even more dismayed than Amsdorf had been.

Again the door opened, ushering in a pale-faced weakly little man, somewhat stooping — that was

Magister Philip Melancthon. He fairly trembled, having recognised Luther's voice on the spot; his was a shy, anxious disposition, and the Doctor had some trouble in calming his apprehension.

Melancthon's news, however, did not add to Luther's composure. The Doctor learned, to his surprise and vexation, that his pamphlet to the Cardinal, to all appearance, was still safe in Spalatin's custody.

That was more than his high mettle could brook; his wrath knew no bounds, quite bewildering his friends, who scarcely understood the meaning. And even when Luther tried to make them see it, they were not quick in sharing his views, doing their utmost, on the contrary, to convince him of the inadvisability of his intention, urging him to withdraw the pamphlet, or at least to take time for re-consideration. The latter point they carried, Luther yielding after much pressure; the pamphlet, then, should be delayed for a while.

Unanimity being restored, the four friends sat in happy intercourse far into the night, early dawn witnessing the departure of the grey-coated horseman with the curly beard.

Proceeding on the road, his thoughts reverted to the promise given to the Wittenberg friends. His own views were gaining the upper hand, and his anger turned against himself for having yielded. His fiery spirit resented the curb; patience and prudence dictated by fear were scarcely suited to his mind.

Suddenly he rose in the saddle, his eyes brightening with newborn intention. "I am not to print, they said; well, then, there is ink at the Wartburg—for Luther's voice must reach thee, Cardinal!"

. . . .

The privy councillor and court chaplain of Cardinal Albrecht, Wolfgang Fabricius Capito, was sitting in his quiet chamber at the Moritzburg lost in study, when a servant came to him with a letter sealed and addressed to his eminence.

He started, recognising the handwriting; there was no mistaking the firm, powerful characters of Doctor Martin Luther.

Rising from his table, he paced the room excitedly. What might not be written in that letter? There was little chance of its being pleasant correspondence, but every probability that it treated of the same matter as that pamphlet in Spalatin's keeping. Should he take the letter to his grace? Was it not far wiser to destroy it at once? But what if Luther should inquire? Capito trembled at the bare thought. He could not, he dared not resist him; it was nothing short of a vision of terror, that Luther, goaded beyond endurance by a second interference with his intention, would not only find means for holding up the Cardinal to the eyes of the world, but his chaplain along with him. He saw no loophole for escaping his unwelcome duty, but took the letter to the Cardinal.

Albrecht was busy consulting with Hans Schönitz; bales of costly silks and Brabant carpets were spread upon the floor. His grace knew no bounds in the embellishing of his new cathedral church, nor need he fear expenses, since the alms of pious pilgrims showed no symptoms of abatement.

"What ill-luck is written in your face, my chaplain?" exclaimed the Cardinal, stopping short in the midst of a dissertation upon tapestry.

Capito vainly endeavoured to look unconcerned,

saying, "I am the bearer of a sealed document; I can only guess at the contents; it is addressed in the handwriting of Martin Luther."

"What is this I hear?" cried the Cardinal. "What daring is this of one who has been found guilty of double ban!"

He took hold of the letter with the tips of his fingers, as though fearing the very contact were contaminating, flinging it from him in high displeasure. Capito did not await his breaking the seal; and the Cardinal, not anxious to learn the contents, reverted to his business with Schönitz.

The latter having retired at last, Albrecht took up the missive, murmuring with every mark of disgust: "This is the third time that the churl dares to address me, his archbishop, and a prince of the realm."

Unfolding the document, his eyes glanced over the contents. A deep flush overspread his features, his eyes began to swim, and crumbling the paper, he sank helplessly into a chair, cold drops gathering upon his forehead.

Recovering himself at last, he glanced about the room uneasily—there lay the letter before him on the floor. He snatched it up, reading now more slowly.

But the process did not tend to his composure. He was beside himself, scarcely knowing what he did. Stamping the floor, and once more crushing the paper, he burst into an exasperated fury against the heretic who again and again crossed his path like some evil spectre, holding up a hand of warning, as though there were no difference between a begging friar and a Cardinal of the Church. "It is beyond mortal endurance!" he cried; "how the churl dares censure one so immeasurably above him; he who is under the ban of Pope and Emperor alike, finding fault with the Primate of all Germany—having no regard even for the sanctity of the purple! Nothing is safe from his degrading touch; the holy relics even must be a butt to his insulting remarks. Be anathema, thou child of hell! for daring to shake the pillars of the Church, for—for—endeavouring to empty my coffers! Good heavens! what has been effected by my publishing the Edict of Worms through the length and breadth of my diocese? Art thou become powerless, Holy Father, and is thy ban as little thought of as the sting of a fly? And thou, Charles, where is the power of thy sword? Dost thou not hear him whom thou hast pronounced an outlaw blaspheme us?"

The Cardinal stopped—another thought came uppermost, shaking his frame as with a fit of ague. He remembered that part of the letter which hinted at his private life, leaving him with the fear that the cloak should be snatched from him in the face of all the world. His eminence was sensible to the disgrace; again the cold dews covered his countenance—the Archbishop gasped for breath.

In order to understand all this, we must quote Luther's letter, long as it is.

"Twice I have written to your electoral grace in the Latin tongue, in the first instance dealing with the deceitful sale of indulgences. I could easily have directed the whole tumult against your grace, but I saved your grace and the princely house of Brandenburg, thinking you did it unwittingly, misled by pickthanks. But my faithful exhortation met with little gratitude. Upon the second occasion I craved instruction, but received only a harsh, ill-mannered, unbishoplike and unchristian answer, referring me to men of the schools. As both letters therefore availed me nothing, I purpose to write a third one in the vulgar tongue.

"Your grace has again raised up the idol which robs poor simple Christians of money and soul, thereby acknowledging openly that it is the Bishop of Mainz who is answerable for whatever Tetzel has done, although at the time I did not impute it to him. Maybe your electoral grace now imagines that I have vanished from the scene—you would like to be safe from me, and have the monk smothered by Imperial majesty. Very well then. Your electoral grace nevertheless shall know that I mean to do what Christian charity demands, not being a respecter of the gates of hell, far less of those who know not, popes, cardinals or bishops. I will neither suffer it nor hold my peace, that the Bishop of Mainz should pretend he knows not, or ought not to give instruction if a poor sinner asks it of him, seeing that he knows well enough, and no shame of his prevents the doing, where his gain of money is concerned. This, then, is my most humble petition, that your electoral grace would leave poor people unmisled and unrobbed, proving yourself to be a bishop and not a wolf. It is full well known now that the sale of indulgences is nought but knavery and deceit, and that Christ alone should be preached to the people; and your electoral grace therefore has not the excuse of ignorance. Let your grace remember the beginning, and the direful fire sprung from the despised little spark, when all the world would have believed that a single poor mendicant was far too immeasurably beneath the Pope, having set about a thing altogether impossible. Yet God has found judgment, making hard work for the Pope and his own; for, against all the world's opinion, He has brought matters to such an issue that the Pope will not easily recover, the rather that each day finds him the worse: the work of God then is plainly to be perceived. That same God is alive still, let no one doubt it; and He understands the art of resisting also a Cardinal of Mainz, no matter how many Emperors may hold a hand over him. He delights especially in laying low the grand cedars, and to humble proud, hard-hearted Pharaohs. Your electoral grace, I pray, should not tempt or despise Him, for there is no end to His power. And let your electoral grace not imagine that Luther is dead; nay, he rejoices to boast of that God who humbled the Pope, and he is ready for a game with the Cardinal of Mainz which may surprise many. Unless the idol be done away with, I must take occasion at it, openly to attack your grace, together with the Pope; I shall speak against it with assurance, laying all past wickedness of Tetzel to the charge of the Bishop of Mainz, and proclaim to the world the difference between a bishop and a wolf.

"Further, I pray your electoral grace to forbear and leave such clergy unmolested who, for the better avoiding of unchastity, have entered, or are about to enter, the wedded state, and not to attempt depriving them of that which God has given them. If this my prayer be not considered, a cry from the Gospel will be heard, how well it would befit the bishops first to cast out the beam of their own eye, and turn out their concubines, before they attempt to separate others from their piously-wedded wives. I pray your electoral grace to keep watch over yourself, that I may hold my peace. For I take no delight in your grace's shame, but I and all Christians are bound to hold by what God has called honourable, even if a poor sinner, not to say a cardinal, should have to be dishonoured. I now pray for and await your electoral grace's proper and undelayed answer within a fortnight from this; for after these fourteen days, unless there be an answer, my little book treating of the idol at Halle shall be sent forth. And if this letter should be detained by your grace's councillors, and not reach your hand, that shall not stop my course. For councillors should be faithful, and a bishop should thus order his court that nothing be kept from him which he ought to see. May God grant *His* grace to your electoral grace for a right-minded will.

"Given in my desert.

"MARTIN LUTHER."

Albrecht sat for a long time debating what he had better do. He at first thought he would keep the letter to himself; but this resolution seemed unsatisfactory. He knew not what course to take.

Rising presently he touched his bell. A valet appeared.

The Elector stared at him absently, and said, gruffly: "You are not wanted!"

The man retired.

But very soon the bell called him back, the Elector had thought of a message now: "Fetch the privy councillor; he is to make his appearance without delay!"

The Elector had so far got over his feelings that he perceived he must take some one into his counsel; and it could only be Capito, with his unoffending amiability.

When the chaplain entered, the Elector had outwardly recovered. And throwing down the letter with a short, "There, read it!" he stepped to a window, turning his back upon Capito, who obeyed the command.

But vainly did he wait for Capito's initiatory remark; he saw he was obliged to take the lead, and said presently, with all the sarcasm at his command: "You seem highly edified, to judge by your appearance."

Poor Capito was only embarrassed, flush and pallor succeeding each other rapidly upon his cheeks. His secret conviction was with the writer of that letter; what could he say?

"It is just like Luther!" he stammered at last. "It is no light matter for any one to incur his anger, for he knows no bounds and respects no man's person."

"Well, but what is your advice?" demanded the Cardinal, sharply; "that is what I wish to hear."

Capito tremblingly made answer: "My advice, if I am to give it, may not be agreeable to your grace, but I know not what else to say. Your electoral grace must try and appease Luther, lest he should do as he has threatened, and send forth that little book, and the cry of the people be louder than ever. Methinks it might be the best way to appease the enemy, to deal gently with him, and give him a soft answer."

"It is a pity you are not an apothecary," sneered the Elector, "since you seem to understand the manufacture of bitter pills."

"Yet bitter pills are more serviceable in illness than sweetmeats," returned Capito, humbly.

"You may retire!" said the Elector, shortly.

The privy councillor was glad to obey, the very ground seemed to burn under his feet.

"My days here are numbered!" he murmured to himself, when the Elector's closet lay behind him. "I must see where I can build me another nest."

Albrecht sat and stared at the clean sheet of paper before him. Highly displeased as he was with his councillor, whose advice he had always found useful, there seemed nothing left but to swallow the pill, bitter as it was.

Again and again he dipped his pen, but the quill seemed refractory, and words would not take shape. Having written a line or two he crumpled up the paper, a second sheet meeting with a like fate. A third time he began, and now he seemed to have found his cue; the quill went over the paper rapidly, nor did he stop till, having ended, the epistle required dating.

This is what he wrote:

"MY DEAR DOCTOR,—I have read your letter, and have taken it in all favour and good-will, considering at the same time that the cause which has moved you to such writing has long since been rectified. It is my desire, please God, to live and show myself as befits a pious, spiritual, and Christian prince, if so be that God grant me grace, strength, and understanding, for the which I will pray Him faithfully, and cause others to pray. For I have no power in myself, and confess that I need the grace of God, seeing that I am a poor sinful man, who may be found in sin and error, indeed, who sins and errs daily. I know that, apart from the grace of God, there is no good in me, and that, like any other man, if not more so, I am but foul and useless dust. I will not deny this, in answer to your writing, in all good will, for I am fully ready to show you nought but good for Christ's sake. Brotherly and Christian reproof I may well suffer, hoping the merciful and gracious God will further grant me grace, strength, and patience in this and all other matters to live according to His will.

"Given at Halle—"

But here the pen rebounded; he was going to put the date, but "No!" he cried; "this is too much of concession to the miserable friar, if I were to keep even his appointed time, as though I, the Cardinal, *could* fear his churlish chastisement. The letter shall go, but not till after the fortnight he has tied me to."

Once more dipping the pen he added, by way of date, the 21st of December.

Now he rose, wiping his forehead. Never in all the thirty-one years of his life had any work been so hard to do as this short letter. He *had* humbled his pride before the mendicant, whom the Pope had excommunicated and the Emperor outlawed. He had done it because he was forced to it, because it seemed the only possible means for averting contumely and disgrace. He had humbled himself, yes, but with clenched fist and grinding teeth, and every word of that letter was blackest hypocrisy. Could he expect to deceive Luther?

Again he stood by the window, gazing upon the wintry scene. "Thou hast forced me to kneel, Augustinian! but dream not that I am defeated; think not thou hast triumphed over the Cardinal! *I will take* up the gauntlet now, and fight thee ; and it remains to be seen who will come forth as conqueror, I, the Cardinal, or thou, the mendicant friar. Behold the steeples of my new cathedral church; how quickly they have grown, how proudly they stand ! They shall be an emblem to me of prophetic meaning, that the Cardinal will conquer thee, Augustinian !"

CHAPTER XIX.

THE GREAT CATHEDRAL.

It was the eve of St. Bartholemew, the 23rd of August, 1523. Brightly the sun had risen on a cloudless sky, a pleasant wind kept fanning the air with coolness of the east. Although it was a working day, Sunday quiet had settled on the fields: no waggon laden with sheaves was on its way to the threshing-floor, no sickle plied, no happy reapers were singing the harvest home. Yet songs rose on the air, deep piety-breathing melody, as pilgrims poured into Halle, country-folk from far and near, the bells of the many-steepled city swelling the sounds of devotion.

The townspeople were about in holiday attire. Shops were closed, the salt-springs left to themselves; rich and poor, old and young, were on foot to assist at the solemn opening of the now finished cathedral.

A considerable group of buildings made up the new foundation, and proudly rose its chief structure, the collegiate church of Sts. Maurice and Magdalene, with her towering steeples, adding importance to the town and quite a halo of glory to her founder.

Albrecht, indeed, had spared no effort to grace his

cathedral, which should rank first after the high Dom of Magdeburg; all the cloisters of Halle, its churches and chapels must yield the supremacy. Convent Neuwerk, which had been foremost hitherto, had been required to cede its judiciary rights; the provost of the new foundation should be archdeacon of the diocese, in whom spiritual jurisdiction henceforth should be vested. There were other rights and privileges which the Cardinal had not failed to procure for his darling creation, on which rested the pride of his heart.

To the Moritzburg, then, the people pressed, for thence the procession should start.

At the tenth hour of morning a flourish of trumpets from within the palace-yard announced to the populace that their time of waiting was at an end. And from the archway there streamed forth a division of the archiepiscopal body-guard with breastplate and waving plume, behind them the school children with wreaths and tapers. Next came the secular clergy decked in all their finery, followed by monks and nuns with cross and banner. Close upon the spiritual worthies appeared the chief officials of the archbishopric, together with the High Chapter of Magdeburg; the Bishops of Brandenburg, Merseburg, and Naumburg preceding the Lord Cardinal himself in purple splendour, and holding aloft the golden crosier. He walked beneath a canopy of gold-broidered scarlet, carried by pages of noble degree and showing the armorial bearings of Mainz, Magdeburg, and Brandenburg. Behind him followed the canons and numerous dignitaries who had been found worthy of being promoted to the new foundation. The knighthood of the diocese, the representatives of the nobility, the magistrates, the chiefs of guilds and corporations terminated the procession, not forgetting a favoured selection of the salt-workers in military trim.

With bared heads and devout looks the people watched the imposing procession. As soon as the train approached the cathedral an anthem resounded through the sacred edifice, causing solemnity to fall upon the gathering crowd; for the doors had been thrown wide, and the people pressed in behind the festive throng.

Splendid indeed was the structure and surpassingly beautiful, fully coming up to its proud distinction as a cathedral of the Primate of all Germany. If wanting in size, so much the greater seemed the richness of adornment brought together within. The very porch was a masterpiece of sculpture, the foot treading upon exquisite mosaic. The pillars and arches showed a profusion of golden arabesques, from between which white marble angels on hovering wing tended to impress an appearance of awe upon the upturned faces of the congregation. Art and splendour, however, culminated at the high altar, to the perfection of which the greatest masters of the age had yielded their best. On the broad marble table rested a shrine with the life-size representations of St. Maurice, St. Magdalene, St. Martha, St. Lazarus and St. Chrysostom, the pictures being surmounted with a statue of St. Maurice of wrought silver, images of other saints surrounding this centre. The walls were hung with Flemish tapestry, the half-length portrait of Charles, the Emperor, and Albrecht, the Cardinal, being added on either side. A thousand tapers lit up this imagery, weaving about it a veil of transfiguring glory, the lights themselves gleaming through clouds of incense as so many stars through the mists of night. Mists of the night indeed!

the Protestant reader could almost imagine Albrecht standing up with the cry, "Great is Diana of the Ephesians." The side aisles of the structure were devoted to the "holy things," that is, the precious relics of which the reader had a vision on a former page, and which by their richness, set forth in the mysterious illumination, were now supposed to have their fullest effect on the minds of devout beholders.

There was a magnificent organ, and a *Te Deum* was sung. The Cardinal thereupon performed service, using a famous missal, the outward beauty of which he had caused to be restored for the occasion by Nicholas Glockendon. The missal was worth untold sums of money, not only on account of the profusion of gold and precious stones introduced into the binding, but even more so because of the artistic beauty of its pages.

Standing on the steps of the high altar, the Cardinal surveyed his handiwork—for such to his pride was the magnificent cathedral. One who understood how to read his features, would have taken his expression as the elation of present victory and hope for the future. He was laying to his heart even now the assurance of a power and glory inherent in the Catholic Church, the pinnacles of which should not be laid low by a mere Wittenberg mendicant, and which in the strength of her long-lived history would yet ride triumphant over the imaginations of a poor monkish dreamer.

The act of consecration being completed, the procession returned to the palace, and the populace dispersed. But the great hall of the Moritzburg witnessed further solemnity. There the High Chapter of Magdeburg assembled, together with the archiepiscopal office-bearers and the dignitaries of the new foundation, which latter numbered some sixty in all. They had gathered to wait for the hierarch who was going to address them upon the event.

And presently he appeared, the great Cardinal Elector, Archbishop of Mainz and Magdeburg, followed by his chancellor. How handsome, how imposing he looked! He had put off the purple and donned the archiepiscopal robe, and now took his place on a throne at the upper end of the hall. All eyes rested upon him. How reverence-inspiring was the dignity of his princely bearing, yet how engaging the benignity of his countenance! There was both authority and graciousness in the sound of his voice: he commanded attention, but there was charm in the listening.

When stillness had spread her wing, settling down with a hush of expectation, he opened his mouth, and his speech flowed forth with a fervour, which was surprising even to those who had heard him before. This is what he said:

"Upon a solemn occasion you are gathered together, most reverend members of the High Chapter and of our new foundation. A building has been raised to the honour of God, a great cathedral has been consecrated. This in itself is a matter of import; it is very meet and right that the people, resting from work, should put on the garment of joy and gladness for the beholding of that which is now accomplished. But it is not the mere consecration which so moves our hearts. There is a deeper meaning, of, we trust, far-reaching consequence. We dedicate this foundation to the warfare with Wittenberg; it shall prove itself a stronghold of our faith. This town of Halle shall be as a city set on a hill; a power shall go out from it which shall take no denial. We will go forth to battle with the heretic, we will fight him with spiritual weapons, since the weapons of temporal power avail not. For he laughs at his enemies in spite of the ban of both Pope and Emperor. If he is to be vanquished, it must be by other means. It is to you, then, we look in this conflict—to you whom we have thought fit to be worthy inmates of this collegiate foundation! You shall be the soldiers we send afield against the heretic. We trust you are prepared to meet him in the strength of the Spirit, and with the weapons of a knowledge rooted in the Church. What is the reason that this Luther has been able to do great things hitherto? Why is it that the people have accepted him so readily, why, I ask? Because the Church has not done her duty, because our clergy have laid up their pound in the napkin of ignorance and sloth. Indeed, we owe this much of gratitude to Luther, that he has roused the sleepers, that he has laid bare the sore in our midst. But now, since we are awake, we will stand manfully at our post, we will defend the walls of Zion against those who would lay them low. For is not this the sacrilegious intention of the Augustinian, to pull down the venerable structure of the Catholic Church, and build up a new church after his own liking? A seditious rebel he is—witness the events of both Zwickau and Wittenberg. To him, and him alone, it is due that fanatical rioters have arisen as a host of wild boars to destroy the gracious beauty of the vineyard. It is Luther who has called up the spirits of the deep. If he had not roused men's minds, sowing the seeds of revolt, such things never would have happened.

Therefore, I say, heresy is the mother of all rebellion, and the world even now hath proof what spirit moves within him whom the infatuated masses worship as a prophet; for it is apparent what must be the consequences, if men dare question the authority of the Church.

"At Wittenberg then are the head-quarters of sedition; let Halle be the place where the means has been found of opposing the wild commotion with powerful reaction; we will meet the rebellion, but we will meet it with reformation. We will arise and seek for a healing of the sores within the Church. True knowledge shall help us; we will return to the wisdom of the fathers—too long has it lain hidden amid the cobwebs of forgetfulness; we will bring it forth anew, it shall testify against the heretic and his fanatical dreamings; it shall prove that we are the true Church, and that he has fallen away grievously. Upon you, Magister Winkler, we would count especially in this matter—you whom we have elected to the responsible position of our court preacher. For you shall not be satisfied with the service at the high altar, we desire you especially to cultivate the influence of the pulpit, and furnish proof that it is but vanity and conceit of these Lutherans to imagine that none but they can open the Scriptures to the people. A great gift of speech is yours, we know, for the fame of your power has gone before you; if then it lies with you to move the hearts of hearers, we enjoin you to let your voice go forth in behalf of the Catholic faith, and for the good of the Church.

"Nor stand we alone in our hopeful endeavour, seeing that his Holiness the Pope has set us a bright example. Truly the Spirit of God is upon him who was raised to the throne of St. Peter at the demise of Leo X.; for clear is his perception concerning the infirmities of Holy Church, and strong is his will to work for a bettering of both head and members. The Wittenberg seducer will lose all ground then for his would-be reformation. With deepest gratification did we listen to Pope Adrian VI.'s declaration given at the Diet of Nürnberg by the mouth of his legate, bravely owning that 'much unholiness had become apparent in the Holy See, for the which it was not to be marvelled at, if the whole body had sickened of impurity; that it was meet to honour God by humbling ourselves, that he himself would not be last, but first in this, earnestly striving to reform the Romish court, so that the spot whence the disease had spread should be the spot also whence healing might go forth and new life for the recovery of the members. To be sure, the healing could not be sudden, for the disease was of long standing and greatly complicated; circumspectly and by degrees, therefore, must be the process of reformation.' Thus the new Pope, and for a truth it is a great word he hath spoken. Let us join him, then, and be found working by his side.

"It is high time, moreover, that a beginning should be made, for heresy is spreading as a very canker in our midst. Is there a town left in the empire where Lutheranism has not its followers? At the Diet of Nürnberg even, to our grief be it owned, heresy opened its mouth, deceiving the people by thousands, and not stopping short of commotion when the Diet attempted to impose silence. And what shall we say of men so gifted or so situated, that they might be shining lights in their generation? Albrecht Dürer, the noble master, has grieved us sadly by his barely-hidden friendship for Luther, while Lucas Kranach quite openly has joined his side. Bishops even might be pointed at for furthering, rather than opposing, this dire evil, seeing that his grace of Bamberg has not refrained from saying that Luther, after all, was not far wrong, half his diocese following the example. Women even have considered themselves called upon to raise their voices in behalf of the heretic; to wit, Dame Argula von Grumpach and her ill-advised composition. Fitly Doctor Eck has endeavoured to remind her of the true vocation of womanhood, by making her a present of a distaff. For surely the days are but evil when women take to the pen. And turning to Switzerland, you all must have heard that Luther has found a fellow-in-arms there who even goes beyond him. Along the Rhine, too, the flame is uprising; Capito, who once stood so high in our trust, adding fuel upon fuel from his retreat at Strassburg. We loved him once, little suspecting what an adder we were nourishing in our bosom; for he actually was a secret adherent of Luther while pretending friendship for ourselves. As far as Austria even, and Hungary, the seeds of heresy have spread, taking root in Bohemia especially, where the secret followers of Huss venture abroad now, extolling Luther as the promised saviour of whom the former heretic had prophesied. And this even is not all; everywhere, in Holstein and Mecklenburg, in Pomerania, Prussia, and Silesia the new teaching is gaining ground, thus spreading its perilous net all over Germany. In France men look up when there is mention of Luther; nay, in very Italy, in the face of the Pope himself, there is a questioning and asking whether this Luther might not have been sent as a judgment upon the corruptness of the Church.

"Let these things then be a sign to you, reverend Chapter and brethren of our foundation, a token of the great necessity that we should be asleep no longer, but take up the arms of knowledge, fighting for the old faith against the new, seeing that even at Halle that has happened which must perturb our pious spirit. We refer to those clergy of St. Gertrude's and St. Mary's who have broken their vows of chastity and have married wives; yea, even the Provost of Cloister Neuwerk, whom we have raised to the position of our privy-councillor, has not stopped short of the like wickedness. Let these be the first and the last amongst us whose sinful defection we have to deplore. Arise then, ye priests of the holiest, ye men of learning, gird about your loins the sword of truth, and fulfil the hopes we have built upon you. We have spoken, and now praise ye the Lord!"

Thus the Cardinal, and piously the assembly bowed their heads.

. . . . . .

This speech, however, was heard beyond the archiepiscopal hall; its import was known in the town by the evening, creating not a little excitement among the citizens. It became apparent soon that Luther had even more friends at Halle than the Cardinal wot of.

At the Ratskeller,[1] especially, disturbance ran high, not yielding to quiet till old Gabriel Burkhardt rose in his seat, and all prepared to listen; for he enjoyed the confidence of his fellow-citizens, who venerated both his

[1] Literally cellars of the council, a social meeting-place of the citizens.

age and his wisdom. "What is this," he said, "that we hear about the Wittenberg rebellion? Has the Archbishop forgotten that Luther has not left the Church of his own free will and intention? Did he rise against its authority in the pride of the flesh? Do we not know that he prayed and conjured the Pope to do away with the great offence, and he would return to his cell and quiet studies? Did the Pope lend an ear to the cry of conscience? No! As a mad dog they attacked him; to the stake they would have dragged him as a godless heretic. What could he do—he whose conscience was astir with the truth, who felt constrained by the Word of God? Was he not driven for the Lord's sake to break with the Church which had thrust him out? Is that rebellion? Is that sedition? Woe unto you, Popes and Bishops, who will not hear the truth, hardening your hearts against him whom God hath sent."

"But, Master Burkhardt," cried a voice among the listeners, "was there not mention in the speech of how the new Pope, and our Archbishop too, are aware of the evils within the Church, and are prepared to set about reforming these things?"

The salt-worker gave a groan. "They should have thought of this before it was too late," he returned. "If our Luther were the Cardinal, there might be some hope, perchance. As it is, I call it barren promises if they talk of reforming either head or members; how should they reform the body if the very life-blood is diseased? Will they cure the deep-seated infirmity with their plasters, or even with the surgeon's knife? It will be well, no doubt, to shake up the lazy monks, better still to forbid the granting of benefices for filthy lucre doing away with the worst abuses within the Church; but what boots even this if root and doctrine cannot be purified according to the Scriptures? This, I say, is the great work of our Luther: that he strives for a healing of the diseased life-blood of the Church,—its doctrine, that is,—showing us the true faith which rests upon the Gospel, and giving us that Gospel in our own tongue, that each of us may read for himself, searching the Scriptures to see whether these things *are* so. Therefore I cannot doubt but that he is a messenger sent from God, in whose name he has gone forth, in whose name he will obtain the victory. In the power of God, I say, the monk will be stronger than Pope or Cardinal. I am an old man, I may not live to see the day, but you who are young, you will see it; a new and purer Church is about to rise on the ruins of the old one; and when the Lord will have brought it to pass, then remember that I, Gabriel Burkhardt, said so."

A deep silence had sunk upon the Ratskeller. The aged believer's prophetic words made an impression which none of the adversaries dared gainsay.

The Cardinal heard of the occurrence, and people watched anxiously lest the venerable Burkhardt should suffer for his Christian manliness. But no harm befell him. Did the Cardinal not dare to call the old man to account who was beloved in the city? Or what was it that held his arm?

CHAPTER XX.

ANOTHER WITNESS FOR THE TRUTH.

The Archbishop had made a happy choice with his new court chaplain. Magister George Winkler was a man well fitted for his post. He had all the qualities that make a popular orator—portliness of figure, a fine ringing voice, geniality of address, and the command of language. Not that he overpowered people with high-flown words of human wisdom; his delivery, on the contrary, was as plain and simple as possible, but all the more lucid, so that even the illiterate could follow, and there was a warmth of feeling in his discourse that went straight to the hearer's heart. People felt attracted by the natural simplicity of speech which avoided all puffing and storming, desirous rather that the Word of God should be its own powerful exponent.

The Archbishop had given him a hint to prove to his hearers that the Lutherans were not the only people who understood the interpreting of the Scriptures. The new chaplain was an earnest man, anxious to come up to his every duty; and in obedience to the Archbishop's desire he set about a special study of the Holy Writings.

But the more he read the more his mind was impressed. A strange unrest seized him; there was a moving in his heart as of waters being troubled. The towering structure of the creed he had hitherto held was giving way; the mortar loosening its hold, the crumbling stones falling to the ground. The teaching of the Church seemed unable to heal the ruin; opposing Scripture rose as in judgment, and Magister George found himself face to face with the question: "Can Luther after all be in the right?"

The very possibility filled him with a quivering dread. "If Luther's teaching be the truth, woe is me! What shall I do? Am I not called hither to bear testimony against him?"

He sent for Luther's books, and read them secretly with a burning zeal. But this only added to his distress, for he found not that on which he could base the slightest refutation. His trouble was present with him in the pulpit, he wrestled with it; but his struggle seemed to react as a kindling power on his sermons, and the result was that the people flocked in increasing numbers to the great cathedral. Whoever had heard one sermon was anxious for another; and every hearer felt that step by step he was being led into new realms of understanding; that the chaplain had a way of breaking seal after seal of the Holy Book; his touch and guidance withal being so gentle that people scarcely perceived the growth, and arrived on Luther's vantage ground without knowing it or ever hearing his name, nor yet suspecting that the truth they drank in so eagerly might have been preached at the Schlosskirche of Wittenberg itself.

Archbishop Albrecht, who was away, assisting at the

Diet of Nürnberg, was greatly delighted to hear of his court chaplain's success, sending him marks of his favour by every messenger he despatched to Halle. Not so pleased, however, were the clergy of that city, whose churches and chapels grew alarmingly empty, their congregations openly forsaking them for the preaching at the new collegiate church. The pressure of objurgation was applied, but in vain. The offended shepherds, as a last resource, took their complaints to the Archbishop.

One of these, brother Bartholomew of Our Lady's, journeyed to Nürnberg and presented his and his brethren's grievance to his grace: Magister Winkler was a wolf in sheep's clothing, he was expected to bear testimony against Luther, but he never as much as mentioned the heretic's name; his preaching, on the contrary, savoured of highly suspicious meaning; he had said things which any heretic might have said, but he had a way of expressing them which sheltered his wickedness; he had quite caught the people, and had simply emptied all other churches at Halle. Moreover there were those among his hearers whose leaning to Lutheranism was notorious.

The Archbishop, perceiving the jealousy, smiled knowingly, dismissing the charge, with the advice that the preachers at Halle had better all try to attract the masses; he, the Archbishop, would take opportunity to inquire into his chaplain's creed.

Nor was this mere putting-off; but the "special report" which reached his grace from Halle seemed not to offer any inducement for censuring his chaplain.

Brother Bartholomew discovered that his journey's end was disappointment: the people did not cease from attending Magister Winkler's preaching, and the collegiate church could scarcely hold the anxious crowds.

One morning this said disappointed brother was on his way to officiate at Our Lady's, when he was met by streams of worshippers evidently flocking towards the cathedral. That was too much for his equanimity: "There they are again, running after that priest of Baal!" he cried, with ill-suppressed resentment. "But see if I don't pay you out! I'll visit your houses, and your womankind shall rue it."

This was intended for soliloquy. But two men passing alongside had sharper ears than he expected. They showed it by a look only, leaving him quickly behind.

The afternoon of that day witnessed a gathering crowd on the market-place. Men stood by twos and threes in eager conversation, and presently the populace moved towards the vicarage of Our Lady's. A tumult rose around the house; there was an attempt at forcing the door, and that not succeeding, stones flew against the lozenge-paned windows. A couple of ringleaders were about to effect an entrance, when the constabulary appeared, forcing them to desist. But the excited crowd would not subside until the sergeant, having learned the cause of the disturbance, agreed to arrest the culprit chaplain, and lead him before the magistrate.

To the ministers of authority the barricaded door could but yield; and presently Bartholomew Mellerstadt, chaplain of Our Lady's, appeared between two officers on his way to the town hall. The people were loud in their indignation, many preparing to wait in the streets for the magisterial decision.

But that was vain: the magistracy was not so eager

to try the delinquent; the case was drawn up for the information of the Prior of Convent Neuwerk, the prisoner meanwhile being lodged in the Temnitz.[1]

The prior's answer was not long in coming, a complaint being returned against the town authorities' arbitrary interference with the rights of the convent: how could the magistracy think of laying hands on a consecrated priest, instead of submitting their charges against him to the prior, his own superior?

The magistracy made excuse that the brother was in the Temnitz merely to hold him safe from the people; if the prior would examine into the case, the accused should be given up; the town authorities at the same time expecting that the convent would hold him in custody against the return of the Archbishop himself, who no doubt was best fitted to pronounce judgment, whereas the prior might be disposed to connive. There had been some talk of sending the miscreant backwards on a donkey across the market-place to the gates of Neuwerk; but, for the avoiding of further tumult, this thought had been relinquished, and he should be delivered quietly to the jurisdiction of his order.

That was done. But the convent highly resented the magisterial bearing. A messenger was despatched to Nürnberg to lodge complaint with his electoral grace concerning the unheard-of demeanour of the town authorities of Halle, interfering with the papal and imperial privileges of the convent, casting slur and insult upon the reverend body and all consecrated clergy; the brethren humbly prayed his electoral grace to exercise his prerogative commanding forthwith that the innocent victim should be reinstated in his cure, abiding his

[1] The "toll-booth" of Halle.

grace's return, when the Archbishop himself should pass judgment according to his pleasure.

The messenger brought back his grace's desire that his return should indeed be awaited, the accused remaining in charge of the convent's custody.

This incident resulted in sending all the more hearers to the cathedral.

The people's love and veneration for the magister grew from day to day. But their tribute added only to their inward trouble. He knew now that he differed nowise from Luther's doctrine, and yet he dared not, openly and before all the people, acknowledge his conformity with him who taught the truth. But was not that deceiving the people? Was it not playing at hypocrisy, if he clothed the Gospel with a veil of careful, if not ambiguous words? He began to feel ashamed of himself. "Where is thy manliness, George Winkler? So many stand up for the Gospel fearlessly; even at Magdeburg, beneath the very eyes of the High Chapter, Nicholas Amsdorf with noble courage dares preach the pure Word of God, while the court chaplain of Halle deals it out but insincerely. Lord, help me to fight Thy battle, showing my colours openly!"

Thus he wrestled day by day, night after night, irresolution holding him her prey. What chiefly prevented his laying hold of true courage, was the oath which bound him to the Archbishop. "I have sworn, as far as in me lies, to help build up and defend the Holy Mother Church. Woe is me, I have fallen from my oath! How shall I meet him who is shepherd over us all, who has shown me nought but kindness and confidence?"

But one morning he came forth from his chamber a

new creature. He had not closed an eye that night, yet he felt like one bathed in strength, for the firm resolve had at last been given him; uncertainty was at an end. He had found his better self. "Why all this needless torment?" he was now able to say. "Is it breaking my oath if I preach as Luther preaches? I am bound to build up and defend the Church—but where is the Church, the true Church? Is it not where Christ is preached? Can that be the Church where He, the One Mediator, is put aside and men are invited to try and gain heaven by their own good works? Can that be the Church where priests step in between the Saviour and the individual believer, saying: No one can come to Him but by us? God cannot forgive thy sins unless thou hast first confessed to the priest? Or again, is that the Church where the 'vicar' of Him who had not where to lay His head clothes himself in purple and fine raiment? Where the 'successor' of Him who said, 'My kingdom is not of this world,' has built himself a throne, assuming a crown fit only for a prince of this world? Truly there is but corruption coming from Rome; it is at Wittenberg where we hear of healing. Luther is the man who in the power of God can build up a true Church on the crumbling ruins. And if I take my place by the side of him, working together with him, can that be breaking my oath? Is it not rather *fulfilling it in its truest and holiest sense?* ... It shall be done then, what must be done; I will obey the voice of conscience. I will speak openly before all the people, they shall hear my confession. They shall know that by earnest study of the Holy Book I have arrived where Luther is; and that he is no heretic, but a teacher of God's own blessed truth."

The court chaplain took his Bible to meditate upon the Word he intended to preach from the following morning. He felt as though his heart were freed from a great burden; his soul was filled with happy hopes, and they radiated from his countenance. With a joyful assurance, such as he had never known before, he ascended his pulpit and gave out his text: "And Jesus said unto him, Go thy way: thy faith hath made thee whole. And immediately he received his sight, and followed Jesus in the way."

The congregation, soon *en rapport* with the preacher, hung on his lips breathlessly; his people felt the moving of the Spirit. It was a sermon full of power, the very words ringing with a clearness of exposition which could not but convince. For the first time, the chaplain mentioned the Wittenberg Reformer by name, not to denounce him, but to say that concerning this man's enemies and persecutors, the Christian could not but repeat the Lord's own words: "Father, forgive them; for they know not what they do!" Those who cursed Luther did not know him; those who knew him could not revile, but must bless him altogether.

There was a movement in the church like the swell of a rising tide; the chaplain had to raise his voice to make himself heard. As soon as the "Amen" had dropped from his lips, part of the congregation rose and somewhat noisily left the building, not awaiting the concluding prayer. But when the preacher retired to his vestry the venerable Gabriel Burkhardt followed him, holding out both hands, and saying with tearful eyes: "God bless you, reverend sir! Now you have spoken openly, giving us the truth with courage. May the Lord of the Church be your own reward, and help you to stand faithfully by your confession, even though the martyr's crown should await you."

Winkler thanked his noble parishioner, and left the cathedral with the joyful assurance that his Master's power would uphold him.

Returning to his home on the Burg, he perceived that most of the episcopal household looked at him askance; his colleagues treated him to silence, the Chancellor Turk only attacked him with the ominous question: "Herr Magister, how could you?"

"I have followed the voice of conscience," replied Winkler, with simple manliness.

"Conscience!" reiterated the chancellor disdainfully; "methinks, then, it ought to have spoken differently. Besides, what of your oath?"

"I deem I have come up to its meaning to-day in its truest sense," said Winkler.

The chancellor looked up amazed, wondering whether the chaplain could be labouring under some sudden derangement. "We shall soon have the Cardinal back," he rejoined presently; "and I would rather not be in your place then. How are you going to face him?"

"In the name of my Lord," said Winkler, with a look of holy confidence. "If God be for me, who can be against me?"

Again the chancellor looked up in wonderment. "And how can you be so certain that God is for you?"

"I cannot doubt it," returned the chaplain. "Those who seek the truth shall hear His voice; the believing heart experiences the upholding of the Spirit, and there is a love of God which casteth out fear."

Turk shrugged his shoulders. " Many a one dreameth it is the Spirit of God within him, and after all it is but his own misguided mind which leads him astray. Have we not heard of the prophets of Zwickau, and what sorry fanatics, to be sure, they are ! "

And saying this the worldly-wise chancellor went his way.

Soon after this, about the middle of October, the Cardinal returned to Halle. The very first morning after his arrival, Winkler was cited to his eminence's presence ; and it was fully two hours before he was seen taking his leave.

No one ever learned what had passed ; but the citizens of Halle vainly waited for the voice of their beloved preacher ; a stranger officiated in his stead.

"Has he been dismissed ?" his friends asked ; and the idea did not tend to move the citizens' hearts in favour of the Cardinal ; people, on the contrary, began to speak of tyranny, and it became apparent that the new preacher must direct his discourse to empty benches.

It was announced at last that Magister Winkler had met with no further mark of episcopal displeasure than being suspended for the space of three months, which time of disgrace his eminence had advised him to devote to a close study of the fathers. Learning this, the people felt hopeful of the result ; a study of St. Augustine, they believed, would not turn Winkler from the truth, but rather yield fresh proof that the Papal Church and Gospel teaching were widely apart. And what then ? " Well, if the time comes when again he may speak to us of the truth," said the venerable Gabriel Burkhardt one day to his like-minded fellow-citizens, "and if the Cardinal should attempt to stop it, then *we* may claim a voice in the matter! We will go up to his eminence and say boldly, 'This Magister Winkler is giving us the Word of God truly and unalloyed; him only will we hear. Do we not know that Nicholas von Amsdorf preaches the Gospel at Magdeburg? and shall that be denied to the town of Halle which the city of Magdeburg is enjoying freely?' Which of you, my fellow-citizens, are ready to join me in standing up for our own beloved Magister Winkler?"

And most of those present held up their hands in token of earnest assent.

CHAPTER XXI.

STORM-TIDE.

HEAVY, terror-boding clouds covered the heavens when the bells of churches and chapels rang in the year of our Lord 1525, and fearfully the eyes of men gazed into the immediate future. It seemed as though there was to be fulfilled what astrologers had read in the stars, what the clear-sighted Luther had foreseen, not needing the spy-glass. War and bloodshed was hovering over the land. It had begun among the peasantry of Franconia and Swabia; but in widening circles horror seemed about to enfold the realm.

"Peasantry" is scarcely the correct expression, seeing there were no peasants in those days. There might be a yeoman or some rustic freeman here and there, but the great mass of the toilers of the earth were serfs—nothing short of slaves—a wretched people, despised and abused. Significantly enough, the tiller of the soil went by the appellation of the "poor man." He seemed created only to work for others; the produce of the field gained in the sweat of his brow he was bound to take to castle or convent, and thank his taskmasters if they allowed him the refuse as his reward. It was his lot sadly to bend the neck and bear all manner of loads—tithes, taxes, tribute, and toll. He must give work without wages, let the deer revel in his sprouting fields, nor raise a murmur should the lordly hunting train tread down his growing corn; and if the more nobly-born had a desire for the gracious gifts of womanhood, woe to the poor man if he dared withstand the sacrifice!

Towards the close of the fifteenth century, then, and at the beginning of the sixteenth, despair had driven the people to attempt a bursting of their chains. In Swabia, in particular, a conspiracy had been formed calling itself the "arme Conrad,"[1] and which gathered round a standard bearing a shoe as their cognisance; similar risings occurring in the Rhineland. These efforts at insurrection, however, lacked unity, being easily overridden therefore by knight and nobleman, who never failed to take dire vengeance upon the unfortunate rebels.

But though successful so far, they could not stamp out the fire, since they thought not of rectifying the grievances; the heaped-up tinder again and again flared up upon the slightest provocation.

Such was the state of affairs when the word "Liberty" was spoken at Wittenberg, resounding through the length and breadth of the land; when Luther stood up against Pope and Bishop, working for a new creation upon the ruins of the degenerate Church. And lo! the "poor Conrad" caught at that word, straightway thinking

[1] *i.e.* Poor Conrad. For such readers as can see German derivation, we add that the appellation is supposed to mean: dem "armen" Mann "kein Rat" (no help for the poor man); the Swabian patois for kein Rat being koan Rat, whence Conraad. We own, however, that this is almost too ingenious not to be an after conclusion!

of the liberty he longed for. Were they going to clear up the rubbish within the Church? Surely it was right and meet then to attack the heaped-up filth in the fair lands of Germany as well. If souls should be free, was it not time then to burst asunder the bonds of slavery that held the body? Men should no longer be worse off than the wild beasts of the field. And there was a heaving and upboiling throughout the land. In the dark of night, in caves and forests, the goaded peasantry would meet, passing the word to and fro on byways and hidden paths, the ominous correspondence travelling through Franconia and Swabia, through Thuringia and the valleys of the Rhine.

And before long they dared to raise the veil of secresy, rebellion walking in the daylight boldly.

The villages of Thuringia were haunted by a man of strangest demeanour. Weirdly glowed the large grey eyes from beneath the bushy eyebrows in a face overhung with wildly flowing hair, and he looked at the people with the power of speech upon his lips. All who heard him seemed helpless against the charm: he appeared as a very Prophet Elias come to show from the Scriptures that slavery was against the behest of the Almighty, that the Gospel required the people to be free, that men were brethren now as in the days of the apostles, when no man called anything his own, but all men had all things in common. Frightful was the sound of his voice when in the strain of a psalm of vengeance; he delivered his woe upon the godless oppressors—the wicked Pharaohs who drove the people to work with lashes, chastising them with scorpions; the bloodsuckers who grew rich upon the sweat of the poor man's brow; the fiends in human guise who took delight in the writhings of the worm at their feet, the cries of anguish of a tortured people being as music to their ear.

Thomas Münzer was the name of this man, the whilom schoolmaster of Halle, who had played a leading part in the rising against Archbishop Ernest, Albrecht's predecessor in the diocese of Magdeburg, a leading part also among the fanatics of Zwickau. Once more he had come to the front, the people gathering round him as their prophet; as a mountain torrent he carried them headlong to the turbulent scene.

More wildly still foamed the waters of uproar in the south, in Franconia and in Swabia. The lawless hordes found leaders there who with powerful arm directed the commotion, rendering it all the more terrible; Florian Geyer, a worthy warrior, giving them the benefit of his generalship, while Wendel Hipler, a well-meaning lawyer and politician, served them with legal advice. Both these men did not join the agitation under pressure, as was the case with the adventurous knight, Götz von Berlichingen; but they of their own free will and with all their soul adopted the cause of the suffering people, ready to yield heart and hand, liberty and life, in purest enthusiasm for the rebellious peasantry.

When such men took the lead, insurrection walked with assurance, and was in a fair way of gaining its end. Very moderate and sober were the twelve articles which at the inspiration of Wendel Hipler were drawn up by the peasantry; and even Luther, who was appealed to, could not but acknowledge the justice of their demands in the main, exhorting the despotic lords to come to an amicable adjustment with the peasants. They claimed the right for each parish to choose their own minister. They agreed to continue giving tithes of the field, but only for the maintenance of the clergy, refusing the tithes of live stock, because God had made the cattle free for the benefit of man. It was against the word of God, too, they added, that the poor man should be barred from his share of game and fish. Furthermore, they demanded that serfdom should be absolutely abolished, for Christ had shed His blood for all men equally. They prayed for the usufruct of forest lands, unless a clear case of right by purchase could be made out, and they requested a reasonable reduction of taxes, a material lessening also of tributary labour.

Luther's admonition, however, was spoken to the winds. The tyrants' pride despised the alternative of a compromise with the peasantry, adding insult to injury.

Then broke the long-suffering patience of the oppressed, the last thread snapping asunder, and their vengeance knew no bounds; the hands which had been folded in petition snatched up the sword, passion rose to the level of madness, overbearing the sobriety of Hipler, the moderation, too, of Florian Geyer; terror had raised her front, ready to fulfil the star-gazers' direst prediction.

As ravening beasts raged the peasants, strangers to ruth. Whatever was owned by nobleman or monk must be theirs now, and what they knew not how to make use of was doomed to destruction, the red blood of murder soaking the land. The Swabian Bund was formed under Truchsess of Waldburg, partial success tending but to a fuller development of the wild-beast nature in man. The angel of humanity averted her face and wept.

As a spectre of hell appears that Jerkin Rohrbach, whose history yields terrible proof that a man may be worse than a tiger, ay, worse than a fiend. He was the ringleader of the bloody Easter of Weinsberg. For on Easter Monday of the year of grace 1525, the rising sun beheld a ghastly scene on the common stretching away from the lower gate of the little town. The rebels had succeeded in storming the place, to the walls of which a great number of the Swabian nobility had fled for safety; they made prisoners of some seventy knights, foremost among them the justiciary, Count Helfenstein, whose wife was a natural daughter of the late Emperor Maximilian. They prepared for immediate execution. Florian Geyer did his utmost to awaken some feeling of forbearance, but in vain; the Black Witch, an ancient hag of a woman, with the face of a screech-owl, who haunted the rebel camp to bless the sedition with her spells, set up a wild howl of revenge, supported by the terrible Jerkin. And fearful was the punishment resolved upon. The hapless prisoners should be driven into the enemies' spears. And forthwith the line was formed through which the victims should run. They were being led to the dismal scene; the Count Justiciary was appointed to the dire precedence, when his wife, the Emperor's daughter, a child on her arm, and about to give birth to another, pressed through the crowd, falling to her knees with anguished cries for pity. The warrior Geyer was moved to compassion, sending a helpless glance along the rebel ranks; but they were dead to the dictates of mercy, Jerkin and the Black Witch pouring oil into the flame, the latter not refraining from dragging the poor wife away by the hair, thus at least sparing her the awful sight. Upon a miserable dung-cart they cast her—Maximilian's daughter—and hurried her away. Count Helfenstein meanwhile was chased into the spears, sinking dead, not uttering a groan. The pitiful execution continued till, in the end, the seventy lay pierced by the lances, the rebels' piper playing merry tunes the while.

A cry of horror echoed through the land at this and similar occurrences. The Emperor trembled in his castle. And Luther? With such murderers he could have nothing in common; he could no longer advocate their claims, but wrote a book "Against the murderous and rapacious peasants," calling upon the princes to rise in common for the suppression of the work of darkness.

And the knights buckled on their armour; but much blood must yet be shed, many a fire flare aloft, many a trophy of human skill sink in ashes, before quiet could be restored.

As a fearful avalanche the rebel army rolled northwards towards the Saxon lands, which had not thought of arms. On the 24th of April the governor of the Wartburg announced to his duke at Weimar that Salzungen had yielded to the insurgents, and that Eisenach was in imminent danger. The selfsame day the lurid flame was seen bursting, Cloister Reinhardsbrunn was afire, the frightened township of Erfurt opening its gates to the rebels.

The seditious hosts had swelled by thousands; from their villages came the peasants, many citizens from the towns, joined by the rabble that had flocked round Thomas Münzer, who had succeeded in planting his standard at Mühlhausen. They swarmed through the country, the wild cohorts, with fire and sword, they spread through the Eichsfeld and the Harz, they overran the golden Aue and the county of Mansfeld. Within a fortnight some forty convents, and a still greater number of Burgen, had vanished from the face of the earth, which was coloured afresh with the blood of her children.

Duke John of Weimar quaked behind his castle walls, Duke George at Dresden sending doleful appeals to the Saxon Elector, who could not help, for he lay dying on his bed. The turreted homes of the nobility were filled with panic, the knights trembled as women, gazing about them dispirited, not knowing where to turn for their lives.

Luther even for a moment had lost his balance. He saw the world reeling on her foundations, he believed that Satan was riding atop of the commotion, that he would succeed in destroying the Gospel, that the great judgment day was at hand. But not for long; the brave courage of his faith returned, he felt ready for a battling with Satan; and since his Elector lay dying, he, Luther, would front the adversary. To Mansfeld then he went alone, facing the insurgents with his thundering voice. But even that voice seemed powerless amid the curses of the maddened host. "Thou hast forsaken our cause!" they cried; "thou hast betrayed us! Get thee gone, lest thou share the fate of the aristocracy, the dogs, to whom thou lendest thy voice!"

And sore at heart Luther retired to his closet, to groan and wrestle in prayer; and again despondency would have him believe that judgment was at hand.

At Halle too the pangs of terror were felt. An

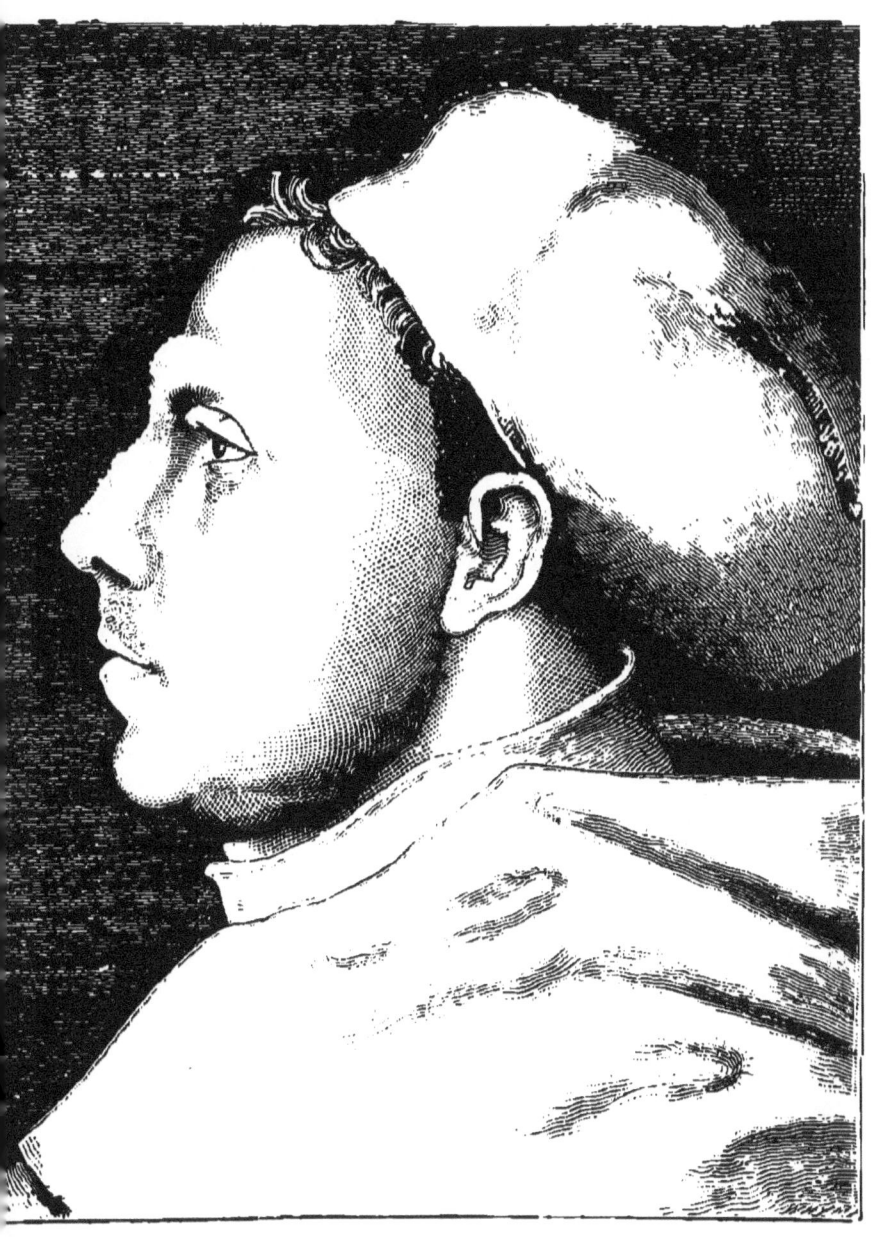

LUTHER.
After Albert Dürer.

oppressive silence had hushed the Moritzburg, the innermost chambers of which hid the Cardinal, for he had lost his head. Ominous was the news he received from his western diocese, Bishop William of Strassburg, his vicegerent at Mainz, despatching more dismal information week after week. A desperate rabble from the Odenwald had overrun the archiepiscopal electorate, swelling in numbers day after day. The little town of Miltenberg, where the Elector's own receiver of revenues headed the rebels, had yielded to the enemy, the distressed vicegerent calling upon the vassals of the diocese to oppose the insurrection. But they were slow of preparation, news of the catastrophe of Weinsberg quite paralysing the knights, and Bishop William was brought to harassing straits. The insurgents made for Aschaffenburg, where he resided, matters taking a most critical turn since the citizens pronounced for the peasants, forcing the Bishop to treat with them. What could he do, poor man, but yield to whatever they demanded? Nor was Mainz more peacefully situated. On the 25th of April, St. Mark's Eve, a crowd had gathered on the oxen market, passing the night under arms, at daybreak forcing the magistrates to give up the town keys; whereupon they released from prison a number of Lutheran preachers, and having possessed themselves of the cannon from the ramparts, they demanded surrender of the Martinsburg. This being refused, they turned the cannons' mouth upon the Martinsburg, to take it by storm; then the Chapter yielded, and were found willing to grant the thirty-one articles setting forth the citizens' complaints.

This was the news which reached the Cardinal from his electorate; no wonder he hid his face, night after night courting sleep in vain. As a shipwrecked man he was, to whom nothing is left but a helpless plank the waves of destruction yawning about him. And even that plank must be snatched from his hold if the storm should dash the commotion upon Magdeburg, upon his very town of Halle!

With his chancellor Turk he had climbed one of the western turrets, anxiously peering along the Mansfeld hills: the news had spread that an armed rabble had been seen approaching.

As far as the eye reached nothing suspicious could be discovered, but a dull noise rising from the streets broke upon the ear.

"What is it?" cried the Cardinal, in alarm. "What can there be within the town? The Lord preserve us, if the people of Halle will follow the example of the citizens of Mainz or Aschaffenburg! I trust them but half."

The chancellor bit his lips, about to descend to inquire into the tumult, when the captain of the palace rushed up the turret stairs, announcing suspicious gatherings about the town.

"Your grace had better anticipate further harm," cried Turk unceremoniously. "A kind word may yet avert mischief; promise them what you please."

The Cardinal stared into vacancy, but coming to a sudden resolution, he cried: "Follow me!"

And hastily the two descended from the watchtower.

A great multitude had gathered in the churchyard of St. Ulrich; debate ran high, but yielded to a hush at the sudden appearance of the Cardinal.

All eyes were upon him, as he raised his powerful

voice: "What is it that moves you, our beloved, our faithful subjects? Has the tumult of this time of wickedness drawn you within its circle? Have you forgotten that justice and mildness govern the hand which rules you?"

There was no answer save a deep, swelling murmur, and quickly he continued: "Which prince is able to please and satisfy his every subject? But if there is aught we have done amiss, such was not our intention. We enjoin you to state any grievance openly, and none shall be blamed for doing it. And we invite you to do so by writing, for the better discharging thereof; it is I, your just and loving ruler, that desires it."

The citizens kept silent, and the Cardinal, taking their passive demeanour for acquiescence, went his way with the chancellor through the Ulrich Street to the market-place, where another crowd had gathered. He repeated the self-same words, also apparently quieting the disturbance. He proceeded to St. Maurice's, with a similar result.

On the following day the guilds and corporations, together with the town council, despatched a deputation to the Moritzburg, submitting an address to the Cardinal, duly stating their complaints, as he had desired. The first clause prayed for the removal of some of the magistrates who had lost the citizens' confidence by oppressive measures.

The Cardinal swallowed his vexation, for the officials in question, he knew, were on his side; but he felt obliged to yield.

The second clause ran thus: "We pray that our gracious ruler may permit the Word of God to be preached to us, pure and unalloyed, and the sacrament to be administered as the Lord Jesus Himself hath appointed." The Cardinal flushed scarlet, but he agreed. The further clauses, being of less significance, could all the more willingly be granted.

The deputation expressed their heartfelt thanks, and left the Burg, holding trustfully by the given promise.

CHAPTER XXII.

POSSIBILITIES.

THE town was quiet, but there was tempest in the heart of the Cardinal, who with his Chancellor Turk, and the newly appointed councillor, Dr. John Rühel, was sitting in earnest consultation.

"These are serious matters," said Albrecht, troubled ; "there is no saying where they will land us. Hear me, Martin Luther!" he cried, with suppressed emotion, "hear me, thou child of disturbance! It is thou who art answerable for all this war and bloodshed, for all the misery brought upon us by men who have become as ravening beasts. It is the spirit of Wittenberg which is upon them, it is thy teaching which is astir in the turbid commotion."

"I venture to dissent from your electoral grace," said Dr. Rühel, speaking courageously. "Martin Luther may provoke many a man's displeasure, but he has not deserved your grace's present accusation. It must not be laid to his charge if the oppressed, untutored masses understand in a carnal sense his preaching of Christian liberty! Do we not know that truth is easily misapprehended, and from high spiritual meaning dragged to the level of worldly abuse? And where, let me ask, has the terrible peasant war shown its wildest excess? Is it not rather in the popish districts? Look at Electoral Saxony, where the Gospel has been received most fully; the people are quiet there, and have no mind for rebellion."

That was true, if boldly spoken. Dr. Rühel was secretly inclined to Luther, but at the same time he desired to be faithful to his master, the Cardinal. Indeed, he entertained that boldest of all ideas—to endeavour to bring about a reconciliation between the two. Albrecht knew the councillor's honesty, and was not inclined to censure him for a candid remark; but he changed the conversation, saying—

"There are more important things occupying my mind, of which I would speak to you, gentlemen. Last night, sleep being absent, my thoughts again and again reverted to my cousin Albrecht, the Grand Master of the Teutonic Order, who, as you will remember, visited me last year. Even then he confided to me a bold plan, which has ripened to fulfilment since, for he has cast off the ragged worn-out robe of his spiritual distinction, turning the Teutonic Mastership into a temporal Duchy. When he first hinted at this idea, I was amazed and full of misgivings, but I view it differently now; in these days of subversion and downfall, when the religious question is endeavouring to change the very face of the earth, a spiritual ruler may well entertain such thoughts; the sceptre seems of more importance now than the crosier. I have heard it rumoured that the Elector Archbishop of Cologne secretly harbours similar longings. What should you say to it, gentlemen?"

The two were not ready with an answer to this most unexpected appeal; Rühel, however, recovering first. "It seems to me," he said, "that your grace's cousin has done wisely in overthrowing a building which was tottering on its foundation; the Teutonic Order has outlived itself, it has fulfilled its destiny, and its days are over. If the spiritual rulership will revive in another form, a new lustre may be in store for it."

"And what should you say?" inquired the Cardinal, turning to the chancellor.

But Turk was circumspect, and answered evasively, "I admire the Grand Master for his courage; for there can be no lack of reproaches and revilings, more especially since it must be expected that as a temporal prince he will see fit to marry."

"My cousin is a prince every inch of him!" cried Albrecht warmly. "He will not be deterred by what his enemies may say, he will do what he thinks right. But if the Archbishop of Cologne were to follow his example, what should you say to that?"

Again Turk took shelter in evasion. "It is but a report," he replied. "Moreover, an Archbishop could scarcely carry into effect what was possible to a Grand Master, whose spiritual dignity was about to be enveloped in ruin."

But the Cardinal was not put off so easily. Annoyed at his chancellor's dulness, he returned to Rühel, whose brain was alight now with a sudden hope. "Do you think his grace of Cologne might have similar courage?"

"Why not?" replied the councillor enthusiastically, "since he also is a prince who will not bow to the fear of man; he might be bold enough to oppose both Emperor and Pope!"

His grace of Mainz seemed flattered by this statement, continuing after a while: "And if two have dared, others may follow. There would be an end then to the Pope's authority in Germany."

"Which would be an advantage and blessing to the realm," added Rühel quickly; "since at Rome lies the root of all evil for this poor land of ours."

The Cardinal raised a finger, smiling archly: "Be careful of your tongue, sir councillor. Silence is gold!"

Again changing the topic, he spoke of matters of government, of a new tax especially for which he hoped to gain the approval of the Estates. Consultation being ended, the officials took their leave.

Albrecht continued in his chair, lost in thought. His cousin, the Grand Master, occupied him greatly; the idea that he, the Cardinal, might possibly follow his example, quite perturbing his mind; the drops appeared on his forehead, and his heart beat in expectation. Might not that be a cure for all his troubles, if he too were to cast off the crosier, wielding the temporal sceptre all the more powerfully? Was it not to the mitre that he owed all his vexation hitherto? His theological learning was but inadequate; it might have served his purpose in days of quiet, but he was not equal to grappling with the overwhelming tide called up by Luther. Not that he owned as much to himself, but the consciousness of deficiency was somewhere in his mind, underlying the desire of following his cousin's example. He resolved, however, to abide the Archbishop of Cologne's example.

But Doctor Rühel, too, was engaged upon the problem. "An unfathomable nature, this Cardinal!" he soliloquised. "Who shall get at the bottom of his heart, and know his mind? His action has ever been mysterious, the very opposite at times of what one would have expected. What thoughts are these now engaging his attention? Why should he have directed us so pointedly to the step taken by his cousin? Has he not betrayed a desire of following the example, and is he not likely to carry such desire into effect? It is the Church, no doubt, to which he, who was but a younger prince, owes all his greatness; but I doubt not he is equal to throwing off the spiritual robe, if he can see his way. He has a dislike to Luther, yet I am not sure but that he will accept the Gospel if it will ease his shoulder from the burden of his spiritual dignity, leaving him the temporal power. Might not this be the opportunity of reconciliation? Yes, Luther shall know of the Cardinal's secret leaning. We must strike the iron while it is hot. Perhaps Luther will succeed with the Cardinal, as he succeeded with the Grand Master. They are Albrechts, both of them; let this be of good omen. Luther will have harder work with the Cardinal, no doubt, for this Albrecht does not ask his advice, as did Albrecht the Grand Master; yet who knows whether the Cardinal will not accept unsolicited counsel, if it falls in with his own inclination?"

And Rühel took up his pen, writing quickly:

"My beloved Doctor Martin!

"Strange ideas seem moving in my master's the Cardinal's mind; he has spoken to us admiringly, nay, almost with envy, of his cousin the Teutonic Grand

Master in Prussia, barely hiding the thought that such example might be worthy of imitation. I will endeavour to keep him to this opinion; but I pray you, much loved Doctor, to send to my gracious master a letter of comfort in these troublous times, which might ease his mind and help him to take the great step; of such letter I would fain have a copy. May the Lord in heaven look graciously to such important work! I trust you understand me aright, since it is not meet to put everything on paper. God be with you and ourselves!

"JOHN RÜHEL."

Far into the night this good Doctor sat meditating on the contents of this missive, which grew in importance the more he thought of it. If it were indeed possible to influence the Cardinal for turning his spiritual power into mere temporal rulership, how far-reaching might not be the consequence! If he, the chief of spiritual Electors, whose dominions extended from the Rhine to the Elbe, were to break with Rome, how many more might not follow, especially as the Archbishop of Cologne seemed on a similar track. And if the first step were taken, the second would come naturally, he would turn his back upon celibacy; and the greater result would be this, that he would throw open the land to the teaching of the Gospel. And if he, the most powerful of the German princes, were now for the new teaching, the empire, no doubt, would be brought to accept the Reformation. And what then? Why, the whole realm would be regenerate; it would rise as an eagle on wings of glory.

The honest Doctor was quite dazzled at these happy

prospects, too exceeding great for fulfilment almost!
However, the letter was written, and it should go. In
these times of wondrous events, of high-going waves
both in religion and in politics, might not the impossible
be possible after all ?

On the following morning a special messenger
sped from Halle to Wittenberg, knocking at Doctor
Luther's door. His urgency, however, had to submit to
delay. The Doctor was not at home, but in his
pulpit at the Schlosskirche, delivering his "Sermon
of Peace," the tidings of victory over the rebellious
peasants having been received the night before. There
was a new hope of rest for the land, the storm had done
its worst, and seemed about to fold its terrible wings,
hearts might look up again with assurance, nor be
deceived of their faith.

. . . . .

But if all the world rejoiced, there was one who
would have liked to defer the good news, and that was
Doctor Rühel; he would have liked the Cardinal to
have a little more of anxiety, for on that anxiety the
honest councillor had rested his hopes. If all trouble
were at an end, it was much to be feared the Cardinal
would think no more of the plans engendered by
that trouble.

With misgivings, therefore, he received the reply to
his letter, in which Luther said: "If you perceive that
the Cardinal takes pleasure in what I have written,
then take the copy herewith inclosed and have it
printed for circulation. And if his electoral grace
should put the question, which has been asked of me
before, why Martin Luther refrains from taking a wife,
seeing that he recommends wedlock to others, you shall

say that I continue doubting my fitness, on account of the great weakness of my perishable body; but if my marriage were a comforting example to his electoral grace, I would not hesitate to trot ahead, if so be that he might follow."

Rühel took the letter to the Cardinal, having carefully deposited the copy in his desk.

He was unfortunate in choosing his time, for in an oriel window of his favourite chamber Albrecht sat chatting with fair Margaret, and interruption was not desired. Rühel put down his letter, retiring quickly, with an imprecation on his lips concerning "that woman," who had more power over the Elector than all his officials united.

Indeed, the Cardinal for quite an hour thought too much of the smiles of his companion to look at any letter; only when she had retired it caught his eyes, and the serene forehead clouded. "What is it?" he cried. "Is that monk at me again?"

He threw down the missive and quitted the apartment.

But the thought of it followed him and brought him back almost immediately. He broke the seal. And presently a smile glided across his features. "Is that it?" he said. "You think Albrecht of Mainz will take the advice, because Albrecht of Königsberg has taken it!"

But as he continued reading, the smile vanished in the gloom of wrath, the hot glow again and again rising to his brow.

He put down the letter and sat thinking. A wrench at the bell, and the valet was despatched to command Doctor Rühel's immediate attendance.

The Cardinal had collected himself, and received the official with dignity. "I have desired your presence," he said; "Luther seems of a mind with yourself."

"Yes, I know," replied the councillor, somewhat hastily, "he has written to me himself."

"Then you know the contents of his letter to me?"

"I do."

"We desire to hear your opinion."

Rühel hesitated, but said after a while: "Though it is Luther's advice, he has not written as an enemy to your grace, but is anxious for your real advantage."

The Cardinal smiled artfully. "Doctor Martin is likely to outwit the rest of us, and he can see from Wittenberg to Halle, even into the Cardinal's inmost thoughts."

Rühel felt ready to triumph, and added rather rashly: "The Grand Master of the Teutonic Order is Duke of Prussia now, and is not likely to forget what he owes to Luther. Doctor Martin trusts your electoral grace will not spurn his counsel; indeed, he has begged me to have that letter printed, as soon as your grace has resolved upon accepting the advice."

"Has he?" cried the Cardinal, with kindling eyes. "Does he imagine it is his opinion I have been waiting for? that he need but pipe, and the Cardinal Archbishop Elector will straightway dance!"

Rühel bit his lips, he saw he had gone too far, and had spoiled what hopes there might have been.

The Cardinal dismissed him coldly, exclaiming wrathfully, as soon as the door had closed upon the councillor: "Fool of a monk, must thou needs again try to lecture the Cardinal? this time thou shalt be outwitted. . . . . But I thank thee, thou hast helped me to shake off the last of uncertainty. I know my mind now, I shall continue Archbishop Cardinal, if only for thy sake sweet Margaret, for I should lose thee did I part with the mitre; the daughter of a baker may be the Cardinal's companion, but never the wife of a prince of the realm! ... And for other reasons I have to thank thee, Luther. Thy letter will be useful; let it be printed by all means, foolish Rühel; let Pope and Emperor see what brilliant prospects the Elector Archbishop of Mainz and Magdeburg has known how to refuse! Both Pope and Emperor will owe me thanks, they will vie with each other to propitiate me, I shall be sure of my reward! Hast thou lessened my revenues, Luther? thou hast tried to make up for it now! The Emperor has plenty of money, and more still has the Pope—it is easy for them to fill the empty coffers of the poverty-stricken Primate of Germany."

The Cardinal touched his bell, Doctor Rühel was sent for. The defeated councillor entered bashfully, but with shining eyes he walked away presently. "The Lord be praised!" he cried, "the storm has passed over. How pleasantly he has spoken—I may print the letter! Then I was not mistaken after all—he will do it. Oh, I must let Luther know immediately; he *must* know it, and sure I am he will do what he can to strengthen this happy resolution, even if he should have to trot ahead, as he put it, that the Cardinal might follow."

Poor Rühel! his fingers trembled for delight as he tried to pen the wonderful news. Could he have cast a look into the electoral closet, his delight would have been drowned in disappointment. For the Cardinal was pacing the floor, proudly conscious that for once he had outwitted the Augustinian to the length even of victory.

And presently, as the news startled Christendom that Martin Luther had married a runaway nun, his enemies made it a grand occasion for venting their venom upon him; but the Cardinal burst into laughter. "Behold the monk!" he cried; "behold him trotting ahead, and looking for the Cardinal to follow!"

And turning to his cash-box, he despatched twenty gold gulden as a wedding present to Wittenberg.

Luther perceived the irony of the gift, and returned it. But for all that the Cardinal gloried in having derided his enemy, and was flushed in the thought of having outwitted him.

Fair Margaret marvelled in her heart at the new tide of affection that was showered upon her. Little she knew how near she had come to being thrust from her height, to quitting the princely splendour for the obscurity of her father's house.

CHAPTER XXIII.

THE PROMISE BROKEN.

It had been a cheap triumph after all. If Albrecht believed Luther had entered upon marriage solely for the purpose of setting an example to him, the Cardinal, he was mistaken. The Reformer had seen that celibacy, a mere invention of popery, was a sin against nature, even against God Himself, who had instituted matrimony as an honourable estate; that it was meet and right therefore to be found in that estate; and believing his death not far distant, he resolved upon a step which he considered his Christian duty, and a testimony to his teaching.

Public events also tended to undeceive his eminence. The news was abroad that the new Duke of Prussia had not only accepted the Gospel for himself, but had opened his dominions to the truth, that his very bishops were zealous in assisting him in the good work.

Nor was this all. The eyes of men were directed to Electoral Saxony. How would the new ruler deport himself with regard to the religious question? It appeared speedily that Elector John intended to stand by the

Gospel even more boldly than his late brother had done. The Papists were dismayed.

But even this was not all. Intelligence had been received from Hesse which must shake the very heart of popery; Landgrave Philip had joined the Lutheran camp. That was good news to all who were zealous for the Reformation. This prince ruled no important realm, but his mind was great, his understanding clear, his heart warm, and unbendable his will. Nor had he accepted the Gospel merely because others had set him the example; but, perceiving the evils of popery, he had searched the Scriptures to judge for himself what truth there might be in the Wittenberg teaching and having satisfied himself that Luther stood upon the Bible, the enthusiastic and high-minded young man had joined the Reformer with all his heart, declaring to his father-in-law, Duke George of Saxony, that he would rather lose life and land than depart from the Word of God.

Luther's enemies were alarmed: the Reformation had gained a champion of champions. Landgrave Philip would prove a patron who might not only stand side by side with Luther in faith, fearlessness and self-surrender, but who, as a political or military leader, had not his equal among the princes of the empire. And what if he were to gain over his father-in-law, that pillar of Rome!

The Roman Catholic Estates had formed a league at Regensburg for the suppression of the Wittenberg movement; there was a power now on the Lutheran side which they could not but acknowledge. Landgrave Philip of Hesse, Elector John of Saxony, Duke Albrecht of Prussia these three alone might suffice to deprive the Romish confederates of their fondest hopes.

Cardinal Albrecht saw it, and his spirits sank accordingly, nor did he conceal his doubts, as together with his brother, Elector Joachim of Brandenburg, and both the Dukes of Brunswick, he sat in consultation at Dessau. "It is a matter of deepest apprehension," he said, "that Philip of Hesse should have joined the Lutheran side; I know him, he has an indomitable spirit, and will soon be the soul of the whole movement. Hitherto the Lutheran princes were disunited, but now, with the Landgrave among them, there will soon be a counter-league opposing our own alliance. It is all very well for the Emperor, elated as he is by his victory over France, to send us word that he means to return now, and speedily root out this miserable heresy, that Germany once more may be at peace. He will be surprised to find that the weeds, in his absence, have grown to the power of forest trees."

The truth must be told that his grace returned to Halle in no pleasant frame of mind. As he drove along with his chancellor, he suddenly turned upon the latter, saying: "Yes, the time has come now, when we mean to pay out the citizens for the affront they have put upon us with their articles of complaint, which in those days of distress we were forced to accept. It was with a heavy heart that we agreed to their demands, quite against our own conscience; and we deem that our promise, not being a free one, can scarcely be binding. We expect of you, our chancellor, to find out for us which of the citizens have had a hand in the framing of those articles. We will give them their due!"

But Turk shook his head. "This would be a most hazardous enterprise," he said. "They would accuse your grace of having broken the archiepiscopal promise, and they will hold out for their rights."

The Elector frowned. "There are means," he said, "for getting over refractory spirits; not that I share your white-livered apprehension! Recollection of how the peasants fared must still be fresh with the citizens."

"Then what are your grace's intentions?" inquired Turk humbly.

"Those who took an active part shall rue it in the stocks," decided the Cardinal. "And now we expect you to do your duty; we desire to know their names."

The chancellor felt real mortification, but he dared not show it.

. . . . .

Just beyond the town, close by the river Saale, stood the vine-covered cottage which was the home of Kaspar Verdigris, with his wife and five children; but poverty dwelt in the house since Kaspar, in consequence of some dishonesty, had been discharged from the archiepiscopal service.

The family were sitting at table, it being supper time, the children looking wistfully into the empty platter, and the customary returning of thanks by no means coming from the little ones' hearts. It was some time since they had enjoyed a sufficient meal.

They were rising from table, when following immediately upon a knock at the door, a short, puny figure made its appearance.

"His worship the chancellor!" cried both Kaspar and his wife, dismayed.

"If you have finished supper, send the children away, and your wife too; I have come to speak to you, Kaspar."

The desire having been obeyed, the Chancellor Turk took his seat upon a wooden stool.

"And how are you getting on, Kaspar?" he inquired sympathisingly.

"Poorly, sir, poorly; my good days are past."

"I trust not, Kaspar. It remains with yourself, I expect, whether you are to be received back to the service. A man after all must carve out his own fortune."

Kaspar was all eyes and ears, but knew not what to say; the chancellor proceeded, "It is only cowards who hang the tail in the hail-storm. A man who knows what is what, bears the brunt, and is the better for it afterwards."

"Surely I am not a coward," said Kaspar. "How would you have me show it?"

"I did not think you were," rejoined Doctor Turk. "You may prove your fitness to his grace himself, and you may be sure of your reward. It lies with you to oblige the Elector greatly, if you like."

"With all my heart!" gasped the hungry Kaspar. "But what is it—no impossibility?"

"Don't be foolish," returned the chancellor; "it is the simplest matter imaginable. You are only to find out which of the citizens framed those articles granted by his grace just before peace was restored. You don't call that an impossibility, do you?"

Kaspar grinned, holding out his hand. "You shall have them, but——" he looked as though he were doubtful of recompense.

Whereupon the chancellor, putting on an expression of severest virtue, "This is doubting his grace and doubting myself. Do your duty, and you shall have your meed."

Kaspar was profuse in thanks, but the little chancellor escaped them, highly satisfied with his evening's work.

When three days had passed the town was thrown into a ferment. Everywhere the excited women put their heads together, the men gathered in alarm, the salt-pans were left unheeded, there was an asking and no answer, "Is it possible? can it be true?"

People would not believe their ears; it could not be true that such a high-born prince and prelate had broken his word, the solemn promise given to his people of Halle.

But true it was; four of the citizens who had been chiefly instrumental in framing the articles were imprisoned in the Temnitz, as though guilty of crime. They had been seized at nightfall, and, in spite of all protestation, in spite of the prayers and tears of their families, they had been dragged away as common felons. Three others, Gabriel Burkhardt among them, were confined within their own houses, forbidden to leave them under pain of further punishment.

The first excitement yielded to a silence akin to the lull before the bursting storm.

It quite oppressed the chancellor; he took opportunity to warn the Cardinal.

"The peasant war has proved it," he said, "that we have more foes than friends, if once the people are roused. We ought not to anger them needlessly."

"Needlessly!" exclaimed the Cardinal. "But it is

very necessary, and I am determined that the town shall pay now for past insolence. How can we rule our diocese if a single town can dare to oppose us? It is necessary, I say, to prove our authority."

At this moment an attendant announced a deputation from the town council.

"I knew it," groaned the chancellor; and turning to the Cardinal he added, not without a touch of bitterness, "The town seems anxious to submit to authority."

Albrecht turned a wrathful brow upon his chancellor, startling the servant with a "Tell them to come some other day."

The man vanished and returned. The deputation was determined not to leave the palace without seeing his grace.

The chancellor smiled sarcastically; the Cardinal, perceiving it, gave a passionate stamp on the floor. "They are a stubborn race, but I will show them who is master! Bring them in."

There was a pause, and the deputation was ushered into his presence, three members of the town council, bowing with cold deference. "We plead forgiveness," said the spokesman, "if the present hour be inconvenient to your electoral grace, but our mission is too important to admit of delay. We have come, humbly praying for explanation why four honourable citizens have been cast into prison at your grace's command, as though they were common malefactors. We would gladly believe that there is some mistake."

The Cardinal's eyes shot fire. "What is this I hear? Since when is it the subject's part to inquire into the ruler's reasons? Asking for explanation, forsooth! These twelve years might have taught you that one

THE PROMISE BROKEN. 259

thing at least—that yours is a just and well-intentioned ruler, if so be that you do your duty and obey the law." But unflinchingly the spokesman made answer, " We crave leave to dissent, electoral grace. Those who have been made prisoners have done their duty, and did so even at the archiepiscopal behest. Your grace requested the township to draw up in writing what might be our grievances; those men did so in our name and in obedience to your desire. Shall they suffer punishment for doing so, and are we to consider this your grace's just and well-intentioned government?"

The Cardinal shook with resentment, unable to speak for a moment. When the power returned, it came with a roar as of thunder; "Hapless mortal!" be cried, " have you come hither to be their fellow in disgrace?"

His eye sought the chancellor, who, understanding, quitted the apartment, returning after a moment with five of the body-guard.

The unexpected appearance dumbfounded the deputation; they offered no resistance, not a word even of protest. The spokesman was handcuffed, the others looking on with a petrified stare.

" In the name of heaven," stammered the chancellor, left alone with the Cardinal, " can your grace be aware—it is daring the utmost!"

The Cardinal laughed harshly. " The utmost indeed —we will dare it. We dare put a bridle upon the restive horse; we will dare even to drive the spur into its flanks. We mean to ride it, and we mean to be master. Our citizens of Halle shall perceive that our forbearance has its limits if they dare require explanation at our hands. To-morrow morning the thumbscrews are to be used; you shall take the prisoners' depositions."

Turk retired horror-struck; he had never seen the Cardinal in such a towering passion.

And on the following morning the Archbishop left for his see of Magdeburg, where he was expected to arbitrate in a lawsuit between the Chapter and the township.

Returning at the end of a week, he took the chancellor's report. "The town is astonishingly quiet," said the official. "There was some attempt at disturbance when it transpired that torture was being applied, but the constabulary, together with the garrison of the Burg, soon quelled the riot."

The Cardinal smiled proudly. "We knew what we were about. One need but make front, and the discontented are as mice flying for their holes. But what of confession has the thumbscrew elicited?"

"Nothing of importance," replied Turk, "except a statement that an emissary of Thomas Münzer had been in the town, secretly attempting to gain over the people to the revolutionary movement, urging them to admit the rebels into the well-fortified city."

The Cardinal's lips quivered as he exclaimed: "And what of your advice now, sir chancellor? where would we be if we had taken it? We perceive we have judged aright, and we will pursue the path we have chosen. Too long have we allowed our leniency to be abused; but we will proceed with severity now, nay, with relentless rigour! And we mean to bring one to judgment who has long deserved punishment, who has indeed incurred our most just displeasure, with whom we have borne hitherto on account of the unsettled times. The measure is full now, and he shall have his meed. I do not intend to quit Halle or the diocese of Magdeburg until I have dealt with that mole. You know whom I mean—Magister Winkler our court preacher—he shall be silenced now. Most shamefully has he abused our confidence. We received him back into favour after those objectionable sermons of his, exhorting him carefully to study the fathers; but he has added new sermons to the old ones, and has even dared in our absence to administer the cup to the laity. Many of the citizens, we hear, have availed themselves of the opportunity—men even whom otherwise one would hardly like to impugn. The very cloisters are not free of the taint of heresy, and scarcely a monk is left at Convent Neuwerk. We have remonstrated with him in all kindness and confidence, pointing out the effects of his preaching; but a strange spirit of contradiction possesses the man who was all meekness before; he has dared to say to our face that he cannot obey us, being constrained by the truth. The magister will have to take his reward now!"

The chancellor agreed with the Cardinal: "He has deserved it, no doubt, for it is most grievous to behold the state of distraction raised by his preaching within the town. My advice has of late not enjoyed much of your grace's approval, yet I must venture to submit the extreme necessity of setting about this matter with all manner of prudence; for those of the citizens who favour heresy simply adore the man, and resorting to violence against him might provoke an outbreak among the people. The flame of resentment is barely kept under as it is. For this reason I would conjure your grace not to bring him to judgment here at Halle, but to take the matter to your western diocese, and refrain from passing sentence yourself, referring the case entirely to the High Chapter of Mainz."

The Cardinal considered for a moment, nodding his head presently. "We approve of your advice; but before we set out for Mainz we must take counsel with Canon Hoffmann of the new foundation; doubtless his information will be of use to the Chapter."

This Canon Hoffmann was the very man to incense the Cardinal against the court chaplain, if this were needed; for his jealous hatred of the popular magister stopped short of no falsehood, and he took delight in calumniating him to the utmost.

Cardinal Albrecht quitted Halle with a splendid retinue, to take up his residence in the archiepiscopal electorate.

CHAPTER XXIV.

A DEED OF DARKNESS.

ONE lovely sun-lit day in June, 1527, the dwelling of the court-chaplain Winkler was surrounded by men and women with expectation in their eyes. The house door was wreathed with flowers and garlands of oak-leaves, and the chamber within was bright, a presentation gift of wrought silver awaiting the return of him whom the people loved and delighted to honour. The brave confessor had decided upon another step in testimony of the truth he preached, not heeding the scorn of those whose hearts were at Rome. He had made up his mind to enter upon the holy estate of marriage, and the wife he had chosen was fully worthy to be joined to him in blessed love. For the Lady Adelaide of the noble house of Raben was not only a pattern of beauty and loveliness, but hers were the higher gifts and graces which are more to be desired than mere bodily charms, and many a noble knight might envy the plain magister who had won so sweet a companion. As for him, his eyes had been directed to the lady chiefly by the holy enthusiasm with which she had accepted the Gospel. Whenever he stood in his pulpit, the upturned face had met his vision, unconscious of aught else but the deep fervour burning within her soul. He had not sought her intentionally, but opportunity bringing them together one day, the hearts of both opened to one another, and they knew that they could join hands for life.

And now the magister was coming home with his espoused wife, and the people were anxious to grace their return.

Nor were they kept waiting long; the sounds of wheels were heard: another minute and the newly married couple had alighted. Cheer after cheer broke upon the sunny air, loving words of sympathy bid them welcome home, and the happy couple hardly knew how to return thanks for so much affection.

Left to themselves at last, the magister drew closer his wife. "My Adelaide," he said, "how full of love and promise is this happy time! The people in this place are prepared for the Gospel; we may indeed say the Lord is adding to His Church daily: soon the whole town will come forth to confess Him, and the Cardinal himself cannot prevent it. Who knows but the Lord may yet turn even his heart, that he will no longer kick against the pricks, but be brought to accept the truth?"

The happy young wife, nestling within her husband's embrace, looked up at him saying: "This is indeed my hope, else I could never cease trembling for your safety. I believe in the power of the Gospel, and that the work will prevail which Luther, the man of God, has begun."

Winkler with happy pride gazed into the face so full of trust and sweetest surrender, saying: "Let us rejoice, then, in hope which maketh not ashamed."

Restful and happy were the days, that sunny month of June. The roses and lilies were abloom, the larks and nightingales sent forth their jubilant song, all nature shed abroad her treasures, and in the humble dwelling two noble God-fearing souls drank in the fulness of His favour, who in the beginning had made man, male and female, and put them into a garden, and blessed them.

There was a blessing, too, upon the magister's renewed labour; the people more and more seemed ready for the Gospel, the convent churches grew emptier day by day, and before long another witness arose, for in a chapel of the 'Holy Ghost's' the Word was being preached also.

Yet this was not all, a special joy was being given to the faithful confessor. Of all his enemies none had been more rancorous than a certain canon, Conrad Hoffmann by name, and even this man was seemingly turned by the Lord; he met the chaplain with invariable kindness now, repeatedly attending his preaching, and occasionally calling upon him, when he would be specially attentive to the Lady Adelaide. True, he anxiously avoided any religious topic, but this might be the shyness of new-born conviction. Winkler took it as such, and carefully refrained offering human assistance to what he gladly believed might be the work of the Spirit, remembering the canon all the more diligently in prayer.

. . . .

At Aschaffenburg, in the castle, Cardinal Albrecht was sitting surrounded by the Chapter of Mainz, which had come to that town by special command.

His grace opened the sitting.

"Reverend brethren," he began, "it may at first sight surprise you that we have called you hither on behalf of a matter which, nowise concerning our archbishopric of Mainz, should rather be settled at Magdeburg, as referring to Magister George Winkler, our court preacher of Halle. But let it not dismay you, seeing that we act upon careful consideration. This man has repaid us good with evil, shamefully deceiving our unsuspecting confidence. Quite forgetful of his oath, he has ventured upon all manner of mischief during our absence; more especially has he dared to administer baptism without the use of the chrism, and to admit the laity to the sacramental cup; entirely neglectful of holy mass, he has directed, moreover, all his efforts to pulpit ministry, misleading the people with all manner of heresy. And not only this, his influence has reached the very convents, actually lessening the number of our friars. But worst of all, since we have left Halle, he has not stopped short of breaking his vow of celibacy; he has married a wife! All these things bear testimony against him, calling aloud for his punishment. We greatly regret that we have delayed it so long, thereby leaving him free for the committing of his last and most shocking offence. But all the more needful is it now to show our entire disapprobation by speedy action; and it is to your judgment, most worthy Chapter, that we have decided to pass over the case. There is another of our preachers at Halle who has begun to follow his example, but with him we have dealt already, commanding our captain of the Moritzburg to turn that miscreant from his cure at once, forbidding him the town. But this matter of Magister Winkler we do not care to touch with our own hands, desiring you to act in our stead, well aware that you will judge him according to his deserts and for the well-being of Holy Church."

The prebends were indeed surprised that the Elector should draw them into a case so entirely foreign to their own jurisdiction, seeing they had more than enough to do to prevent the spread of heresy within their own domain; however, the Archbishop having spoken, they could not but express their subservience.

Three days later the Chapter met for deliberation; there was difference of opinion, but a resolution was carried at last that the heretical court preacher should be immured for life within some monastery.

The meeting was about to rise when an underling announced the arrival of one who craved immediate admittance. The reverend members were tired of long consultation, and would far rather have gone to solace themselves with meat and drink, but the request was urgent, and the stranger was suffered to enter. He was no other than Conrad Hoffmann, canon of the new foundation of Halle, who prayed for a hearing.

The prebends reseating themselves, Hoffmann began: "Having been secretly informed by the captain of the Moritzburg, that his grace's court preacher is to be judged by the reverend High Chapter of Mainz, I have come hither to offer my most humble information, well knowing how difficult it is to arrive at a correct estimate of one not personally known. Magister Winkler is no stranger to me, I have had opportunity of sounding his evil-working heart. He goes about in sheep's clothing, but he is a ravening wolf disturbing the flock of Christ. Far too mildly has his grace dealt with him, not suspecting in his pious mind the court chaplain's desperate wickedness. Far too long, also, has he delayed punishment; for if this man had been brought to judgment sooner, great offence might have been prevented. My humble advice, therefore, is this: that the High Chapter should nowise spare the miscreant, seeing that forbearance towards such a one is actual sin."

The provost waved his hand: "You might have saved yourself the trouble, brother canon, seeing that the Chapter has arrived at a sentence without you, and the punishment methinks is sufficient; the court preacher will be rendered harmless by lifelong detention in a convent prison."

The canon bit his lips, silent a while, and then he resumed: "I respect the wisdom of the High Chapter, but I crave leave to say the punishment is not sufficient, since it cannot render the man harmless! If the reverend prebends knew him as I do, they would know that in wickedness and evil intent he is nowise behind Luther himself, wherefore he is justly guilty of a like punishment."

"What!" cried the provost, amazed, "shall we ask both Pope and Emperor to fulminate the ban against a nameless chaplain?"

"Perhaps not," said the wily tempter. "May it please the Chapter to let me finish! I was going to add that such men should be got rid of. You little guess how the town of Halle, ay, the whole archbishopric of Magdeburg, is endangered by Winkler's influence, else you would not hesitate one moment. Convent walls and prison bars are no safe keeping for a man of such perversity; think ye he would not find a way out in spite of your watchfulness? Better by far to think of another expedient. I would propose that the magister be cited hither to appear before his grace and your reverence; let him off with a reproof; there is no reason why he should not meet with an accident on the road, and his face be seen at Halle no more."

The prebends started from their seat. "Assassin!" cried some. "Ruthless rascal!" another.

But the canon, immovable, continued blandly, "I crave your pardon; is he an assassin who would free the Church of a heretic? Were they assassins who brought John Huss to the stake? Is it not rather our bounden duty to extirpate heresy, no matter by what means?"

The provost, who was known for his zeal in this latter respect, left the chair now, taking the canon aside to confer with him privately. Returning to the table after a while, he said, "Our brother's advice is not altogether to be despised, the rather that he is prepared himself to take the avenger's part, if we provide him with some men-at-arms. I request the reverend members to reconsider the resolution arrived at; I move acceptance of the canon's offer."

The prebends remained silent, but eventually eight rose for "Ayes," four only keeping their seats in token of "No!" Winkler's mortal enemy had triumphed. Jealousy, wearing the mask of zeal for the Church, had whetted the dagger, and was ready to plunge it into the chaplain's faithful heart.

. . . . . .

On the 19th of August, 1527, two travellers on horseback entered the town of Aschaffenburg.

"God be praised that we have reached our journey's

end!" said the one who evidently stood in the relation of master to his companion. "I am tired to death. The air is sultry and oppressive; ever since yesterday the horizon is heavy with thunder-clouds, the very look of which is a weight to one's weariness."

"It is well we are under shelter now," responded the servant. "The storm is about to break, methinks; see how low the swallows are flying, piping timorously, and I noticed a lurid flash of lightning but a minute since."

The two were passing beneath the archway leading to the Elector's castle, and dismounting, left the bridle to some attendant grooms.

"I fancy you had better make sure of the horses' comfort, Nicholas," muttered the gentleman; "these fellows don't look over-anxious to bestir themselves."

"Never fear about the horses, sir," returned Nicholas. "I wish I could be as easy concerning yourself. God save your reverence!"

Shaking the dust from his mantle, the former replied with a sigh, "I own I am oppressed, yet I will not fear, for the Lord is my defence. If He holds me safe, men cannot harm me."

Nicholas was left alone, and waited a long time for his master's return; there was a positive foreboding of trouble weighing upon the faithful servant's heart, which he tried to shake off, entering into conversation with the electoral grooms. They were anxious enough to learn all about him, and he saw no reason to hide the fact that he was in attendance on his master, the court-preacher, Magister Winkler of Halle, who had come hither at his grace's desire on important business. Concerning the nature of this business, however, he was silent, and was glad to withdraw presently, preferring a lonely saunter about the town.

Returning, he recognised his master's figure in the courtyard, and hastened up to him. "Oh, sir, how did you fare?" he asked.

The court chaplain looked another man, holding out his hand to the faithful creature with a reassuring smile. "All is well!" he said. "His electoral grace has received me most condescendingly, speaking to me in all kindness; I have been desired to refrain from preaching for the present, but it scarcely amounted to a reproof. Nor has there been any reference to my marriage—the fact may not be known here yet. After to-morrow we will turn our horses' heads homeward, I hope."

But Nicholas looked full of diffidence, remaining silent.

"What is the matter?" asked Winkler. "I thought thou wouldest rejoice at the good news?"

"Oh, yes, I do," replied the man, absently. "I feel strangely heavy at heart."

"It is the thunder, Nicholas; a refreshing rain would do us good."

"Yes, yes," said Nicholas, casting a troubled look about him, adding, after a pause, "might the canon, Conrad Hoffmann, be here too?"

Winkler looked up surprised, "Hoffmann of Halle? How should he? Why, he saw us off on our journey, wishing us God speed! Nor do I know what could bring him hither."

"Neither do I, sir. But as I strolled about the town just now I caught sight of a figure in the distance so like the canon, but it vanished."

"Does that trouble you? even if it had been friend Hoffmann; however, it is scarcely probable."

"But——" replied the man, a tremendous flash of lightning cutting him short; the courtyard seemed enveloped in flames, an uproarious clap of thunder burst overhead, master and servant running for shelter within doors.

All through the night Winkler lay restless on his couch. The events of the day kept passing and repassing through his mind, holding sleep aloof. His thoughts grew anxious and troubled; his gladdened hopes had fled; there seemed other things to be set over against the unexpected leniency of his reception. If Nicholas had seen right, if Conrad Hoffmann, the canon of Halle, had really followed his footsteps, arriving before him, what could it mean? What business had he here, of which he had not hinted a word at their parting? And again, the Elector's clemency, the more than mildness of treatment he had met with at the hands of the Chapter, how was he to take it? If that was all they desired his presence for, what need was there to summon him to Aschaffenburg? Was it possible that all this was mere disguise, could more and worse be behind?

The more he thought over these things, the less chance of rest he found; his veins throbbed, his heart beat anxiously, he could not shake off the feeling of some unknown fear.

Towards morning he slept, but only that dreams might add to his distress, vision chasing vision through his soul; at one time he saw his wife putting on her mournful weeds; and looking closer, it was not she, but the canon in knightly accoutrements, and baring the sword; and then he felt as though fleeing for life from threatening danger, but attempting to run, he was rooted to the ground; wanting to cry for help, he could not produce a sound. Bathed in anguish, he started up at last, and was thankful to see the morning.

Towards noon a Dominican friar came, requesting his attendance in the provost's cell.

Complying on the spot, he found his reverence and three of the prebends seated with bottles of wine. Invited to join the jovial company, he could not but sit down, but the fiery Cyprian of the electoral cellars was as poison to his lips. Nevertheless, the merry brethren knew how to draw him out, talking of this and that, quite getting the better of his dejection.

It struck him to ask what they knew as to the canon's presence in the town. But the provost shook his head with all possible unconcern. "Who did you say? I know no one of this name."

Honest Winkler was misled. "I have wronged them, after all," he said, and felt ready to ask their forgiveness.

They inquired when he intended to quit the neighbourhood, and learning that he hoped to set out the following morning, they tried to dissuade him. "He had better enjoy a little rest with them," they said; meeting his objection that he was being expected at home by saying "Then let your servant ride in advance of you and announce your coming."

He did not like the proposal, but somehow they managed to prevail.

They kept him all that day, making their company as pleasant as possible. Again he thought: "Surely I have wronged them in my heart!" But looking for his servant in the evening, the same strange apprehension haunted him, needing an effort to master it.

"Get thyself ready for the morning, Nicholas, to return to Halle," he said.

"Myself?" echoed Nicholas, looking up wondering. "And what about yourself, sir?"

"You may ride in advance of me," returned his master.

"What is the matter, your reverence? You look sadly put out!."

"I hardly can tell you; depression will get the better of one sometimes, you know!"

"But why should you part with me? Let me remain—let us journey together."

"Are you afraid to ride by yourself?"

"Do not make it a matter of jest! It is not about myself I am fearful—but you, sir, you!"

"Set thyself at ease about me; one of the Elector's men is to see me home."

"The Elector's men are not your Nicholas."

"Yes, yes, thou faithful soul, but let it be. It seems a settled matter; go thy way then, and take a greeting to my wife."

The chaplain turned quickly like one not certain of himself and walked away.

Nicholas with drooping arms gazed after him. "I do not like that; there is more behind. I do feel badly. It can't be the thunder, for that is passed, and the sky is blue enough. I wish we were safe at Halle, both of us."

The honest servant heaved a great sigh, and went to look after his horses.

The following morning, mounted and ready to start, he lingered in the courtyard, looking wistfully at his master's window, anxious for a parting sign. The magister, as though sensible of the gaze in the depth of his chamber, came to the casement, waving his hand.

And slowly Nicholas rode from the town—speed seemed not his desire.

How happy looked the world at early dawn, each little flower sparkled with laughter, though tearful with the dew of conquered night. Nicholas saw it, but no brightness rose within him; trouble gathered at his eyelids, and he cared not to brush away the glistening tear.

. . . .

Two days later there was again a departure at early dawn. He who now rode forth from the electoral archway at Aschaffenburg turned his horse's head in the same direction as Nicholas had done. He rode alone, but was followed at some distance by one of his grace's grooms.

The traveller seemed anxious to gain ground; the day proved hot, but he thought not of saving his horse, and the man behind him kept cursing his hurry.

At noon a wayside inn offered refreshment, but the halt was of the shortest possible duration.

At sunset the churlish groom rode up alongside, saying: "Lessen your speed, sir, for there is need to think of the night's lodging. There is neither town nor village within reach now, and I know of no inn within miles; but a keeper's cottage must be hereabouts, where we might find shelter, this being electoral forest."

"Thou art mistaken, friend," returned the traveller. "I rode this way but shortly, though in opposite direction; we cannot be far of a certain village. I was the vicar's guest coming hither, and promised him to avail myself of his hospitality on my return. He will be glad to take us in, I know."

The groom gave a growl. "If you are so certain of the way, sir chaplain, my attendance could have been dispensed with."

Winkler pulled up, saying after a while, "Well, then, take the lead."

The groom spurred his horse, the two riders disappearing in the dark of the crime-haunted Spessart.

The moon stole up the sky, casting quivering beams through the pine-wood, the shadows gliding like spectres between the boles. On and on they rode, but no keeper's cottage beckoned welcome through the dismal night.

"I seem to have missed my way," muttered the menial at last. "We must make the best of it!"

"But I had rather not camp out," returned the court chaplain, plainly. "I can still hold out—let us push on."

"I follow your pleasure," said the groom, "*I* am not tired;" and he pulled his horse's rein.

There was a sound as of breaking brushwood, sending a shiver through the chaplain's frame.

It was but a deer, startled from its lair, bounding across their path.

Another minute and the same noise was repeated—not by a dappled fugitive this time; there were sounds of horses' hoofs and a clanking of armour. Three horsemen broke from the underwood, the fitful moonlight giving but uncertain outlines.

Magister Winkler peered at the shadowy apparitions; they were upon him, and pierced by their swords he sank to the ground.

One of the murderers, jumping from his horse, bent over him, hissing, "God's justice confound thee, hateful heretic!"

"Ah, is it you, Conrad Hoffman?" gasped the bleeding chaplain. "May He have mercy on your soul!"

Another thrust, and the martyred confessor was with his Lord.

Silence was left to guard the spot—the tree-tops bending their heads to the wind, the moonlight casting a glory on the forsaken corpse.

. . . . . .

The Lady Adelaide, the magister's newly-wedded wife, sat lonely in her chamber awaiting her husband's return. Day after day passed, and the minutes were as hours to her longing love.

At last, on the tenth day after her lord's departure, she beheld Nicholas riding up the street.

She started in happy delight. But what can be the matter? It is Nicholas by himself, coming slowly, not raising his head.

A cry of anguish burst from her lips, she dared not run to meet the messenger, although the latter seemed hours in ascending the stairs.

At last he entered; a terrible fear clutched at her heart, overspreading her face with a ghastly pallor.

"Where is your master—my husband?" she gasped.

The faithful servant could but cover his face, sobbing like a child.

But he must not give way to his own grief, the

poor young wife had to be thought of who lay fainting at his feet.

It was long before she recovered. Her sorrow-boding heart had guessed the worst before the servant found strength to open his mouth. But no—his account, given at last amid sobs and tears, was far beyond her most fearful apprehension.

"Unwillingly I did his bidding," said Nicholas, "when he commanded me to ride in advance, to return without him. My horse made way but slowly, I did not care to spur it on. Having arrived at the second night's quarters, I resolved not to proceed further, but to abide his coming—he had said he would come after me shortly. But a day passed, and another day, and he came not. On the third morning I could rest no longer, I returned on my steps; and behold, at no great distance, where the gloomy forest skirts the high road, I came upon a crowd of villagers: 'A man has been found murdered in the wood!' they cried—'look, where they bring him!' I went nearer—and looked him in the face—and——"

Adelaide gave a heart-rending cry: "My husband—murdered—ah me!" A merciful swoon enveloped the broken heart.

CHAPTER XXV.

CONSCIENCE.

" WHAT news is this, provost? Is it thus you misunderstood and abused our trust? An honest verdict I requested from the High Chapter, a straightforward judgment, however severe, but not secret assassination. All the world will point at the Elector of Mainz. Luther especially will roar louder than ever—methinks I hear him already."

With these words, and feeling anxious not a little, Cardinal Albrecht burst into the apartment of the provost of his cathedral at Mainz.

This latter worthy must have been prepared for some such greeting, for he was not in the least disconcerted by the sudden reproach, answering blandly: "Your electoral grace wrongs me, surely, and entertains most needless anxiety. I have not decided on the matter by myself, the whole Chapter did sit in judgment, and the verdict was not given without fullest consideration. Indeed, our first resolution had been to the effect that the heretic should be immured for life in some convent, when a canon of Halle arrived, Conrad Hoffmann by name, who made us view things differently, offering himself to carry out the sentence. Your grace is right in this, that it was done in the dead of night; but, I would ask, has not the Vehm itself again and again made use of the secret dagger, nor ever lifting the veil from her jurisdiction? And yet the people call it the *holy* Vehm. Supposing a hue and cry were raised concerning the matter, suspicion would never touch your electoral grace! All the world knows that the High Chapter of Mainz was intrusted with the business. If any have to bear the brunt, it is we, and not your grace. But who will dare to attack even the Chapter? Can we not prove that the accused left us unscathed to return to his home? People will have to be satisfied with the apparent fact that the good man fell a victim to some murderous highwayman of the Spessart, or, it might have been, to private revenge. The Lady Adelaide whom he wedded has brothers, we hear, who hated him for the marriage, seeing that they are of ancient nobility, and he was a nobody. There are all sorts of possibilities, you see, why the man who had left us should never reach home."

The Elector was not exactly satisfied with this argumentation, nor could it allay his fears. People most probably would point to him, he repeated, and Doctor Martin would do so for a certainty.

He retired to his innermost chambers, communing with solitude. Margaret only dared venture near him, and it added to his oppression that even she had no comfort in his strait.

His nights offered no solace, for sleep was troubled, and dreams were alarming. He tried to quiet his conscience with all manner of subterfuge, but conscience spoke with a voice of its own and took no denial:

"Thou art guilty of this man's death," it said, " or at least thou hast brought him to it ! Why wouldest thou not judge him in his own place? why didst thou call him to Aschaffenburg? Yes, why?"

His distress only increased, his courage forsook him. "Send for Doctor Rühel," he said one morning; "I want him."

He could hardly await the councillor's arrival, and no sooner was he present than the Elector plunged into matters. "You must write a letter to Martin Luther, in order to anticipate the storm he will most certainly raise; he will be sure to attack me all the more unsparingly, now he has the semblance of right on his side. Write forthwith, and despatch our fleetest messenger!"

Rühel obeyed the behest. He was glad to hear the Elector assert his innocence; and being himself on a friendly footing with Luther he hoped the best of the letter in question. But all at once the thought struck him as strange that the Elector should take matters so quietly and do nothing towards bringing the murderer to justice. He was courageous, or, as it might be, audacious enough, to express his doubts to Albrecht.

The Elector was taken aback, but said, after a moment's reflection : "Do not imagine that we are inactive, though it should appear so. We believe to be more certain of results by means of secret investigation."

Rühel was satisfied, although he might have noticed the Elector's diffidence. The latter, however, took the councillor's hint, and determined to cite the Canon Hoffmann to his presence, in order to take his deposition himself, feeling somehow distrustful of the provost's account.

That same day an archiepiscopal messenger was despatched to Halle.

He must have been well mounted, for as early as the sixth day he returned, presenting himself to the Elector.

"Where is the canon?" demanded Albrecht hastily.

The messenger with an obeisance made answer: "So please your grace, I could not but come without him. For learning your desire, the canon grew white, but promised to prepare himself for the journey without delay. But on the following morning, as I stood waiting for him to join me, I perceived a sudden commotion among the people, there was a running to and fro, and terror spoke from all faces. Presently one of them came to me saying: 'You must return by yourself, master. Canon Hoffmann has just been found with a broken neck.'"

The Elector shook perceptibly, his lips blanching. But Margaret held up her hands, exclaiming: "God's justice in heaven! The world will know now who murdered the chaplain!"

The Elector gave her a half-smile, but seemed hardly to share her satisfaction. The shadow was not lifted from his brow when he retired to his solitude.

. . . . .

The whole of Halle was overcast with sorrow at the news of the ruthless deed. The house of the murdered man seemed a very place of pilgrimage; all were anxious to express their sympathy to the widow, tears flowed abundantly, and the cry of mourning went up to heaven. The flock who loved the Gospel had lost their shepherd, their stay on whom they leaned, and reproachful words were spoken of the Cardinal. Even such of the citizens who remained in the bonds of popery felt aggrieved and walked in silence.

It was towards the end of September when the people pressed to the "Ratskeller," women and children even joining the gathering of men, for it had become known that there had arrived from Doctor Martin a "Consolation to the Christian People of Halle concerning the death of Magister George, their Preacher."

The assembly listened in breathless silence when the venerable clerk of the council read the letter with ringing voice.

"Grace and peace in Christ Jesus, our Lord and Saviour. Amen.

"I have intended for some time to write to your love, exhortation, and comfort against the trouble which Satan hath done to you by the murderous death to which he brought the good and pious Magister George, robbing you thereby of your faithful minister, and of the Word of God. I have been prevented hitherto by various reasons, more especially by my weakness, and although I have hardly got over it, I cannot delay further. And albeit we would not console ourselves concerning such matter, it would on the other hand be most unrighteous to pass in silence this infamous and treacherous murder, to bury as it were the blood that was spilt which is a witness for the Word of God. Therefore I will put it into writ, helping it to call and raise up a cry to heaven, that such deed of murder be never suppressed until God, the Merciful Father and righteous Judge, hath heard the cry as He heard the blood of Abel, and until He hath righted the cause, avenging it on the murderer and corrupter, the old enemy who hath done this; and until He hath so ordered it that the blood of Magister George be a Divine seed bringing fruit an hundred-fold, so that in the place of the one murdered George there be a hundred preachers of righteousness, who will do a thousand times more grief and hurt to Satan than the one magister has been able.

"But to you, and all of us, dear friends, shall be this comfort: firstly, that we should nowise be surprised concerning such murder and evil deed upon earth, for the devil is a murderer and a liar from the beginning. Let this be the first part of our consolation: that we do know who is the real murderer, although we cannot know for certain who are the men that commanded it, or whose are the fists and weapons which did it. For I hear much talking concerning the innocence of the Archbishop of Mainz, which I heartily desire may be true, and will so accept it. Indeed, I rather believe it is the Chapter of Mainz which brought about this murder; seeing that they have had in their mind much greater murder, intending in their deadly counsel to set the German princes at one another, by means of the Emperor Charles, drowning the whole of Germany in murder and in blood. Now those who would not hesitate to bring a whole country to murder and bloodshed, will take it lightly that a poor magister should be brought to death. Such are they, those ghostly holy folk, who with their masses and prayers will keep up Christianity, and yet are able to sacrifice the whole world to the devil, who is the murderer of old. It was by the work of such assassins, I deem, that many priests have been found drowned in the Rhine, no man knowing who did it. Continue your work, then, ye murderers and assassins, ye follow a righteous road, even as Cain did! Was *his* deed suppressed in silence? It will be with you then, as it was with him, whoever you be, your murder will be kept dark and secret, known by no one save those who now know the murderer of righteous Abel. Well then, this I mention, it is Satan who hath done it; the Chapter of Mainz I cannot accuse for a certainty; but I will say this: unless they do their utmost that the true murderer be looked for and brought to justice, they will be guilty of the deed, if they have not actually commanded it. Let them laugh at it if they can. They shall be called assassins and murderous thieves; villains they are who have broken the public peace, if they let a man be murdered without trial and judgment, and do nothing to avenge it.

"We have comfort, secondly, in this: that the pious Magister George fell a victim to his obedience to authority. It was his master who had summoned him away from Halle, and he counted not his life, although evil forebodings would dissuade him; in this we may say that he followed his true Master, the Lord Jesus Christ, and like Him was obedient even unto death. Yea, not only was he obedient, but he loved and honoured his earthly master faithfully with body and life; for I have heard tell how wondrously true he was to his bishop in the peasants' rebellion, and that he, the Archbishop, fairly loved him for it. This then is the good man's reward!

"But, thirdly, he hath been murdered not only in obedient service of his earthly ruler, but hath died for the Gospel, for that part of it chiefly which would have the sacrament administered as the Lord hath commanded, not forbidding the cup. A great fire must flare up at this, for Satan and all his murderers see the need of stopping such proceeding; so they enticed him away beyond his own diocese of Magdeburg, into another to whose jurisdiction he nowise belonged, and not only this, but have him murdered secretly and treacherously on the way.

"I pray you, therefore, and exhort you, to commit this matter, for which you justly grieve and are troubled, to Him who judges right, even as St. Peter saith that Christ Himself hath done; bear ill-will or hatred to no one, speak no evil, curse not, and desire not revenge, but pray ye for the murderers.

"Let your love accept this exhortation in good part as I give it; Christ surely will direct your hearts and advise you by His Holy Spirit, teaching you what to do now and alway. For it cannot be otherwise than what saith the Scripture: 'We must through much tribulation enter the kingdom of God.' It cannot be that our Lord Christ should die on the cross and wear the crown of thorns, and we be saved straightway in sheer pleasure and delight. Christ, our Lord and Saviour, be with you with His grace! Amen."

"Amen!" responded the assembly, separating in silence, Doctor Martin's comfort accompanying them to their homes.

. . . . .

But if the Christian people of Halle were cheered by this letter of Martin Luther, it nowise tended to edify the great Cardinal, who heard of it; yet in his heart he could not but be thankful that Luther had not dealt worse with him; and Councillor Rühel was taken into special favour.

But the Cardinal's lightness of heart would not come back to him—it was a lingering shadow which the dreadful deed trailed behind it.

What bodes the light in the castle of Aschaffenburg, gleaming from the chamber where she sleeps who is Albrecht's darling? Why step her women so fearfully? What is it they whisper of the dread in their hearts? What is it that has hushed those halls, where joy and pleasure dwelt, and trouble seemed forbidden to enter? Margaret has been struck down in the freshness of life, suddenly and without a warning; the fire has gone out from those eyes, the roses have faded from her lips; on her cheeks they linger, adding bloom to bloom; but the physicians do not like that brightness, watching the fever in helpless despair, yet showing the face of hope to the anxious Cardinal. But two days since she was in the very flower of youth and happiness, Albrecht's delight, smoothing away care and trouble from his forehead by her sparkling gaiety, ever ready to enfold him in the sweetness of her charms—and now? What is life, indeed, and the beauty and power thereof?

The Cardinal held by the falsest of hopes, he would not, he could not think that it might be an illness unto death. Yet so it was—early in the morning the dreaded spectre broke upon his slumbers—"She is gone," they said.

He tried to rouse from what he believed a fearful dream. "She is dead!" they repeated.

Albrecht was terribly shaken; the strong man could scarcely summon strength to go to her chamber. In silence and with bloodless cheeks he sat by the couch of death; none dared approach him, none dared offer a word of comfort. Part of the following night, too, he spent in a lonely watch by the dead. With myrtles they had decked her, and the lonesome light of consecrated tapers lit up her shroud.

"How he must have loved her!" his people whispered. "How pitiful to see the strong man cast down with grief!"

But little they guessed what was the sorest sting of his grief! Little they knew that there was more than the loss of her he had loved; that the heart could not bear up under its trouble, because *conscience* stood by his dead, showing him the loss in the light of punishment—he was overtaken, the voice said, by the Avenger of blood.

Sadly the bearers had clothed themselves in the garb of mourning, the last of autumnal leaves fell slowly to the ground, some few remaining flowerets of the season stood shrivelled by the wayside—fit witnesses of the sorrowful procession on its way from Aschaffenburg to Halle. Slowly and sadly they bore her through field and forest, whence the glory had departed. Once more and for the last time the Cardinal took her the well-known way to his eastern residence. More splendid than ever was the pride of her surroundings, but the golden shell was a coffin, the costly silks a shroud; her eye saw nothing of it all, she was gone, and for ever.

Mournfully the procession moved through the streets of Halle towards the magnificent cathedral. The citizens stood aloof, silent and thoughtful. The venerable clerk of the council, meeting a like-minded friend, said reverently, "He that hath ears to hear, let him hear, for the Lord hath spoken."

CHAPTER XXVI.

FRESH ENDEAVOURS.

Two years had passed. During the Cardinal's prolonged absence the good seed had grown and multiplied at Halle. The murdered witness of the Gospel had not found a successor in the city itself, but round about the Word was being preached; at Eisleben, at Brehna and other villages, the glad tidings could be heard, and thither went those whose hearts were prepared for the truth.

The Cardinal perceived the increase, and again he determined with spiritual weapons to fight the Reformation; he had first made the effort when the collegiate foundation was called to life.

At the hostelry of the "Golden Lamb" one hot July day of 1529, two worthy citizens of Halle were sitting on the window bench, looking abroad through the lozenge panes. The eye commanded a considerable prospect, from the new cathedral in the foreground to the gloomy walls of the hospital of St. Cyriace beyond.

"There, you see now that they are going to do it," said the one, a stocking-weaver, to his companion, a blacksmith. "They are beginning to pull down the hospital. Surely the building might have served a decent purpose for many a year to come. But, since the Cardinal has procured the Emperor's patent of nobility for Schönitz, appointing him his lord chamberlain besides, a desperate spirit has taken possession of the trader; he must aye be pulling down, and building anew, not by any means to the certain gain of the city."

"Yes, yes," replied the blacksmith. "Schönitz is the incarnate wandering Jew of late, he cannot rest for a moment. I dare say the Cardinal finds him useful, for he is ever ready to procure money; and he has a knack of pleasing his master, pandering to all sorts of amusements which one had better not mention. Many of our people have taken a dislike to Schönitz, and he has made himself downright enemies by his wheedling St. Lambart's out of the Cardinal, turning the ancient chapel into a dwelling-house for himself. The Lords of Hagedorn and Gumprecht especially hate him for it, for they loved the little chapel which had been endowed by their ancestors. It is a shame, too, that the very place which once echoed with pious chanting should now be the all-powerful chamberlain's residence—a proud residence, forsooth, to which he has added a secret entrance for the Cardinal, leading to a private chamber of surpassing splendour, they say. Heaven knows what that may be for, and why his grace should need a secret entrance! The people have taken offence too that the Cardinal will no longer have the dead buried in the time-honoured churchyards within the city, but has ordered a cemetery to be erected right away on the Martinsberg. The dear old churchyards of

St. Mary's, St. Gertrude's, St. Ulrich's, and St. Maurice's have actually been levelled, the town's traffic now passing over the resting-place of her departed children. It is sacrilege, I say."

Master Isaac, the stocking-weaver, shook his head. "No, I would not blame that," he said. "I have been told, and can well believe it, that it is bad for the living to have the dead buried in their midst. Those which are gone care little where they sleep; they are very peaceful, methinks, in the new cemetery. But I agree with you concerning that business of St. Lambart's. It is not well that his grace thus deals with consecrated ground. I have heard it rumoured that Schönitz is to have St. Nicholas's as well."

Simon, the blacksmith, struck his fist upon the window-sill, so that the panes quivered and the mortar crumbled from the walls. "This is beyond endurance!" he cried; "the town council must interfere!"

"Much interference there will be," interposed Master Isaac, "while Peter Silktail is in the chair; he is too anxious to please the Cardinal, I know."

"Then the citizens must interfere," continued the blacksmith angrily.

The stocking-weaver smiled grimly. "It will be no use, I tell you. How should the Cardinal reward his faithful servant? Money is scarce, so he pays him in chapels."

A tremendous crash here disturbed the speaker.

"Look there!" he cried, "the roof will be down in a minute."

A man entered the room, asking for a drink of beer.

"We make you welcome, Master Builder!" exclaimed the smith sarcastically; "Master Puller-down, we should say. I suppose it is warm work, and you find you are getting dry?"

"To be sure," returned the builder; "one has to swallow a good deal of dust when such walls are giving way."

"And why should they give way?" queried Simon sharply. "They would have stood well enough but for your crowbars."

"I dare say," said the work-master, paying attention to his beer.

"I should like to know," continued the smith, "what will be the upshot. Is the foundation going to be enlarged?"

"Indeed it is," was the answer; "a university is to be added. I understand it is a pet plan of his grace's."

"Ha! ha!" laughed Master Simon. "I see! I see! My Lord Cardinal thinks it a pity that the lecture halls at Wittenberg are full to overflowing; he would kindly make room for some of the students here. Is that it?"

"That is not my business," returned the builder testily; "my duty is to see to the work being done."

"Yes, yes; build away!" sneered Simon. "The owls and crows will thank you for a place they can haunt."

But now the work-master rose in a passion. "Take care of your tongue!" he cried. "You might rue it if his grace came to know."

He emptied his jug and walked away without taking further notice.

"Indeed you had better be warned," remarked the stocking-weaver; "it is unwise to say all one thinks. Look, there goes the lord chamberlain and the work-master at his elbow; see if he does not repeat to him every word you said!"

"I don't care!" cried the smith. "I don't care a fig for Schönitz!"

The two men left the hostelry.

They directed their steps towards the market-place. Arriving near the lord chamberlain's house, they came upon a crowd of people gazing at the roof of St. Mary's. Astride on the backbone of the church sat some men beginning to take off the tiles.

"The foul fiend fetch them!" cried Simon, with terrific intonation. "Is the whole town to come down, or what is it? Is it possible that they are pulling down St. Mary's as well?"

"It would seem so," said Isaac quietly; "and sure it is a pity. What can his grace be thinking of to destroy so fine a church?"

"What is it to him," returned the smith petulantly, "so long as it pleases his fancy?"

The two men joined the crowd at the base of the building. The mass of the people were of the smith's mind, and were loud in disapprobation, those of the Elector's party not daring to raise a word of contradiction, there being many among the dissatisfied whose position entitled them to respect.

. . . . . .

At an upper window of the lord chamberlain's house sat Dame Magdalen Schönitz, the wife of the Elector's favourite, a lovely woman with auburn hair, and large, wondrously thoughtful eyes. Her garment was of the simplest kind, a white lace ruffle brightening the plain woollen tire, a neat little cap confining the wavy tresses. She had her youngest child on her lap and gazed dreamily upon the market-place.

"Look, mother, there are men upon the roof," said the curly-headed boy, "what are they doing?"

"They are beginning to pull down the church," replied the mother.

"But why?" asked the little fellow wonderingly.

"Mother cannot tell you, my child," said Dame Magdalen wistfully; "you must ask your father."

Schönitz had just entered the room, smiling upon wife and child.

"Did you hear the question?" asked the young wife. "I should like you to tell us both, dear husband. How can the Elector pull down the church which is an ornament to the town? It makes one's heart ache to see it."

"Don't let it ache, wifie," said Hans von Schönitz pleasantly. "Enough that it is the Cardinal's desire; no doubt he knows what he is about. See how the two churches, St. Mary's and St. Gertrude's, are standing in a row, separated by a passage merely, as though they had been shot out of a double-barrelled gun; it is surprising that those who built them could do such a foolish thing. One of them must go. Our Lady's is to make room for St. Gertrude's enlargement. You will be satisfied presently."

But Dame Magdalen shook her head. "St. Gertrude's is far more fit to give way, decrepit with age as it is. Why don't they rather think of enlarging that beautiful church of Our Lady's?"

"How should women understand?" said Schönitz impatiently.

But Dame Magdalen would have her say. "Look at

the people," she went on, pointing to the crowd beneath, "they do not seem to like it any more than I. And it is not only the plain citizens; I perceive there are magistrates and members of the nobility among them. I see the venerable Lord of Hagedorn, who still is aggrieved concerning St. Lambart's, and there——"

"Do leave them alone," interrupted Schönitz, showing annoyance. "We all know that Halle is full of people ready to take umbrage at anything the Cardinal might decide upon."

But still Dame Magdalen continued: "That may be so, and yet I cannot approve the Cardinal's action. Is it wise to be pulling down when the old faith everywhere is shaking on its foundation? St. Maurice's has been despoiled of its riches, Cloister Neuwerk has been forced to yield its authority, a number of chapels have been demolished, St. Mary's is in a like damnation, St. Ulrich's to all appearance too. Whither are we going?"

"You talk as a foolish woman," said Schönitz rudely. "Better keep to your own concerns, and tell me whether my commands have been obeyed, and whether the private chamber is quite ready now. Have the Flemish carpets been laid down?"

"Not yet, my husband," replied the lady, somewhat embarrassed. "Surely the Elector is not thinking of returning just yet."

"But I desire my behests to be carried into effect without delay," said the chamberlain overbearingly. "Follow me; you will see to it at once. I am anxious to have the place completed."

Husband and wife, through a long dark passage,

reached the side wing of their dwelling and entered a spacious apartment, the splendour of which outshone every other room in the house, although there was no lack of comfort or even luxury in the whilom chapel. The ceiling was richly carved, a deep red crystal chandelier hanging suspended from the centre. The walls were covered with frescoes, Bacchus and Aphrodite being the ever-recurring theme. There was a table in the midst, with twelve chairs of finely carved oak, soft velvet ottomans filling every available space, white damask curtains half hiding the entrance to a smaller apartment.

Two servants now brought the Flemish carpets intended to add comfort to the floor, which consisted of square flags, blue and white.

Dame Magdalen viewed the preparations silently, casting shy glances at her husband, who seemed to enjoy the prospect. "The Cardinal will take pleasure in the sanctuary raised for him by the hand of his servant," he said, quite elated.

But the wife answered, with a sigh: "Do you call that a sanctuary, where the Lord in heaven can never be worshipped, since it is destined to the lusts of the flesh?"

Schönitz frowned. "You seem particularly bent on annoying me!" he cried. "There are sanctuaries of all kinds; Bacchus and Venus have theirs. And if great rulers delight in aught, it is not the business of such as you and I to inquire too closely. If there is a responsibility, let it be theirs."

"True," replied the wife, "we need not be responsible. But how if we pander to their desires? And there is another thing troubling me—that the Elector should make an instrument of you for the filling of his pockets; that he is deep in your debt is the lesser grief, but the constant taxation you have recourse to has gained you much ill-will, and I doubt me how you may fare, if ever the Estates should demand a rendering of accounts. Supposing they thought of examining the exchequer; and if there should be discrepancies, whose do you think would be the blame? Oh, my husband, great is the favour you have attained, but do not lay it to your soul too fondly! The love of princes is no enviable possession; how many a favoured one has lived to rue it!"

But that did not serve to smooth the husband's ruffled temper. "Leave me alone!" he cried; "your head is full of maggots to-day. I tell you the Cardinal is a gracious master, and just to boot. The world would come to an end before he proves false to his trusted servant. And moreover, he has too often taken me into his secret, he owes me too much too, to be able to cast me off. That alone is a safeguard."

Dame Magdalen could but sigh, and presently left the chamber to return to her children.

Hans von Schönitz continued in thought. His wife's warning had made a deeper impression than he cared to own. He felt oppressed, the room seemed stifling. "What if there were a danger after all?" he soliloquised; "is it not written somewhere, 'Put not thy trust in princes'? But no, this is foolish woman's prate. Art become a woman too, Hans von Schönitz?"

He shook, holding forth his hands, as though to ward off the imagined catastrophe, and left the chamber quickly. At a front window he stood presently, watching the workpeople dismantling St. Mary's. The crowd had dispersed, a few loiterers only remained in the market-place.

"The populace is easily moved," he said to himself, "but their excitement is as a straw-fire, which is soon burnt out. We will hurry on matters now, and begin to improve St. Gertrude's, that the Cardinal may delight in returning to Halle, and praise his faithful chamberlain."

CHAPTER XXVII.

TIGHTENING THE REIN.

THE Cardinal's had been a prolonged absence, and great things had happened. The Imperial Diet had sat at Spires and again at Augsburg, the Gospel at both gaining ground. At Spires the popish princes demanded of the Lutherans to abstain from all further attempts at reformation; but the lovers of the Gospel came forward with a solemn protestation, whence the appellation Protestants. Their enemies meant it in sarcasm, but they themselves accepted the designation as their badge of honour. The document was signed by Elector John of Saxony, Landgrave Philip of Hesse, Markgrave George of Brandenburg, Prince Wolfgang of Anhalt, both the Dukes of Lüneburg and fourteen towns.

The Emperor imprisoned the deputation sent to him with the memorable document; but he was mistaken if he believed thereby to intimidate the Protestants. They repeated boldly that they had bound themselves together as one man to stand by the truth for better or for worse.

The rescript inviting the princes and Estates to meet at Augsburg in 1530 struck a note of conciliation; once more the Emperor would try to come to terms with the Protestants. Whereupon the Elector of Saxony called his theologians to Torgau, that they should draw up a set of clear, concise articles giving the chief points of Protestant faith and longing: the Emperor should know plainly that the Lutherans were not guilty of the black wickedness imputed to them, but men who cared for religion truly. Thus originated the Articles of Torgau; and as the Emperor delayed his arrival, Melancthon worked them out further, producing a full confession which should be read at the Diet of Augsburg.

The Emperor, however, meanwhile had yielded to the instigations of those about him; he began by refusing a hearing of the said articles; the Protestants should be satisfied with his arbitration. But they were not satisfied, and the Imperial Majesty was obliged to give way.

On the 25th of June the famous confession was read, not, however, in the great hall of the Diet, but in the chapter-room, which was not large enough to admit many of the estates. The two chancellors of Electoral Saxony, Doctor Beier and Doctor Brück, stood up at the bar, the one with a German, the other with a Latin copy of the document. The Emperor desired a reading in Latin, which the Elector of Saxony opposed with the courageous words: "We are Germans on German soil, and hope your Majesty will allow us to speak in our own tongue."

The confession being read, the Emperor took both copies into his keeping, not a safe keeping, since they were lost, and not a trace of them could afterwards be found.

Those present had listened attentively, many a frown

CHARLES V.
After Titian.

giving way to an expression of relief, for Melancthon, the prudent man who could step so gently, had framed the articles of Protestant belief in such a manner that only those could be offended whose hatred sought for offence. There were many who owned it openly that they had lost much of their prejudice against the Lutheran faith, William of Nassau joining the Protestants on the spot. This confessing of their faith in common greatly tended to strengthen and uphold the Protestant princes; they felt they had spoken, had shown to the Emperor and the assembled Estates that they were no rebels and no heathen, but faithful subjects and true-hearted followers of the Gospel. That fearless confession, moreover, reacted as a power of growth on the Protestants; it created a bond of brotherhood among them, and a feeling in each individual believer that he was personally bound to the great cause, at any cost, at any sacrifice.

For the present their courage had gained them the Emperor's unwilling respect; he did not venture to break with them openly.

Charles V. indeed was anxious to arrive at a compromise; but efforts in this direction remained abortive, the matter being finally dismissed with the decision that the Protestant rulers should have time for consideration until the 15th of April ensuing; that meanwhile they should not permit further books to be printed, they should not prohibit the mass in their dominions, and should give up all Church property. The Edict of Worms, it was plain, should be carried out to the full now, and the disobedient must expect to be dealt with accordingly.

Most of the Protestant princes had quitted Augsburg, not waiting for any final decision, showing thereby that

U

whatever conclusion might be arrived at, it could not hinder them from doing what their conscience and the Word of God demanded.

The Emperor went his way nowise rejoicing, the Catholic princes too looked glum. But the Protestants everywhere, in church and market-place, sang a song to the Lord their God, the great battle-song of the Reformation, which Martin Luther, absent from the Diet, though present with his spirit, had written at Castle Coburg to cheer the confessors, the hymn which has ever since been the key-note of Protestant praise and thanksgiving—*Ein' feste Burg is unser Gott.*

. . . . .

It was on the Friday before the Fifth Sunday in Lent, 1531, that Cardinal Albrecht, after an absence of nearly two years, returned to his town of Halle.

Solemn was his reception, far more solemn, indeed, than he could have expected from the reports which had reached him at various times concerning his well-beloved citizens. Yet, nevertheless, here they were meeting him in due procession, amid the ringing of bells and the singing of songs, accompanying him to his very Burg, where the town council had gathered to offer him with the expression of their submissive attachment a large golden tankard filled to the brim with four hundred gold gulden.

The Cardinal was positively startled by these obedient advances, and turned questioning looks upon the councillors. But only when they had left, his eyes were opened by the shrewd chancellor. "Your grace should remember the time-honoured saying," remarked Doctor Turk, "that bacon is useful for the catching of mice. That well-filled tankard is to save the citizens from the consequences of their misdeeds, for much has happened in your absence. They know it, and are humble accordingly. They know that they have furthered heresy in every possible way, and have long trembled at your coming. If I may offer advice to your electoral grace, it will be well to show them the high hand, and call back the recreants peremptorily to the forsaken Church."

The Cardinal approved, and Doctor Turk was charged to draw up a declaration which in the great hall of the Moritzburg, should be read to the magistrates the very next day. Meanwhile the provost of the foundation should attend, his grace being anxious to learn what progress had been achieved by the new university.

The dignitary in question appeared, greatly satisfying the Cardinal by his report: "With all speed the structure arose which is intended to be a nursery of true theology and Christian learning. Four spacious buildings lift their front, forming a noble quadrangle, where, in the shadow of growing lindens, the disciples of knowledge shall dwell. All is ready, awaiting the papal sanction. Yet, sure of the same, I have already entered upon a course of studies with a number of undergraduates; we are at work even now upon St. Paul's Epistle to the Romans, Canon Crotus, my colleague, lecturing upon the doctrine of Christian faith."

The Cardinal gave vent to his delighted satisfaction, expressing the hope that the time was not far distant when those at Wittenberg would raise the cry, "Alas, that Halle should have supplanted us!" And he added: "We are quite certain of the papal privileges; indeed, we have the sure promise of the nuncio Campeggio that they shall be granted speedily. We have resolved, therefore, forthwith to elect a Chancellor for our new university, and we know of none more capable or more worthy than yourself, who are a pattern of learning and wisdom, and of that fidelity which fears no sacrifice. As soon then as the Pope's privileges have been obtained, you shall be invested with the dignity."

The provost expressed his deepest sensibility of this mark of favour, sincerely anxious to meet the great trust. The choice indeed could be called a good one, and if there were any hopes for the prosperity of the rising college, the conciliatory Doctor Vehe, as learned as he was good, was the very man to ensure fulfilment.

On the following day twelve members of the town council arrived at the Moritzburg, in obedience to a special summons to take the great Cardinal's opinion, given by his chancellor's mouth.

Doctor Turk received the deputation with freezing gravity, and read to them what he had been careful to put to paper: "His electoral grace," the manifesto ran, "has been pleased to accept the present offered by the worshipful council, taking the same as a voucher of dutiful submission; his grace is anxious to continue a merciful ruler, if so be that the city will show itself deserving of such good will. The Elector desires the worshipful council to take note, firstly: Whereas it has been resolved by the Diet of Augsburg that in matters of religion the old usage and papal institutions of Holy Church are to be followed, such decree has been duly made known to the worshipful council of Halle, his grace looking to the same for ready obedience. It is a matter of sorrow therefore to our electoral ruler to perceive that nothing as yet has been done to justify his expectation, but that the citizens of Halle seem bent upon their own wilful course. They have laid themselves open to well-merited punishment. But my Lord Cardinal is anxious to let grace guide the hand of justice, that the citizens might accept his fatherly exhortation, and, desisting from their unchristian ways, no longer run after strange doctrine, nor take the sacrament after the fashion of heretics. You shall prove your subjection to the old faith in these coming Easter days, you shall take your places in the cathedral, and receive the host at the hands of the Cardinal himself. None of you shall be absent, the rather that the magistrates shall be willing to be an example to the citizens. Such compliance will tend not only to your eternal salvation, but also to your temporal welfare, since all disobedience up to the present shall in that case be forgiven and forgotten; whereas if you continue in the same punishment will meet you unsparingly.

"Secondly: Since it has been decided by his electoral grace to hold a solemn procession on Palm Sunday, it has also been decided that the worshipful council take a part in it to the honour of God.

"Thirdly: The worshipful council shall appoint some wardens to see that the clergy suffer no insult at the hands of the populace.

"Fourthly: The worshipful council shall further appoint six citizens of good standing to carry the canopy over the host. Barely three have appeared of late, and these only of the commonest among the saltworkers or other disreputable folk, who showed little reverence for the sacrament, but treated it with contumely. I have now informed the deputation of my lord's the Archbishop Cardinal's desires."

The delegates had listened. They declared their

readiness to be the council's faithful reporters, adding the assurance that each member would act as their conscience would justify before God, before the Cardinal and to all the world.

The next meeting of council was stormy in the highest degree. The deputation had reported. A certain Jonas Berbig fought hard for the Cardinal's claims, and did his utmost in reviling the Lutherans. His eloquence prevailed with a great part of the council, and upon division it became apparent that more than half of the magisterial body was yielding to pressure, and ready to stand by the Cardinal. But all the more boldly the opposition held its ground, declaring themselves wronged, if they were accused of disobedience for refusing to do aught against their conscience.

A second deputation, about to be despatched, was anticipated by an archiepiscopal official with a further and more urgent demand for obedience. Some of the Cardinal's adherents had forwarded a report of the council's proceedings. Indignation at their treachery ran high, and his grace received no further answer but a repetition of the assurance already given: that no one could be constrained to act against the voice of conscience.

Palm Sunday arrived. It was a clear, promising spring day; the sun smiled brilliantly on the city, casting a wealth of light on the gorgeous train on its way from the cathedral to the market-place. The procession was headed by the great Cardinal himself in the archiepiscopal robe; he was followed by the dignitaries of the cathedral and all the monks and nuns of the place—a goodly number still, but nothing like the show of former times.

On the market-place the secular clergy, together with the school-children and a great crowd of people, surrounded a tabernacle of painted boards which contained a life-sized image of the crucified Saviour lying on the ground. On the platform of the town hall stood the pipers and trumpeters giving forth a solemn strain.

The procession arranged itself in front of the tabernacle, the whole assembly chanting the *Gloria laus;* whereupon the Archbishop advanced to the crucifix, and after the customary genuflection, lay down flat on the ground, covering the image. Two priests now struck him with slight batons, reciting the while, "I will smite the shepherd, and the sheep of the flock shall be scattered abroad" (Matt. xxvi. 31; Zech. xiii. 7).

During this remarkable proceeding a voice rose from the crowd, an irreverent salt-worker crying, "Better take a flail instead of them little sticks!"

The Cardinal himself had not heard it, but officious tale-bearers were not wanting, and the occurrence did not tend to smooth his feelings of resentment against the citizens.

The chancellor tried to point out that it was but a low salt-worker who had made the wicked remark; but the Cardinal wrought himself up to the belief that the man's sentiment echoed the secret wishes of all the Lutherans, and retired sullenly to his chambers, hiding his face till the Thursday when the great Passion should begin.

He had determined to conduct everything himself, and he did so.

With great solemnity he consecrated the chrism

on Holy Thursday, beginning as early as four o'clock in the morning, continuing for five hours. At ten he distributed the sacred oil to the clergy of Magdeburg, Halberstadt, Meissen, Merseburg, and Naumburg, for all these were in the habit of coming to Halle for their supply of baptismal ointment. It cost the town two barrels of olive oil every year. In the afternoon he performed the emblematical washing. Girt with a towel and carrying a basin, he appeared in the cathedral, washing the feet of all the canons, but the hands only of the lower clergy.

On Good Friday he conducted an elaborate service. Behind the high altar an artificial cave had been constructed representing the holy sepulchre. A procession advanced towards it, singing with hushed voices, the Cardinal, carrying the Saviour's image, taking the lead. Several times he sank beneath his burden, apparently mindful of the approach to Calvary, and arriving at the place of burial his eyes quite glistened with pious emotion.

On the Saturday there was high mass. He was assisted by no less than sixteen priests and acolytes, adding greatly to the show of solemnity.

The town council had appeared in full force, Albrecht's devotion not preventing his counting heads; he was glad to see there was thus much of obedience.

The sacrament was reserved for Sunday, a great crowd approaching to receive it at the Archbishop's hand. But his eye was watchful; he knew that some eight or ten of the council refrained from partaking. He looked across to the magisterial pews, but the absentees were not there, they seemed to have given the slip to the cathedral altogether.

On Easter Monday the recorder of the city was admitted by the Cardinal to a secret audience. This man, having received the communion at various times according to Protestant rite, had incurred the archiepiscopal displeasure, and was deposed in consequence from his honours as saltgrave.[1] But having at the late occasion returned to the sacrament of Romish institution, the Archbishop now smiled graciously upon the repentant sheep.

"It has been well pleasing to us," began his grace, "to see you breaking the fetters of heresy and come back to the bosom of Holy Church. You shall have your reward. We will reinvest you with the saltgraveship, which had been forfeited by your former forsaking. And we will moreover appoint you president of the council at the coming election."

The recorder did his utmost in bowing his thanks for such gracious forgiveness; it was beyond his most ardent hopes; yet, his humility suggested, no saltgrave had ever aspired to the magisterial presidentship.

"Let the ruler decide!" interrupted the Elector grandly; "the archiepiscopal desire may supersede usage. We shall do as we see fit. The council shall know who is lord paramount. But we look to you to try and keep those from office to whom we have reason to object. We desire to have as many of our adherents in the council as possible. You can help us in this."

And, intoxicated by the newly-gained favour, the turncoat of a recorder threw into the balance all the power of his eloquence, influencing the election considerably. Before long he could inform the Cardinal

---

[1] Inspector-general of the salt works.

that his grace had more adherents now than opposers on the magisterial benches.

Albrecht's spirit rose high, and the very next day following the election an archiepiscopal official announced from the balcony of the town hall that his electoral grace had decided to act according to the decision of the late Diet in strict pursuance of the Edict of Worms.

A sound arose from the market-place as of distant thunder, flashes of lightning too forking up here and there, threatening speeches reaching the ears of the official, who, when stones began to fly, hastily withdrew from sight. Nor could he venture to show himself in the public thoroughfares, but, protected by the beadles, returned on by-ways to the Moritzburg.

The citizens showed their further intentions by going all the more diligently where they could hear the Gospel preached, great masses Sunday after Sunday filling the village churches round about in the Mansfeld and the Saxon districts.

CHAPTER XXVIII.

BEHIND THE SCENES.

More than a year had passed, again it was autumn. Dame Magdalen gazed absently through the window. She was alone, save for the little boy, who looked at her wistfully. "When will father be back?" the child asked, breaking the silence. "How long must we wait for the sweet honey-cakes he has promised to bring us from Nürnberg?"

"I cannot tell thee, my child; he has never stayed so long, not even in visiting the more distant Netherlands. I grieve lest anything have happened to him!"

"Do not look sad, little mother," entreated the child. "If you cry, I must cry too."

"You are mother's own little boy," she said, smiling brightly. "What will little Charley be when he grows to be a man?"

"What father is!" cried the boy, unhesitatingly.

But Dame Magdalen shook her head. "No, child, no! You will think differently by-and-by. Go now and play with your brothers."

The poor wife was left to herself. But the quiet she had longed for soon grew oppressive, and with a sigh of relief she welcomed Mistress Kunigonde, the wife of the captain of the Moritzburg, who looked in presently.

"I thought you might be lonely, and have come to cheer you," said the visitor.

"I am truly glad to see you, I sadly need a little company," owned Dame Magdalen.

"But what is the matter? you look quite worn," inquired the friend, sympathisingly.

"I am anxious about my husband."

"Has aught happened to him?"

"I cannot tell—that uncertainty adds to my trouble. These five weeks he has been gone, and there is no sign of his returning. He has journeyed to Nürnberg, as you are aware, to procure a loan for the Cardinal from some Jew. He went but unwillingly, for he begins to feel matters irksome. The Estates have come to hate him, believing him to be a bloodsucker; nor is it a pleasant thing to have to do with Jews, for they are an artful people, full of wicked wiles, and greatly despised. Again and again my husband has prayed the Cardinal to relieve him of his service, that he might return to his former vocation and live more for his family; but his grace will not hear of it. He cannot do without Hans von Schönitz, it seems, who has come to be his right hand in most things. Nor could his grace easily repay the sums of money he owes to my husband—some ninety thousand gulden, I think. I am full of anxiety at this prolonged absence."

Mistress Kunigonde gave an odd look at her friend, saying, after a pause: "You speak of Nürnberg only, as if he had not gone farther; are you not aware——"

"What!" cried the wife, alarmed. "He has only spoken to me of Nürnberg!"

The friend was sorry to have betrayed what evidently was not supposed to be known. But how could she guess that Schönitz had any secrets from the wife for whom he had an honest affection? But the word, however, having slipped her tongue, she could not keep the truth from the anxious dame, but was obliged to tell her that her husband had gone across the Alps on the Cardinal's special business.

"Across the Alps!" repeated Magdalen, with widening eyes. "And what for? Has he gone to sue the Pope himself for money?"

Mistress Kunigonde smiled at the harmless suggestion, taking refuge in allegory, "When an evil spirit troubled Saul," she said, "the fair son of Jesse was sent for to stand before the king with an harp."

"Yes, yes, but what of it? I do not understand!"

And hesitatingly the visitor continued, "The Cardinal too has his times when the evil spirit is upon him. For hours he will sit alone, nursing his gloomy thoughts. He has failed in many things, his opponents are victorious, and he is grievously disappointed. In his struggle with Luther, the heretic, he has suffered defeat after defeat, and the knowledge of it eats into his very soul. The citizens too get more and more unruly, not heeding his desires, the number of Lutherans, or Protestants, as they call them now, increasing daily. The very council is fast becoming Lutheran, there are not many of the Cardinal's friends on the bench now, and those who remain are ill-fitted to bear up against the growing influence. The Cardinal's hopes of the new university also have been sadly dispelled; the number of students is small, not likely to win great battles against the heretics of Wittenberg. His grace hoped the Wittenberg students would come pouring into Halle, but he was mistaken, and it weighs upon his spirits. Your husband has been sent to Italy therefore to fetch hither the fair musician who shall stand before his grace with song and lute. It seems that at the Diet of Augsburg the Cardinal fell in with a lovely Italian, who has wondrous charms, they say, and a voice like a nightingale; and in order to gain her my lord chamberlain has crossed the Alps."

But the chamberlain's wife heaved a groan, covering her face with her pure white hands. " Alas ! " she cried, " has it come to this ? Shall my husband be known and hated as the willing pander to his master's sin ? It has always grieved me to hear the Cardinal's evil passions spoken of; all good people abhor it, and the others laugh at it. Is he not a spiritual lord, a very head of those who are appointed by the Church to stand between God and man, and who should be far above the weakness of earth-born humanity ? His predecessors knew how to keep themselves unspotted. And look at the Lutheran clergy about us ! Call them heretics if you like, but their fair fame in this matter is beyond reproach."

Mistress Kunigonde looked virtuous. "No doubt, dear Magdalen, no doubt; but you must judge men by their equals. His grace of Halle is not singular in this respect; and I say it is not he that is to blame, but the wicked institution of celibacy itself. It is nature's revenge upon a foolish vow."

But Dame Magdalen kept to her own view. The ladies continued a while in serious conversation till the hour of evensong reminded the visitor it was time to take her leave.

The anxious wife had another week of cruel uncertainty before her husband returned, safe and sound, it is true, but with gloomy brow; and the children found he had not thought of the honey-cakes. He seemed irritable, and Magdalen dared not inquire into the results of his mission.

The following day he had an interview with the Cardinal, who was away at Magdeburg when Schönitz returned.

Albrecht's face beamed with satisfaction, and he showered praise upon praise upon his faithful servant. "What a treasure you are, Schönitz mine," said his grace good-humouredly. "You are worth your weight in gold, I declare! I shall be rid of all my cares now in the delight of beholding the signora, and listening to the charm of her voice. The shade of poor Margaret even will yield her the palm." He quite forgot to inquire into the more important mission to the Jew of Nürnberg.

Schönitz reported concerning the Italian acquisition, and continued: "But if I was successful at Milan, not so at Nürnberg. I have managed the money, that is to say; but the Jew is a worse usurer than most of his race."

This remark roused the Cardinal; he took revenge in reviling the children of Israel: a very thorn they were in the nation's side!

"May I crave a favour of your electoral highness?" asked Schönitz, when the outburst had subsided.

"To be sure," said the Cardinal pleasantly.

But the chamberlain seemed embarrassed, humming and hawing a little; presently he said:

"It is nothing new. I have repeatedly prayed for

release from the electoral service. I trust your grace will at last turn a favourable ear to my humble request. I cannot keep up to the duties any longer."

The Cardinal looked annoyed. "Have I been mistaken in you, Schönitz? I believed you to be my faithful servant. But is that true fidelity which is ready to quit me at a moment when more than ever I am hedged in by difficulties? What is it that makes you desire a change of our relationship?"

Schönitz looked gloomily to the ground and said: "Things have reached a terrible pass, accounts are hopelessly entangled, debts and liabilities are beyond one's grasp. Again and again I have begged your electoral grace to command a general overhauling of affairs, but you have never believed in the necessity of following such advice. And the worst for myself is this: I have received a warning from the Estates—I pray your grace to excuse my speaking thus plainly, but I had better say it—Schönitz, they say, look where you tread: if there is a smash, it is you who will have to bear the brunt."

"Who dared say this?" exclaimed Albrecht, flushing purple. "It is vile calumny! Here is my hand, dearest Schönitz; your fate shall never be separated from mine. Whatever there might be to bear the brunt of, we will bear it together. But it is nonsense! Am I not strong enough to shield my trusted servant? You and I, we have got into the muddle together; let us come out of it together; none shall say that we separated! It is adversity that tries men, and friends too. Let me make sure of it, then, that I can trust thee in all things, and at all times, and see if I fail thee!"

The Cardinal spoke with such a vehemence of

persuasion that Schönitz found it impossible to resist. And if his master meant all he said, he need not fear. "We have got into it together; let us come out of it together;" these words kept ringing in his brain, acting as a sort of moral narcotic. And he declared, tamely enough, he was sorry he had spoken, and was anxious to continue his grace's reliable servant.

. . . . . .

On the evening of that day, the high windows of the secret state-room in the chamberlain's house were lit up, the strains of music being heard in the streets. People took little note of it; it was known well enough that the Cardinal, when he had borne the burden and heat of his day, thought fit to live for his pleasures, throwing a veil over it forsooth!

The hidden chamber harboured select company. A few of the Cardinal's most favoured officials were there, together with some of the neighbouring nobility; and, that fair flowerets might not be wanting, there were present in silks and satins, decked with plumes and, pearls, those whom the luxurious hierarch loved to look upon. Nor was he himself the centre of attraction today, but all eyes were drawn to the stranger by his side.

Deep into the night they sat, and when the party broke up his grace felt flattered with success.

But Dame Magdalen in her modest chamber courted sleep in vain, lying awake and troubled. She heard the sounds of music, and they were as daggers stabbing her to the soul. She was deeply incensed that *her* house must offer shelter to the Cardinal's voluptuous delights, yea, that her own husband assisted him in satisfying his dishonourable tastes. He had become a

x

slave to the Cardinal—a stranger almost to wife and children. And yet how they loved him; how gladly they would have tried to please him, if they knew but how! Even the little ones perceived that the father did not give them what he might, ay, should have given. Little Magdalen cherished it in her baby heart as the rarest of treats when he took her to his knees or fondled her curly head—not often, indeed. Poor Schönitz seemed to have no time now for such delights.

Midnight had long passed when the sounds of her husband's approach at last broke upon Magdalen's ear. She had all ready what she meant to say; but when he came her heart closed with anguish, and not a word could she find.

At breakfast only she met him with the saddest of looks; he understood her well enough, and took her hand. "Never mind, wife; it cannot be helped. Nor can I explain very well, and you would not understand if I could. Let be, then, and take it not to heart."

CHAPTER XXIX.

CHASTISING WITH SCORPIONS.

It was early in the morning on the first Saturday in Lent, 1534. The newly-elected town council was being sworn in; crowds of citizens meanwhile stood waiting about the market-place, anxious to learn how far the Cardinal might have succeeded in packing the bench. The ninth hour pealed at last from the belfries, and according to usage the clerk of the council made his appearance on the balcony to give out the names of the newly-elected members, recommending them to the prayers of the community.

Great was the people's applause on learning the welcome result: five only of the Cardinal's adherents were on the board, all the rest, more than three times their number, were known to be for the Lutheran faith.

The people hoped great things, since the adversaries were so few in number. Perhaps the mind of the Cardinal himself was being changed, perhaps he would give up now kicking against the pricks.

But that hope was vain: his grace did not hide his annoyance on learning the defeat. The religious peace which two years previous had been concluded between the Catholic and Protestant princes of the empire had displeased him from the first, since it only tended towards the increase of the new faith. In his own town of Halle even the number of heretics augmented daily, their courage, or defiance, as he considered it, growing in proportion. Twice he had attempted to assert himself by issuing a peremptory mandate, ordering the sacrament to be taken according to Romish rite, and forbidding the town to Lutheran preachers; but on both occasions the effort had served only to add fuel to the fire. For the third time now the command should be repeated, as the very utmost of the Cardinal's forbearance.

The newly-elected council was yet sitting when the archiepiscopal official appeared demanding a hearing, that he might inform the members of his grace's desires.

The council hesitated, but could not refuse to listen, whereupon the official read with pungent voice:

"It is our pleasure that each one of the newly-elected councillors present himself on Easter day, to take the sacrament according to the way approved of by the Romish Church, showing thereby his opposition to corrupt Lutheran practices; for surely *we* know that the old way is the right way, for the which we pledge ourselves and our life. We desire and command therefore that each of you return to the rites of the old Church, and be willing to hold the faith we ourselves hold."

Deep silence ensued, the Catholic members casting gloomy eyes upon their Protestant colleagues; one of whom, Hans Wahle by name, presently broke the silence: "We acknowledge it to be our duty to obey his grace in aught we are able and see right; but since we have been in the habit to partake of the communion as appointed by the Lord Christ Himself, we consider ourselves pledged to God in this matter, and it would be against our conscience to return to the practice of Romish institution. I speak not for myself alone, but for most of those here present, although we have not as yet consulted together. I call upon them to give their opinion."

Unanimously the friends of Protestantism cried: "Hans Wahle has spoken the truth, we support him!"

"Then I prepare you for his electoral grace's direful wrath!" said the official, and left the hall.

There was no great perturbation, the Protestant councillors hoping that consequences in the present instance would be no worse than upon the two previous occasions. Hans Wahle, however, requested the chairman, who was of the Cardinal's faction, to convoke a special meeting for debating on the withholding of obedience in the matter. The presiding magistrate could but yield.

The very next morning the sitting took place, Hans Wahle again taking the word. "We hold there are three points in our favour. In the first place, it is a fact that the Cardinal some years ago allowed the preaching of the Gospel by the late Magister George Winkler in the new cathedral, even in his very own presence, his electoral grace having upon various occasions listened to such preaching, dismissing the congregation with his blessing. By the grace of God many citizens of this town of Halle have accepted that preaching, recognizing it as the truth; they are unable therefore to deny it, but will stand by it in life or death. Secondly, an Imperial mandate has been placarded at this very town hall, clearly announcing that each to each, from the highest to the lowest, in matters of faith, should keep the peace, abiding an œcumenical council. We intend to keep such peace, looking to his electoral grace's protection until the aforenamed general council. Thirdly, each one of us acknowledges himself in duty bound in all temporal things humbly to obey his electoral grace, as the ruler set over us by the Lord Himself; but in matters concerning our conscience and the salvation of our souls we hold we must obey God rather than men. We request the chairman to inform his grace of this our well-considered and immovable opinion."

. . . . .

A painful quiet brooded over the town, when day after day passed without an answer from the Moritzburg. Rumours were current calculated to discourage the councillors; but they thought not of yielding, strengthening one another by brave example.

A full fortnight had elapsed when they were called together again, the chairman meeting them with a declaration in the Archbishop's name.

"His electoral grace does not admit," the statement ran, "that the late Magister George Winkler preached Lutheran heresy in his hearing, although he did at times hold forth concerning the sacrament in a fashion unapproved of by the Church. His grace upon those occasions did not consider it meet to object to such pulpit oratory in the presence of the congregation, but the magister, nevertheless, was taken to task, and received strict warning to desist from such preaching. It became known afterwards that he disregarded such warning, going upon Lutheran lines more and more, yet never in the Archbishop's presence, and still less with his sanction. His grace therefore considers the first point disposed of. As for the second point, concerning the Imperial mandate, you have misunderstood its import, which applies not to subjects but to those in authority. And you will scarcely arrogate to yourselves the duty of explaining the same for his grace's acceptance. Regarding the third point, and that you consider yourselves in duty bound humbly to obey his electoral grace save in matters concerning the salvation of souls and involving your conscience, when you would obey God rather than men, his grace invites no one to do aught against conscience, advising you rather to flee your present abode, seeking for places where you may be free entirely. The Cardinal, however, will not be hindered in conscience either, which tells him that the old faith is right; and since he is the shepherd and bishop of your souls, he will not allow a departing from the faith. His electoral grace is glad to remember that you have in all other things been peaceable and well-behaved citizens hitherto; feeling loth therefore to bring you to account in this matter, and pitying you, would rather be able to retain you and your children, than bring separation upon his dear town of Halle; yet he too feels constrained by conscience. Withdraw now, and consult amongst yourselves what answer you desire to make to this gracious exhortation."

The councillors retired, remaining in deep silence, till Hans Wahle lent expression to their feelings: "We are brought to a serious decision, my friends," he said. "Who hath ears to hear, will have understood from the

Cardinal's message that he intends to banish us from our town of Halle. Indeed he knows how to punish us grievously! To be banished from house and home means to be shut out from happiness. Here we were born, our life is rooted fast in the soil of this place; here alone our days can prosper—banishment will be a slow death to each one of us. The Cardinal knows this, he has hit upon the most exquisite means of coercion. But what think ye, my men? Is there one among you who for fear of the punishment will turn from his faith, let him speak now; but who can be true to the Gospel in the face even of sorrow and tribulation, let them show it by stepping to my side."

And one after another the men pressed round the speaker, clasping hands in token of a common vow. One only, a weaver, Laurence Faust by name, hesitated, but he too followed the example, giving his right hand to Hans Wahle in affirmation of good resolve.

With heads erect they returned to the hall. Hans Wahle declaring in unflinching courage: "Since we know, and faithfully believe it, that the teaching called Luther's doctrine is the true Gospel and the Word of God indeed, we will not depart from the same, and having received Christ, we will not deny Him."

Whereupon the Cardinal's final decision was made known. Thus it ran:

"Since you choose to continue in your rebellious demeanour, it has been resolved upon by his electoral grace, that by Whitsuntide you shall sell your goods and houses and depart from this place. If you desist from your evil intention, and will prove it by presenting yourselves at the sacrament upon Easter day, as appointed, his grace will not withhold his forgiveness."

The chairman added that he, as representing the council, would do his best towards moving the Cardinal to leniency.

But Hans Wahle stood silent, all eyes were upon him awaiting his reply; he had none to make. And finally one of the opposition requested the chairman to intercede with the Cardinal, as he had promised.

The meeting rose, the Protestant members shaking hands once more in the firm resolve to stand manfully by their conviction, and suffer hardship if need be.

The occurrence soon spread about the town, producing a passionate outburst among the citizens. Threatening speeches were heard, some not refraining from accusing the Cardinal of tyranny openly.

But this only tended to aggravate matters.

"I will teach them how to speak of me!" thundered Albrecht, on learning the frame of mind of his citizens. "Have they called me a tyrant? then I will be one! They shall know that the time of mercy is at an end; rebels they are, and I will chastise them accordingly!"

That selfsame day it was made known, that not only the offending councillors, but their wives and children even, should be banished from the town. If, on the one hand, this was a lessening of sorrow, since they were spared the grief of separation, it added to their trouble, on the other hand; for they were obliged now at any consideration to sell their houses and goods, which might have been obviated by the wives continuing at their homes, hoping that their husbands might be pardoned and return some day.

The order was couched in words inexorably hard; yet they prayed for that much of mercy that the families of the banished men might remain until they had succeeded in disposing of their property; and a respite was granted till midsummer.

Sadly Whitsuntide approached. The time when all nature is filled with gladness, when trees and meadows are abloom with joy, was a time of sorrow for the town of Halle; tears were her portion, and she cried to the Lord her God. Sixteen of her most respected houses were not wreathed with the boughs of rejoicing, for there the little ones pressed round their fathers, and the wives clung to their husbands. The strong men even broke down. A man driven from the home of his youth, from the natural soil of his growth, is as a flower torn from her parent stem; you may put it into water, it may live a while, but the hand of death has plucked it, it fades and never yields fruit.

Great was the sympathy of the town, people looked upon them with awe, for martyrs they were to their faith, and they stood firm to the last, willing to bear the cross.

The Moritzburg seemed prepared to quell a rebellion, for her men were under arms, reinforced by the constabulary; but that was needless precaution, the banished councillors themselves endeavouring to quiet the people both by their pious submission and by reminding them of St. Peter's injunction: "Be subject to your masters, not only to the good and gentle, but also to the froward."

The Tuesday in Whitsun-week brought the final wrench. In a body the banished men walked from the town; fellows in sorrow, they would be fellows in bearing it.

The Cardinal that afternoon sat with his chancellor and the captain of the palace, recapitulating recent events. "We feel relieved," he said, "and are satisfied with ourselves for having set an example. Let us hope for good results; since we could not succeed with forbearance, we mean to proceed with strictness now."

"Who are those coming hither?" exclaimed the captain, sitting near the window and overlooking the approach to the Burg.

Both the Cardinal and the chancellor hastily came to his side; a number of women in the garb of mourning were seen moving slowly up the palace yard.

"What the devil are they about?" cried Doctor Turk, savagely. "I recognise the wives of the banished men; they will expect your grace to listen to their whimpering."

"Certainly not!" growled the Cardinal, with hardening features. "I shall not receive them. Go down, captain, and show them the way. You, Turk, may tell them to-morrow that the punishment shall be carried out to the last."

The captain met the women at the entrance. They fell upon their knees and lifted their hands in mute anguish.

The captain's heart was more pitiful than his master's, but, in obedience to that master, he turned them away ruthlessly, telling them they might come the following morning to hear the Cardinal's pleasure.

With bowed heads the women walked away, scarcely hoping that the morrow would lessen their grief. But they came to receive at the chancellor's hands the Cardinal's final decision: They need not have hoped by supplication to alter the sentence, they were told, the electoral grace had been wantonly played with, and there was every reason to suspect that they had encouraged their husbands in rebellion. The men should never return, and the women had amply deserved to share the punishment. In consideration of his grace's mercy and pity, however, they might defer their departure until the eve of St. Bartholomew, after which they should follow their husbands, and not show their faces again at Halle.

The women turned, not uttering a groan—they had done crying—commending their trouble to God; they sold their houses, and with their children went to share their husbands' banishment.

The Elector of Saxony and Prince Wolfgang of Anhalt personally interceded with Albrecht for the troubled families, but in vain. The poor people appealed to the Chapter of Magdeburg, and to the Estates of the diocese, but all the answer they received was: "Renounce your heresy, and we will see what can be done."

One of the banished councillors, Laurence Faust, secretly returned to Halle, did penance and recanted; whereupon he received forty strokes with the rod, and was taken back to favour. All the others remained true to their conviction, three of them dying before ong of a broken heart.

CHAPTER XXX.

RUPTURE.

"There is no help for it, we must sue the Estates for a fresh tax," said the Elector to his confidant, the chamberlain, one day in August that same year. "Michael, the Jew, is getting quite intractable, he insists on having his loans back, the rascal! as if he could get better interest anywhere than we have to pay him. He has doubled his moneys with us, I should say, in sheer usury. And now the Count of Mansfeld and the Markgrave of Brandenburg are also pressing for payment, there is no way out of the difficulty, if it be not that we manage another tax."

Hans von Schönitz moved uneasily, answering after a while: "The Estates have little pleasure in beholding your grace's chamberlain, to judge from the expression of their faces whenever they see him! It will be an unpleasant task to confront them once again; but I will try it, since it seems the only expedient. I must pray, however, for your grace's written warrant."

"You shall have it this very day, dear Schönitz," said the Cardinal, quickly; "let us lose no time, and good fortune speed thee!

At the archiepiscopal castle of Kalbe on the Saale the Estates of the diocese were gathered for the usual session. They were deep in debate when Hans von Schönitz presented himself, praying for a hearing in behalf of his master. The matter in hand was broken off; but it was not with good grace that the Estates prepared to listen, for they knew what to expect whenever the Archbishop's favourite made his appearance.

"I have come hither, authorised by his electoral grace, to submit to the honourable Estates an archi- episcopal request."

Speaking thus, Schönitz handed up to the chair his master's writ.

The document was accepted with ill-suppressed aversion, and having been cursorily examined, the president said to Schönitz, "It needs little guessing what will be the nature of this present demand, since we have been used to the like year after year!" And, turning to the assembly, he continued, "The question is, Shall a new tax be granted to his grace? Will the Estates deliver their opinion in presence of the electoral envoy?"

A deep murmur arose, members exchanging their views with bated breath; one of their number rising at last to give expression to what appeared to be a general feeling—"Since to the demand of unbearable imposts there is no end, I move that the present request be not granted until a clear statement of accounts be laid before this house concerning the revenues of the two latest taxes; we may be forgiven if we desire to know to what use the money has been applied."

Several others added their opinion, and when the question was put to the vote, it was found that the assembly was unanimous in desiring a rendering of accounts.

Schönitz was charged with a message to the Elector to this effect.

Troubled at heart the Cardinal's favourite had set out upon his mission, more troubled still he returned. The idea that an account at last must be given was not a comforting one. He had dreaded the possibility for months—how should he manage it? "How can I unravel the muddle? How can I speak the truth without exposing his grace? Shall I reveal to the Estates what incredible sums have been swallowed up in the recent embellishments of the Moritzburg? Shall I tell them how much money alone I carried across the Alps to pay for the acquisition of that Italian songstress? Shall I tell them how money is wasted and eaten up in the kitchen department? Shall I —— but no, I cannot; it is too shameful, too terrible! It would be betraying my master, for after all he trusts me, and I should despise myself. But if not, no further tax will be granted, and we shall get deeper and deeper into the mire of distress. Shall I make up false accounts?— good God! I cannot—what shall I do? I cannot unburden my heavy heart, not to my wife, not to any one! God help me, and show me the way I can go!"

The Cardinal was pacing his apartment; his face was flushed, the veins of his forehead were swollen. The result of his chamberlain's mission had alarmed him greatly. What! he, the Archbishop, should be asked to give an account, to let all the world see to what use great sums had been put! What was this but expecting him to publish his own disgrace?

The room seemed to go round with him, he felt utterly lost and undone. With a sudden thought he remembered Luther, and the flush faded from his countenance, giving way to a deadly pallor—he fancied he heard the voice of judgment in the distance.

He panted for breath, he staggered on his feet, and at last sank down on a chair in helpless despondence.

But not for long: at length he jumped up with distorted features, a terrible light burning in his eyes. It was a fearful aspect, if any one could have seen him, standing erect with staring eyes, groaning hoarsely, "*He or I*, there is no other way. One of us must fall! Farewell, Schönitz! I am sorry for thee, Schönitz, for thou hast been a faithful servant to me in many things, and I owe thee thanks. But only thou canst save me from utter disgrace even at the cost of thyself; bear the brunt of that which weighs upon us both, though thou art the less guilty. I *am* sorry, poor Schönitz, but after all I must think of myself first. If I am to continue the Archbishop Cardinal, thou must—there is no other way. . . ." He could not put it all into words, shaking as one in a fit of ague.

. . . . .

On a Saturday early in September the special committee appointed by the Estates for the examining of the archiepiscopal exchequer arrived at the new palace, the building, that is, where his grace's most recent creation, the university, should flourish.

The gentlemen were ushered into a comfortable chamber, where a board was spread with the most exquisite fare: they should appease their hunger and slacken their thirst before attacking the labour of sifting unsatisfactory accounts.

The Cardinal himself appeared, a picture of benignity, to discharge the duties of an amiable host, urging the committee to taste his most precious wines, and quite oblivious, to all appearance, of the object which gathered them under his roof.

Yet presently the chairman of the select committee remembered the duty they had come to perform, begging the Cardinal to send for his chamberlain and privy-councillor, Hans von Schönitz.

Albrecht paled, but conquering himself with an effort he expressed his willingness to assist the committee to the best of his ability.

The gentlemen retired to an adjoining room, where a long table, piled with papers, seemed to await their inspection.

Half an hour had passed when Schönitz made his appearance. The Cardinal took his place beside him, considering his presence needful, lest the chamberlain should entangle himself in suspicious statements.

Matters at first ran more smoothly than the Cardinal had anticipated ; the committee was not nearly so intractable as might have been expected—thanks to the electoral malmsey perhaps, or the venison, so deliciously choice.

Presently, however, confusion supervened, the examiners of expenditure before long finding themselves in the muddle hinted at by the Cardinal on a previous occasion ; one thing only appearing to stand out clear —some fifty-three thousand gulden were missing, and could not be accounted for.

The Cardinal fixed a piercing look on his chamberlain. Schönitz understood, and assisted not in unravelling the mystery.

Y

"Your attendance is no further required," said the chairman, presently; "you may retire, sir chamberlain."

Schönitz only too gladly availed himself of the permission, breathing more freely when the door had closed upon him: "The saints be praised!" he ejaculated fervently, "it might have been worse! About a miserable matter of fifty-three thousand gulden they will make no fuss, when hundreds of thousands had to be accounted for. And at the worst—have I not his grace's promise that he will not leave me to battle it through alone!"

Schönitz was very cheerful that evening, quite enjoying his wife's society and intercourse with his little ones; they had not been used to much notice from him lately, they had seen the cloud on his forehead, and had scarcely dared look up in his face.

Dame Magdalen felt the change with a grateful heart. She asked for no explanation, since her husband had not thought fit to let her be privy to his trouble. She had known with the instinct of love that trouble was upon him, and had taken refuge in prayer that it might be averted. It seemed as though an answer had been given; her husband had not appeared so light-hearted for many a day.

The following morning, it being Sunday, Hans accompanied his family to service, offering up thanks not less fervently than his wife.

In the afternoon, still mindful of pleasing the children, he proposed an expedition along the river to enjoy the fields aglow with the warm tints of early autumn. Sunset saw them home, and supper was welcome to the little ones.

They were about to return thanks when heavy steps

resounded in the vestibule. The door was opened, admitting the well-known figure of the bailiff of Castle Giebichenstein, followed by three warders.

Parents and children started dismayed, little Magdalen running for shelter to the folds of her mother's dress.

"There is no occasion for alarm," said the bailiff, looking unconcerned; "my appearance may frighten you, and my commission may seem scarcely pleasant, since I have come to take you, sir chamberlain, a prisoner to the stronghold of Giebichenstein: yet be assured that such arrest shall nowise aggrieve you in body or estate, the rather that it is intended as a safeguard to your honour."

"You speak in riddles, master bailiff!" cried Schönitz hoarsely. "At whose command are you here? Have the Estates despatched you on this mission?"

"By no means," returned the officer, blandly; "the Archbishop himself has resolved upon this expedient yet not in anger, but in loving care of you, anxious you should be taken to a sure place, where no one shall trouble you, just as Frederick the Wise, of blessed memory, carried his beloved Luther a prisoner to the Wartburg."

Schönitz smiled a smile of relief, and, going up to his wife presently, who sat in her chair as one turned to stone, he stroked her hair lovingly, and said: "Fear nothing, dear Magdalen; there is nothing to be afraid of. If I am carried off at the Cardinal's behest, it will be well, I know."

He kissed his wife, who remained motionless; he kissed the children, who cried, "Good-bye, papa!" and followed his captors with a trusting heart.

CHAPTER XXXI.

COMING TO HIMSELF.

THE excitement in the town was great when the occurrence was known. People did not know what to make of it. If the Moritzburg herself had given way on her foundation, it would have surprised them less than to see the chamberlain fall from the Cardinal's favour. What crime could he have committed to bring him to such dire judgment?

The chamberlain's kindred, two lawyers among them, sought the presence of the all-powerful ruler, praying earnestly that the disgrace of jail might be taken from the family; let Schönitz be held a prisoner within his own house, and they would all go bail for him, and answer for any deficiency of accounts.

But the Cardinal received them ungraciously. The case must run its course, he said. If the prisoner were innocent, his innocence would free him speedily, and no one need go bail for him.

Therewith he dismissed the petitioners, who in the antechamber gave vent to their just indignation.

The Cardinal was informed of this by an officious valet, but he could scarcely find fault with the supplicants, since that very day more weighty intercession was made in behalf of the chamberlain, both the Counts of Mansfeld, together with Count Barby, sending a special embassy to urge his release, but in vain.

Albrecht felt himself driven to a corner, public opinion on the one hand and his conscience on the other; but he met both with defiance, making an effort to silence, at any rate, the voice within. He gave strict orders that no one should be admitted to the prisoner. "No mortal man shall see him again," he said to himself; "it is the only way now for saving my reputation; even if the accounts could be brought right, Hans von Schönitz must be silenced."

The Moritzburg after this seemed the centre of a very whirl of pleasure, visitors upon visitors at the invitation of the Cardinal assisting him to keep up the excitement. The Archbishop seemed to thirst for excitement, for the noise of pleasure about him; quiet and loneliness being insupportable. And yet he had to face his seasons of quiet—those silent hours when the stifled voice would still be heard; sleep fled his couch at night when conscience strove with his soul, but he had lost the power of turning upon his sin, he lay awake and groaned.

And what of that other one lying wakeful many a night, innocently imprisoned, yet face to face with the consciousness of sin? Alas, what sorrow he had come to—cruel walls about him, mouldering straw his couch, impenetrable darkness his coverlet! How should he sleep, not knowing when he might see the fair daylight again, not knowing what avengement of wrong was upon him? He was a victim of the cowardly selfishness of the great Cardinal, truly he was; but what of his deeper innocence, or rather his guilt, in the face of the searching Judge above? As he lay day after day, and night after night, alone with himself, with the conscience bearing witness and the thoughts accusing one another, the voice within again and again would cry, "Thou sufferest rightfully!" If not guilty of great wickedness in the eyes of men, was he not guilty of having pandered to the wickedness of another —dragged deeper perhaps than he had intended, yet unable to turn back on the slippery incline, though he had made weak efforts to do so! For the sake of worldly gain, even the great man's favour, he had been the willing servant of his master's iniquity, all these years since first he had yielded himself to provide the means for sinful luxury by assisting the setting up of the idol for the worship of misguided men. And if the punishment had fallen to him, who had the lesser guilt, was it not because perchance he had yet a soul to save? Might it not be the Good Shepherd bringing him thus low for very love's sake? Poor Schönitz came to see he had deserved it all; but how grievously, how thirstily he longed for release!

His sorrow truly was great. Who shall realise the misery of one sitting day and night, or rather in continuous night, in a dungeon deep below the surface of the earth, not knowing whether the fair sun is shining or storms are raging, whether it is the season of violets or of the ripening corn, whether men are plying their weekly labour, or meet with folded hands in the Sabbath sanctuary? And what poignant grief to the poor prisoner to think of his dear ones, of the faithful wife and the little children who would be longing for him as he longs for them! He would fain send them messages of love, write them a letter; but how should he? he has neither pen nor ink; and if he had, the pitiless gaoler would never let the missive go on its way.

The dungeon was a very grave, full of sadness, almost of despair. Hope would raise her shining front at first, at times at least. "It cannot last long; the Cardinal is my friend, he will never break his promise, he will stand by me!" But days passed, weeks passed, and no one came to say, Thou art free!

A little light was allowed him presently, more sad almost in its ghostly glimmer than the hiding night had been. And one day the bailiff appeared, followed by two caitiffs carrying dismal implements. Poor Schönitz, who had jumped to his feet, sank back dismayed, hope fading from his soul.

What did they come for? The bailiff never once pronounced the sweet word of liberty, but with all manner of wiles tried to gain the confession that was needed by the Cardinal in order to satisfy the Estates and clear himself to boot. Wiles availed not, let cruel force do her part! The thumbscrews were applied.

Hast thou hidden thy face, O Justice, that a man should be cruelly tortured to confess himself guilty against his knowledge!

The bones cracked, but the unhappy victim opened not his mouth—at least he said not what his tormentors were anxious to hear, and they left him after a while.

Again they appeared after a couple of days, and again they put him to the cruel test, eliciting no confession, Schönitz protesting his innocence as before.

There are wondrous tales of poor prisoners who, in

spite of pitiless walls, in spite of doubly closed doors, yet find ways and means of communicating with the outer world. In a hard and cruel sense, too, necessity is the mother of invention.

Schönitz, then, found the possibility of exchanging letters with his wife—he writing his with a bit of red chalk, and hiding them in the bundle of linen he sent home at stated intervals.

Several times he had thus despatched news and received answers in return. His faithful Magdalen had informed him that the Cardinal's party sought hard for a cause against him, accusing him of all manner of fraud, but that his own brother Antony zealously strove to vindicate him, that he had even dared to attack the electoral councillors with the question—Whether the Cardinal had power to imprison and hang all those who had grown rich in his service? For if this were the case his brother Hans would have many a fellow in grief. Was it not rather a patent fact that the Cardinal expected high living of his servants, that by their very appearance they might show forth his greatness? His brother had been a rich man originally, but he had often complained of late how dearly he had paid, even as a matter of money, for the favour he enjoyed. And concerning that deficit of fifty-three thousand gulden—why did they not ask his grace himself for an explanation? In all probability he knew best how the money had been spent!

The poor chamberlain rejoiced in having so bold and loving a brother, hoping much of his courage; but fresh clouds of sorrow descended on his buoyant expectation—his wife's letters ceased.

Bundle after bundle arrived, but, anxiously as he

examined the linen, there was nowhere a vestige of news. Had the secret correspondence been discovered? Necessity again taught him invention. He tore a strip from a linen shirt, writing upon it with his bit of red chalk: "My own wife, I suffer agony for absence of news. They intercept our letters. Let us be more cunning still. Examine the sleeves. If you find a red cross send no news. If you find two crosses it purports I cannot write. A rent crossways shall inform thee that they apply cruel force to extort confession. A rent lengthways shall say I am dangerously ill. Three crosses are as good news as I can give in my sorrow."

This strip the prisoner fixed within the folds of a sleeve, and despatched the bundle in hopes.

Nor was he disappointed, receiving an answer in a similar manner from the hands of Dame Magdalen, telling him that his signs would be understood.

Correspondence was resumed, and growing bold by success he from time to time added more complete communication.

"The bailiff has been here," he wrote one day, "urging me to appeal to the Cardinal for pardon and grace; but I shall not do it, since it would be owning myself guilty. I need no man's pardon—not the Cardinal's—but God's alone. I know now what stuff the Cardinal is made of; I know now his mind and heart. He trusts in the power of his arm, and thinks he can crush me. The Lord knows I am innocent of what they accuse me—yet not innocent in His sight. May He have mercy on me in my deep distress!"

But mercy was stayed; week after week passed, month after month. Winter came, and was succeeded by spring; the violets bloomed, the larks rose on joyous wing, but the prisoner continued in the mouldering dungeon. Hope forsook him, and the strong heart grew faint.

Once again he wrote to his wife, with a message to his brother Antony: "I demand an open trial; I will render account to the best of my knowledge before the Cardinal himself, to the town council or to the Estates. But not to adversaries alone; I must have some friends to try me—some just men at least, if right and justice shall not be wronged. If I cannot gain a hearing by trial I shall never leave this place of death! Woe is me, my sorrows are grievous; more merciful it were to let me die! The Lord has brought me to such ignominy that my innocent children even will suffer for it!"

A mercy it was that his poor wife could not see him; she would scarcely have known him again, for he was but a living skeleton to look at. The bailiff himself shook with compassion at the pitiful sight: hollow-eyed despair seemed all that was left of the man whom he had brought thither in the strength and beauty of life—he was but six-and-thirty when they took him. If right should not yield to might, if liberty once more should smile on him, it must be soon—it would be too late ere long. In the meantime the nearness of death worked upon the chamberlain's soul—he was coming to himself.

CHAPTER XXXII.

BROUGHT TO THE GALLOWS.

AT the bar of the Imperial Chamber stood a man who had come to accuse a great prince of the realm— a hierarch of the Church. Right is trodden under foot, and those in power think they can sin with impunity. Yet the high court of the Holy Roman Empire of the German nation will lend an ear when the oppressed one shall be pleaded for. Hope smiled upon the benches.

"Let the plaintiff lodge his complaint."

And the man raised his voice : " Against the Cardinal Elector Archbishop of Mainz and Magdeburg I have come to cry for mercy. The four-and-twentieth tax he has imposed upon his diocese, plundering his people as pitilessly as the invading Turks might do. And now, to cover a discrepancy of accounts, he has thrown into prison his former chamberlain and favourite, submitting him to torture, since he cannot own himself guilty of the imputed fraud. I humbly pray the Imperial Chamber to command that the said prisoner, Hans von Schönitz, be set at liberty and allowed to take his trial in due course of law, lest he perish and be silenced for ever in the dungeon."

"The matter shall be considered," said the president And the man retired.

Within two days from this Cardinal Albrecht, in a high state of alarm, was holding consultation with his confidant and familiar, Doctor Turk. A courier had arrived with a behest he had never anticipated: the prisoner Schönitz should be released within three days, the Imperial Chamber demanding his trial at law.

"What shall we do?" groaned the Cardinal. "Who can have dared to sue the high court against the Prince Primate of Germany?"

"Who else but Antony Schönitz?" replied the chancellor bitterly; "it might have been expected."

"But what shall we do?" repeated the Cardinal.

"Do? We must defy the Chamber!" returned the chancellor unmoved.

"Must we?" echoed the Archbishop helplessly.

"Indeed we must," reiterated the relentless Turk. "Hans von Schönitz must on no account leave his place of confinement. Let me see to it, your grace."

And without awaiting the stricken hierarch's consent the chancellor went forth on his mission; the Cardinal knew it, and did not call him back.

. . . . . .

Hans von Schönitz crouched on the miserable straw, and was just trying to write to his wife—a real labour, in spite of the prompting desire, when the door opened, admitting two hangman's assistants with new implements of torture. The bailiff remained outside. He was not a soft-hearted man, but he could not witness the renewed agony, giving over the prisoner to those who were more cruel than he.

He heard his cries of anguish, growing more faint at last, and dying away in a pitiful moan.

When the servants of torture returned to the daylight, the one remarked : "He will have had enough of it now, unless he be more than human."

But he had not enough. Nature had not come to her last ; he woke from his swoon, though the prayer had been loud in his heart for death to release him.

. . . . .

Four weeks had passed. Again the Cardinal was holding consultation with his chancellor, in still greater dismay, if possible, and even Turk seemed ready to lose his head. A second courier had arrived with more peremptory orders : unless Hans von Schönitz were set at liberty, and allowed to take his trial without delay, the Emperor himself should be appealed to.

How indeed might the Elector's reputation be saved ! But, strange to say, now that the wily chancellor was ready to despair, his master found a cruel courage, to which even the hard-hearted Turk did not reach. Bursting from his seat, he cried with a voice hoarse with the inward emotion : " Has he strength to withstand the torture, then let him try the gallows ! If he cannot confess, he must be silenced, there is no other way ! " The cold drops stood on his forehead.

But the chancellor shook his head. " Who shall pass sentence ? " he queried.

The Cardinal was disconcerted. In his madness of self-preservation he had not thought of that. Of course no properly constituted jury would sanction the proceeding, yet some show of justice must be preserved. " The peasants shall sit in judgment ! " he cried.

" It is not the peasants' business," returned Turk gloomily.

" It shall be then for the nonce ! " exclaimed the exasperated hierarch. " Have I asked you to make more difficulties than there are? Hans Schönitz shall die before the Emperor can hear him!"

"It will be an evil hour!" groaned the chancellor; but Albrecht quitted the apartment.

. . . . .

It was on the Monday after St. Vitus's, the 21st of June, 1535, at three o'clock in the morning, that the bailiff entered the prison cell, followed by a warder bearing a pail of water and a brush and a comb.

"Make yourself tidy, Hans von Schönitz, and follow me to the daylight."

The prisoner stood as one spellbound, unable to take in the news. "God in heaven, is it true?" he cried at last. "Is the hour of release at hand?"

"It is at hand," returned the bailiff significantly; and poor Schönitz clasped him in a transport of gratitude.

The officer pushed him away, not unkindly, urging him to make ready at once. This done, the warder produced a pair of handcuffs, to manacle the prisoner.

"What are you about?" cried Schönitz, trying to free himself. "What is going to be done to me now?"

"You are going to be brought to judgment," explained the bailiff.

The fettered man followed his guide, stair after stair, for his prison was deep under ground.

At last the daylight appeared, and Schönitz closed his eyes—the long night had unfitted them for the sun.

In the castle yard about a hundred peasants stood waiting in a circle; they had come at the archiepiscopal behest to pass sentence on Hans von Schönitz. A couple of lawyers were present in behalf of the Cardinal.

The hangman was called, and with bared hatchet he

accused the chamberlain of delinquency guilty of death, the prisoner interrupting him.

"What is it?" he cried; "are you about to murder me?"

He was seized and dragged to the rack. There was little power of resistance after months of cruelty, but his shrieks for pity were heartrending. And in the agony of most exquisite torture his would-be judges closed round him, urging a confession of his guilt. Schönitz gave a groan; they averred he had said "yes."

The peasant jury was asked whether they found the prisoner guilty.

"Guilty of death!" they echoed, in awful chorus.

"It is murder!" cried Schönitz. "I have not confessed—I have nothing to confess—I ask a proper trial, these cannot judge me."

"You are judged, and you shall die!" yelled the ruthless cohort, the hangman and his fellows preparing to take him to the gallows.

To men he looked in vain for pity, but a power not of man's giving upheld him at the last. He folded his hands, his lips moved in prayer. "Lord Christ!" he said, "hast Thou gone to Calvary? let me follow Thee, and have mercy on my soul!" And gazing upward he repeated the fifty-seventh Psalm with steady voice.

The executioners were more humane than the Cardinal; they were not long about their dismal duty. Within a quarter of an hour the silence of death had settled on the yard; of men only the bailiff was left, who, in accordance with ancient usage, muttered a *paternoster* beneath the gallows for the soul they had sent to its account.

CHAPTER XXXIII.

LUTHER RISING IN JUDGMENT.

CARDINAL ALBRECHT was absent from Halle on that fatal Monday; he had seen fit to travel to Halberstadt, although nothing in particular had called him thither.

Returning on the fourth day, his eye from afar sought the Giebichenstein: the black flag was hoisted, he saw that the work had been done, that the mouth was silenced which, had it spoken, might have cost him both cardinalate and electorship.

But entering his town of Halle, he perceived at once that no peace awaited him. In the first place, public jurisdiction felt itself aggrieved by the recent lawless proceeding, and threatened to lodge complaint with the Imperial Chamber. In the second place, and that was more alarming still, Antony Schönitz had taken forcible possession of his murdered brother's papers, containing compromising letters from the Cardinal to his former favourite, accounts, too, of doubtful nature; while Hans lived they had been under seal at the electoral office, now they should be published and his grace should be sued.

How might he escape it, if it were not by dealing with Antony as Hans had been dealt with?

One sin is the parent of another; this is part of its curse, and who has done the first wrong will do the second more easily.

Antony's movements were watched. One day, as he rode to the Count of Mansfeld, three men-at-arms following him placed themselves in ambush against his return; but their intention was foiled, he went back by another road.

The Cardinal meanwhile put on the mask of innocence, and, by way of proving to the world that his late chamberlain had received the wages of iniquity, he confiscated his every possession, Antony appearing at the Ratskeller one evening in a fury of indignation. "The knavery is beyond conception!" he cried; "not satisfied with having made the poor wife a widow and the children fatherless, the rapacious Cardinal now takes their sustenance, the very playthings of the little ones—everything is carried from the house! People are to believe this is because Hans Schönitz owed great sums to his grace, whereas it is the very contrary: I hold written proof that the Cardinal was deep in my brother's debt. Yet wait, Cardinal, justice shall mete thee with her measure! I know the man who before now has been able to pull off the mask of virtue from thy face; he shall do it again—he shall light a fire that may prove hotter than thou wouldst expect!"

And that selfsame day Antony Schönitz, followed by well-armed servants, rode towards Wittenberg.

In his heart's excitement he never thought that the expedition might have to be paid for with his life; for the plague raged at Wittenberg to such a degree that even the university had quitted the place, taking refuge at Jena. Luther, however, stood manfully by his post, upholding his people through terrible days.

Antony entered the death-stricken town, the streets were deserted, scarcely a sound was to be heard.

Not till he entered the cloister yard of the Augustinians, a human voice fell on his ear; it was Mistress Kate busy with her chickens.

"Is Doctor Martin at home?" he inquired, hastily; "can I see him?"

"To be sure, dear sir," replied Luther's helpmeet, pleasantly; "you will find him in his little study—this way."

Antony's heart beat loudly as through the long dark passage he approached the chamber of the great one, a stranger to him in more ways than one. His hand even trembled as he knocked at the door, yet Luther was his only hope.

"Who are you, my friend, and what brings you hither?" inquired Luther of the stranger who stood reverently by the door. "Come nearer, you are welcome."

"Antony von Schönitz is my name," replied the visitor.

"Ha!" cried Luther, starting, "that is the name of the unhappy victim whose story has been told by Ludwig Rabe at my table this very day. Are you one of the family?"

"His own brother," replied Schönitz eagerly, "and I have come to you, much honoured Doctor, to pray for your help against the murderer."

"Sit down, dear friend, and tell me all. My Kate shall give you a drink, for you must have had a hot time coming hither."

Before Schönitz could answer, the hospitable Doctor had disappeared, returning with his wife presently, who carried a silver tankard with foaming Torgau beer, which she offered with a courtesy, prettily foretasting the beverage, after the fashion of those days.

"Take and enjoy it," said Luther, kindly; "it is my own Elector's gift."

A film overspread Antony's eyes as he looked at the Doctor, and his heart went out to meet him; was this the man of whom the world was full? How simply human he was, how loving withal, nay, a man as the prophet of old described it, who might be as an hiding-place from the wind, as the shadow of a great rock in a weary land.

It is wonderful, yet very natural, how those whose utter trust rests in the Lord their God, invariably inspire their fellow-men with confidence in themselves. Antony had come prepared to unbosom his sorrow to Luther, but he did not expect he could do it so fully, that he could lay open his heart so entirely as to a brother. When he left Wittenberg his soul could rest in trust.

Not many days, and a broadside startled the world, startled the great man at Halle whom no one dared accuse, though many in their secret hearts believed him guilty of innocent blood. The fearless Luther once more opened his mouth, every word bursting like thunder over the head of the Prince Primate of Germany; all the country heard it, and stood breathless, waiting what might follow.

This was the letter :—

"Repentance and forgiveness of sin to you, most

noble Elector, most gracious Lord. I am constrained to address this to your Cardinal Holiness, not for the hope of doing good to yourself, but to satisfy my own conscience. For Ludwig Rabe has shown me a missive in which your Cardinal Holiness threatens him for having spread certain news concerning Hans von Schönitz. Now since that same Ludwig Rabe is my table-fellow, it seems to me that your Cardinal Holiness intends that letter as a stab at myself, for sheer annoyance that I and other good people must hear such news I can testify to it with a bold conscience that Ludwig Rabe sits at my table bashful as a maiden, and is not likely therefore to spread vicious tales of his own invention. Indeed, the town was full of it before I learnt from Ludwig Rabe what I could not believe my ears to be true, that Hans Schönitz, the much-loved servant of the Cardinal's Holiness, had been suddenly brought to the gallows by yourself. Nay, Ludwig Rabe has not made up such tale, and my Lord Cardinal's name was spit at and desecrated barring our invention. If then that missive was a hit at myself, I pray your Cardinal Holiness to leave those unmolested who sit at my table. Indeed, I will be free to hear and believe what honest people tell me concerning that same Hans, and I will venture to speak of such things as I hear. Surely I have not been called to Wittenberg to hush up all those who dare speak good of Hans Schönitz and evil of the Cardinal's grace, and indeed I trust you will not bring me to the gallows, as you did Schönitz, for holding such views. I will be free therefore to think and believe what is true. In sooth, if your Cardinal Holiness felt inclined to hang all those who venture to speak evil of the hell-deserving bishop, there might not be ropes enough in all Germany. However, not many might be hanged so easily as poor Hans was hanged. If Schönitz had been judged anywhere but under his Archbishop's auspices, he would be free and alive this day. And if the Archbishop had our Ludwig Rabe at Halle he would no doubt hang him, and silence him, as Hans Schönitz was silenced. But if the Cardinal's Holiness is anxious to know the goodly reports current about him in German lands, I beg to remind him of things done fifteen years ago, meaning the indulgence and other stories, although one would hardly advise your grace to stir up the muck which we trust is covered, though not forgotten. If your Cardinal Holiness would stifle such reports anywhere out of Halle, the very ban-bull of the Pope might not do it. At Halle these things are smothered under pain of death, but that cannot hurt Hans Schönitz, neither his name nor his cause; and the Cardinal's evil report is added to daily by a calling and crying for vengeance; even as the blood of Magister George—which at the time I was anxious to turn away from the Bishop of Mainz, laying it rather at other doors—is crying the longer the louder, and I for one will not be silenced till it be heard and avenged.

"This letter I have writ to your Cardinal Holiness, even as Elijah the prophet wrote to Jehoram in the Second of Chronicles, chapter the twenty-first, holding myself excused thereby before God and all the world. And I take comfort to myself that ye wrathful saints, cardinals and others, will not hang every one who opposes you, but that you will spare the knocker at least at the Lord Almighty's church door, and that some few of us may escape till the great hangman confound you at the last. So be it.

"Given at Wittenberg, this 31st of July, 1535.

"DOCTOR MARTIN LUTHER."

As carried by invisible hands, this letter sped through the length and breadth of the land, and the people read it.

And what was the Cardinal's reply? Silence. He took it all, not uttering a sound. "He is guilty," said the people.

But Luther was not put off so easily. "He takes no notice, hoping to drown it in oblivion; but he shall not succeed this time, if he succeeded before!"

And again Doctor Martin took his inkstand, filling it deeper still.

"Grace and peace in Christ our Lord, and my poor *paternoster* for mercy. It has come to my knowledge, most gracious Cardinal, how your electoral grace is trying hard to cover up the blood of poor Hans, as you did cover up the innocent blood of Magister George, for the which even I lent you my foolish service, thinking too well of the Bishop of Mainz, and laying that blood at the door of the Chapter. But I see now that your electoral grace relies on this, that haply you might escape unscathed and honourably from both cases, heaping all disgrace upon the dead; I send tidings therefore herewith inclosed, from which your electoral grace may gather that the blood that was spilt is not so silent in German lands as it may be beneath your grace's roof among the pickthanks. I trust your grace will have to say yea and amen, if much against your will. However, I know apart from these tidings that your Cardinal Holiness is guilty of having hanged Hans Schönitz, without the knowledge of his family or of the town of Halle—moreover without granting to the poor man just trial or defence, as had been doubly meet in his position. People speak the truth surely when they say that because your grace could not make good the deficit, poor Hans had to pay for it with his death ; and yet no bishop has power to take life. Again, I have read that your electoral grace is trying to put the blame upon the murdered man's own relatives. Now for a certainty, and though I have heard tell many an evil deed of cardinals, I could never have believed your grace to be such a vicious worm as to be able to mock and insult the very people against whom you have sinned. And since your grace defies the Imperial Chamber, and has robbed the town of Halle of her right of the sword, the Lord God will hear our prayer and cause the Cardinal's Holiness to sweep out the dirt himself. If Hans Schönitz had been a thief (which I do not believe), the Cardinal of Mainz would have to be hanged ten times over upon a gallows thrice the height of the Giebichenstein, for who like he has so shamefully wasted St. Maurice's, draining the diocese with riotous living, continually robbing his people ? Is there not Elsa von Kolze, of unhappy memory, who has lost fair fame and riches for him ? are there not the churches and convents he has spoiled, the citizens of Halle he has driven from house and home ? and the like praiseworthy deeds untold ? I will announce to you then what I mean to do, as one who rues his foolish writing concerning the death of Magister George, more especially as I have given cause to the Chapter of Mainz to accuse me of having wronged them. I will make known to all the world the dying cry of the murdered Hans, when he called aloud for mercy against violence. I will do so, and make a merry Shrovetide for your electoral grace, so help me God!

"DOCTOR MARTIN LUTHER."

Albrecht was furious. If he had met Luther face to face, who knows but what he had not carried out upon him the Edict of Worms with his own hand?

Turk urged him to go to law for libel; but the Cardinal moved not.

"Where shall we get to, if your electoral grace takes it all in silence?" cried the impassioned chancellor. "It must not be, indeed not! An appeal to the House of Brandenburg might stop the calumny. Your august relatives may apply pressure to the Elector of Saxony, and the slanderer will have to yield."

The Cardinal caught at this. "You are right," he said. "The princes of my house will stand by me, where the common people blacken my name. They will resent it, that a mere churl of a faithless monk dares lift his unmannerly fist against the Cardinal who is a born Markgrave of Brandenburg."

Messengers then were dispatched to Berlin and Königsberg, finding a willing ear at both courts. The Elector of Saxony was appealed to to use his influence with Luther.

And he did so, powerfully supported by Albrecht of Königsberg, the whilom Grand Master, now Duke of Prussia, who had some weight with Luther—but not in this matter: the sturdy Reformer insisted on his right, nay, duty, of upbraiding the sinner, if no one else did it.

They tried to find out from him what further writing he intended to fulminate against the Cardinal; but the only answer they could elicit from Wittenberg was to this effect: "What is that to you? The Cardinal has been allowed far too long to scorn the Lord Christ, and vex poor people; it would be a more praiseworthy attempt to try and improve him than to inquire into my writing. It is not I, but he, the Cardinal, who disgraces your princely house. I have done nothing but told the truth to an arrant knave. No house so royal but it may bring forth an evil scion. Go to law with me, an you please. I will not fail to appear. I have already put in writing what shall justify me. Two letters have I writ: that which I now hope to send forth will not fall dead, please God."

Upon this information, Albrecht of Königsberg personally reasoned with Doctor Martin: he was right, no doubt, but let him not judge too harshly. Abuse of spiritual power was an open sore; one could but hope for better times with patience; he prayed urgently Luther should put by the intended pamphlet—the need of its publication might lessen, perhaps.

Said Luther: "I do not blame your cousinly sympathy for taking the part of the Bishop of Mainz; but even your princely grace could not think well of him. far less speak for him, if you knew all I know against him. He is surpassingly wicked and froward. Your princely grace may remember that at the recent meeting of Brandenburghers with the Elector of Saxony, one of the former remarked: 'Would to God the Cardinal were not a prince of Brandenburg!' I can only repeat my former request to your grace: get the prelate to go to law with Luther. I wish him no harm, but he shall have his due."

A more urgent appeal was returned from Königsberg: let Luther remember that there were broken pots everywhere!

Doctor Martin was brought to consider: "Well," he said, "I will put by what I have writ; the time will come to send it forth."

And behold before long the Cardinal found courage to move. There appeared an archiepiscopal official at the Augustinian monastery at Wittenberg, delivering a request from the Cardinal that Doctor Martin himself should act as arbiter.

Luther for a moment was puzzled; but he soon perceived the trick of the wily hierarch. "Indeed," thought he to himself, "and does the Cardinal ask that of me which he knows I cannot do? If I send a refusal, he will imagine he has done his duty, and be rid of the matter."

And turning to the messenger he said: "Tell him who sent you that he has mistaken his man: Luther is unable to arbitrate, since it is unheard of that the accuser should at the same time be judge."

When the official had departed Luther turned to his cupboard: "Come forth, my little book," he said, "come forth to the light; the time has come to dispatch thee. . . . . Yet no! Once more I will make the attempt and preach repentance to the Cardinal. If he does not hear me now, the little book shall go its way."

And with all speed he wrote a letter, sending it after the messenger.

The Cardinal lay sick on his bed when that exhortation reached him. Illness had wrought a change, his spirit was broken, a wave of contrition swept his soul moistening his very eyes with emotion. Conscience was at work, holding up the past. "I will meet his advice," he murmured, "I will show him that I have yielded to brotherly counsel. I will take up the bones of him who was buried beneath the gallows, and will entomb them with all honours in my own cathedral. I cannot do more—but surely that will be enough!"

The proud man had laboured to come to this resolution, but the idea quite cheered him; he rose from his sick bed, hoping that surely now Luther would hold his tongue.

Vain hope! How should the honest-hearted Luther be satisfied with such poverty-stricken repentance—unmanly, not to say unchristian? So far from buying silence, it broke the last tie that withheld the little book.

And the third thunderbolt struck deeper than anything that had gone before.

"A cry goes up from earth to heaven," it said, "the cry of innocent blood. I am not his judge, but a messenger I am of the great Judge: it is not I who call him a murderer and thief, but the Judge above does so. To the light, Bishop!—Nay, the Bishop shuns the light. He could not permit his chamberlain to render full account, but hang him he could! Aha, Bishop! It is better to die on the gallows than to be thrust into hell. .... A rich man, that Cardinal! but let him have a hundred thousand advocates, honest lawyers or pettifoggers, to help him to clatter and spatter, we owe it to God to hear another man. Where is that man? On the gallows. Righteous God, who has hanged him? The Bishop. And for why? The Bishop would have the field to himself, none should stand up against him, the Bishop will preach to fools. And what does the Lord say to it? The Cardinal representing the one side shall not be believed, until he produce the man who can stand for the other side..... Where is the natural law? Why, his princely grace has offered to face the law at the Imperial Chamber. Has he? When Hans Schönitz was alive and could have confronted the Cardinal, his grace shunned the light; now that Hans is dead, he is willing to come to the Chamber, and make fools of all who will hear him. Such wily wisdom the Lord has known how to confound; the living Cardinal must hold his tongue; and dead Hans speaketh by the blood-right of Abel, crying vengeance on his murderer. Behold the holy folk of popedom: they like to be Cardinal, they like to rule the Church, but they despise the Word of God, and would fain overthrow it. Very right and meet it is that they come to grief to their own hurt, like the Cardinal with his sycophants. Would I could touch his conscience to righteous repentance! Would to God that the Cardinal could be brought to know himself, to kneel for God's mercy, then I should have gained a great and happy end by my harsh and scolding writ. But if he will not hear me, I have at least done my duty by Hans Schönitz according to Christian charity; and after my death my testimony will be worth more than the Cardinal's, who even in his lifetime is falling into unsavoury repute. One more true and faithful counsel I would give him, if so be that his majesty will stoop to take it. What saith the Lord in the fifth of St. Matthew: *Be reconciled to thy brother!* The Cardinal then should go to the wife and mother of Schönitz, humbling himself and praying them for God's sake to forgive him all the sorrow, grief, and loss he has brought upon them, and which he would like to make good. This is fine counsel, which the Lord Christ Himself hath given, yea, a command it is which He, Christ, puts upon all. The Word of Christ will remain, not one jot or tittle shall pass from it, but the Cardinal and we all shall pass away. God knows we have all of us our grievous weight of sin, and should not make Him a liar and a cover for our wickedness who is willing to forgive sin. That would be blaspheming the Holy Ghost, for the which there is no forgiveness. Lord help us to be pious sinners and not holy blasphemers! Amen."

The word was spoken, the people heard it, and so did the Cardinal. God once more thereby knocked at his heart; but he had hardened his heart, and it was more hardened still.

CHAPTER XXXIV.

THE LAST STRUGGLE.

ONCE again distress in the archiepiscopal exchequer had reached its height, once again no hope remained but suing the Estates for a tax.

The Chancellor Turk himself undertook the mission, prepared to do his best in matter of management, and, strange to say, he was successful. The assembly granted five hundred thousand gulden, to be raised by an extraordinary impost throughout the diocese. The town of Halle came in for twenty-two thousand gulden.

On the Monday after the Fourth Sunday in Lent, 1541, the town council called together a meeting of citizens to announce to them the decision arrived at.

A deep murmur arose when the fact was known, and the citizens requested time for consideration.

There was nothing to consider, said the recorder; and since it was a settled matter, it behoved the people simply to obey; but they insisted on their right, and time was granted.

The citizens thereupon went into committee, each of the four parishes on its own account, to consult about the proposed tax and in the name of the township to treat with the council.

Excitement ran highest in the parish of Our Lady. There the venerable Wolf Steinbach stood up with all the weight of his influence, and this is what he said: "The time has come now, ye men of Halle, when we may obtain what we have prayed for this many a year, the pure Word of God. Let us stand firm, and refuse the tax until the council grant us a Protestant preacher and schoolmaster. Then we will submit to the Cardinal as dutiful citizens. Listen to me, my brethren! I am an old man: I have watched from the first the great struggle between Albrecht the Cardinal, Prince Primate of Germany, and Luther, the prophet of the High God. Hot indeed has been the battle, and many a blow has fallen. The Cardinal at first believed he could look down with a supercilious smile upon the humble barefooted friar; he brandished his sword, thinking he could never be vanquished—he, the most powerful of German princes. Yet see, even he had to accept it that the Word is a power, stronger than aught besides; that swords and crowns even must yield it the victory. Step by step the Primate lost ground to the monk. As the Gospel has spread victoriously throughout the length and breadth and beyond the confines of the land, so it has entered the diocese of Magdeburg, and the Cardinal could not forbid it. Town after town, village after village, has fallen away from him. His steps have been uncertain; and since he has soiled his hands with the blood of Schönitz, an evil conscience has led him into much folly. It was upon that occasion that Luther dealt him the heaviest blow, shivering his proud sword to pieces. He can but fight with the broken weapon now, and he does it with an obstinate, desperate defiance: if aught fails, he will keep one shred of his power, one stronghold of popery within the diocese—he thinks he is sure of his residence at Halle. You know how, again and again, with a hard heart, he has refused to give us what he has been obliged to yield to other towns of the archbishopric—the preaching of the Gospel. Year after year he has succeeded in getting those into the town council who assisted him effectively; and ever since we lost our beloved Magister George we have been obliged to worship away from our own tôwn. Now at last the hour has come when we may force him to give us what from the first he should not have denied. Let us refuse the tax, then, till he has heard our prayer. It will not be quite easy, since now also the president and sub-president of the town council are his creatures; but if the citizens are of one mind we may gain the victory. Let those who agree with me step to my side."

The committee of Our Lady's parish was unanimous, solemnly vowing to stand by each other, and stand by the faith.

And upon inquiry it was found that of the other three parishes, all, some few excepted, were of a similar mind.

A deputation then waited upon the council to announce the citizens' desire and intention; and having done so, they were told to await decision in the lobby.

More than an hour they were kept waiting, and began to be fearful of the result. To their surprise, however, the recorder made answer: "A well-instructed Gospel preacher you have asked for, and a Protestant schoolmaster besides. This is a request both needful and redounding to the honour of God. The worshipful council has agreed, therefore, speedily to look for a preacher who is well-mannered, pious and learned, and firmly planted in the Gospel, as you desire. An able schoolmaster also shall be inquired for. It is not meet, however, for the Council to act arbitrarily in this most important matter; it has been resolved, therefore, to appeal to the Cardinal, who, as you know, is even now assisting at the Diet of Regensburg."

But Wolf Steinbach interposed : "Not so, your worship ! The citizens cannot accept such conditions. There is no need to appeal for the Word of God to any one but to the Lord Himself, who is the Word. We have often prayed the Cardinal for a Protestant preacher since the days of Magister George, but in vain. Let the worshipful council remember how many poor people have since been left to hunger for the Gospel !"

The council retired to consider, and again the recorder spoke forth : "It shall be done as you would have it ; but if the council thereby should incur the Cardinal's displeasure, you shall promise that the citizens will bear us out."

This assurance was given, and after some further debate it was agreed that Doctor John Pfeffinger, a Protestant divine of Leipzig, should be waited upon with a call to Halle.

The joy in the town was great that the council should have yielded so readily. Wolf Steinbach, however, shook his head, expressing grave doubts to his friends : "I distrust this willingness of the council," he said ; "I fear me there is knavery behind ! What if they are reporting to the Cardinal behind our backs ? If such were indeed the case, we must keep our eyes open, lest the second Protestant preacher of Halle share the fate of the first one. Since Hans Schönitz was brought to the gallows, the Cardinal might be capable of anything."

People thought that was going too far in suspicion, the Cardinal was at a great distance, moreover; but the venerable Steinbach kept to his own opinion: "Sleep if you like," he said; "I shall watch."

On the following Sunday, with the early dawn, an open chaise drove from the Gallowgate, taking the high road to Leipzig. The occupants were two town councillors and two of the committee of Our Lady's; an outrider led the way. The horses were kept at a quick pace, the little party being anxious to arrive at Leipzig in time for morning service. The deputation wished to hear a sermon from the preacher they were about to invite to Halle.

But untoward interruption was at hand; they had not proceeded far when the outrider pulled up sharp: "Look yonder!" he exclaimed, pointing to a copse at a little distance. "I see the glitter of arms through the underwood—there is a man on horseback, and another. Good heavens, it is the garrison from the Giebichenstein!"

"Treason!" cried one of the deputies. "They have broken their word, they have betrayed us to the Cardinal!"

It was indeed the bailiff from the Giebichenstein, with twelve horsemen. Those in the chaise heard him interrogate the outrider as to who was in the vehicle and what might be the object of their journey.

The little party bravely resolved to drive on, nor were they hindered; the outrider was released, having given his information.

Wolf Steinbach that same morning, about breakfast time, was startled by a ponderous knocking at his door. Two of the salt-workers had come, anxious to see their master.

"Important news, though little pleasing!" cried the men, as soon as admitted. "The bailiff of the Giebichenstein with his men has been seen stopping the deputation."

The old man received the news with dismay. "I knew it—I expected it!" he cried. "You shall be rewarded for your watchfulness."

But the men declined; they had not done it for gain, they said.

That same evening Wolf Steinbach convened the committee and other leading citizens, to inform them of the occurrence, the evident treacherous intent calling up not a little wrath. Measures were resolved upon to anticipate any evil designs, the people guarding their suspicions and preparations strictly.

In the night of the following Thursday a band of salt-workers, with halberds and truncheons, gathered quietly round the springs, a body of citizens armed in a like manner collecting about the Gallowgate. And presently, in the dead of night, the united force, some two hundred stalwart fellows, moved from the town with faces set towards Leipzig. The gate-keeper tried to refuse passage, but was forced to give way.

The town council being informed, forthwith summoned the committee, taxing the citizens with insulting distrust, as though the presiding magistrates themselves had ordered abroad the garrison of the Giebichenstein.

The charge was quietly accepted, leaving each and all free to think as they pleased.

The excitement in the town was great; no one thought of work. Old and young, rich and poor, men and women pressed about the Gallowgate, anxiously peering towards Leipzig.

It was noon, and nothing was to be seen. The afternoon waned, and many of the watchers had retired to their homes when a body of armed men became visible through the rising dust. The citizens of Halle returned from their expedition; they had met nothing suspicious, they said; but neither had they fallen in with the deputation.

Fears and surmisings passed about the town, the presiding magistrates being reviled freely for whatever of underhand designs they might be guilty of.

The following day only, at nightfall, the deputation returned, safe and sound, but without the expected preacher.

They repaired at once to the town hall to report; Doctor Pfeffinger truly was a learned man, with a heart in the right place, and a tongue that could speak; he was of the Gospel faith, and much respected by the good folk of Leipzig, who no doubt would not care to part with him. The reverend Doctor, however, was of a fearful mind. Upon learning that he might have to go through much tribulation at Halle, he had prayed the delegates to take their offer to one more fit than he.

The town council accepted the information in silence; but not so the citizens, who hesitated not to hint very broadly that the magistrates apparently knew beforehand what result to expect of the deputation.

The people of Halle before long, however, found reason to calm their ire, as the news was passed from house to house that the deputation had more to tell than they thought well to impart to the adverse magistrates. This is what they reported further : since Doctor Pfeffinger had declined, they had driven straight to Wittenberg, and had been received most warmly by Doctor Martin. "Indeed, and you shall have a preacher," he had said : "I will send you one who not only has a tongue to speak like an angel, but teeth wherewith to bite, and the heart of a lion as a true champion of the Gospel; he will not fear the Cardinal. I make a real sacrifice in parting with him, since he is one of my truest friends and fellow labourers at Wittenberg. But I delight in sending him to the town of Halle. Return to your own, and the Lord be with you ! I will lose no time in sending you the man who may serve you—my beloved Doctor Justus Jonas."

And the town of Halle lifted her face with thanksgiving, many of her children kneeling to their Father in heaven with a song of praise on their lips, that after many days of darkness He had made His sun to rise— the Sun of Righteousness, with healing in His wings. The true Gospel henceforth would illumine the believer's heart.

CHAPTER XXXV.

CONQUERED.

THE Diet of Regensburg was over. It had need to sit long. Much had to be seen to, and lengthy had been the debates about Church and religion. The Emperor longed earnestly for peace and for a settling of those matters of faith which so long had troubled the realm. Not heeding, therefore, the opposition of Catholic princes, he had commanded a religious disputation, himself appointing the theologians who should carry it on. And very careful he had been on both sides to select men of charity rather than contention, hoping thus to arrive at the desired result. Indeed, it appeared for a time as though the Imperial wishes should be realised, on several points of doctrine an agreement being seemingly arrived at. But when they came to dispute about the Church, a common understanding appeared anything but possible, the question of the sacraments entirely rending the bridge of concord so anxiously contrived. On that ground the theologians parted company, and eventually the princes and hierarchs returned to their people.

Cardinal Albrecht set his face towards his town of

Mainz, where his presence was urgently required. But remembering Halle on the road, and the reports that had reached him from that place, he changed his course. "Let the good folk of Mainz possess their souls in patience; methinks I am more needed at Halle, lest the last of my diocese of Magdeburg he wrenched from my hands." Yes, Alhrecht had need to return to Halle.

The folds of night were mantling the place as he reached it, and he was well satisfied it should be so. He felt averse to be received by the citizens with a show of homage. Quietly he entered his Moritzburg, and, weary with the journey, he at once sought his couch.

But the following morning the sun lit up his chamber. The windows looked south, and commanded a view of the collegiate foundation.

He walked to the casement, became pale, and staggered. Ye saints! what is the matter with the steeples of my cathedral?"

He pulled his bell passionately, inquiring almost with a scream of the valet who hastily appeared, "What are they doing? Dismantling my towers!"

"So please your electoral grace," said the man, half frightened; "they are taking down the belfries, the foundation is giving way."

The Cardinal could only wave his hand; the man retired. Alhrecht sank into a chair, covering his face. "Woe is me, my towers!" he groaned; "my towers, in which I heheld an emblem of the invincible glory of the Church, a token of her victory over heresy! The foundation is giving. Give way then, my hopes!"

He sat as one petrified, motionless, overwhelmed with thought.

Rising at last, he again neared the window, the tears of disappointment in his eyes. His own cathedral! The people in festive apparel were running to and fro. The Cardinal saw it, yet somehow he did not seem to take it in till after a while, when the sight, as it were, struck his soul. "What is it?" he cried, "what solemnity moves the people?"

Again the valet was rung for, and hoarsely the Cardinal inquired: "What is it that moves the town?"

The valet trembled at the question, and answered slowly, "Justus Jonas has arrived to preach the Gospel."

The Cardinal's face grew ashy, and scarcely master of himself he burst upon the harmless valet: "Get thee gone, wretched menial! Is that all thy news?"

With beating heart Albrecht paced his room. There was a conflict in his soul, and he fought it out on the spot. He stood still presently, stretching forth his hands. "Fare thee well, Halle!" he murmured; "thou shalt see my face no more. Old things are passing away, new things are bursting to life—*and thou hast conquered, Augustinian!*"

THE END.

LONDON: R. CLAY, SONS, AND TAYLOR, PRINTERS.

www.ingramcontent.com/pod-product-compliance
Lightning Source LLC
Chambersburg PA
CBHW030400230426
43664CB00007BB/677